THE WORLD'S GREATEST
CLASSIC CARS

COMPLETE HISTORIES
WITH UNIQUE CUT-AWAY DRAWINGS

Grange
BOOKS

© Orbis Publishing Ltd 1995

Published By Grange Books
An Imprint of Grange Books PLC
The Grange
Grange Yard
London SE1 3AG

This edition published 1995

This material has previously appeared in
the partwork *The Car*

ISBN 1 85627 715 1
Printed in the Republic of Slovakia
51638

— CONTENTS —

ASTON MARTIN

DB2/2-4

When David Brown bought Aston Martin and Lagonda, his ambition to build luxury sporting cars resulted in the classic DB line, founded with the superb DB2 and 2-4

IN THE 1930S, Britain swarmed with small, specialised sports-car manufacturers. When the smoke of the World War II began to clear, it became obvious that few of them were going to survive. The most significant of those that did – if one excepts Jaguar, MG and Triumph, none of whom was small or specialised to that degree – was Aston Martin.

Aston's survival was by no means a foregone conclusion. It depended heavily on the intervention of one man, the wealthy enthusiast David Brown whose family fortune was founded on the more prosaic activities of gear-cutting and (like Lamborghini twenty years later!) of tractor manufacture. It was also vital to the way things turned out that David Brown bought not only Aston Martin, but also Lagonda, because with the latter company there came the classic 2.6-litre twin-cam engine designed by W.O. Bentley and intended to power the company's post-war luxury car range.

Brown's original plan was to operate Aston Martin and Lagonda as the sporting and luxury marques respectively of his car-building operation. Once he had acquired the assets of both former companies he moved them into almost adjacent premises in Feltham, Middlesex and at this point it must have become obvious (if it was not so already) that the dohc Lagonda engine was a much better bet for a sports car than the pushrod ohv 'six' which Claude Hill had designed for the post-war Aston Martins.

The decision caused Hill to leave in something of a huff, but not before he had laid his own part of the Aston Martin foundation, a chassis which was reasonably light, exceptionally rigid and which offered excellent handling. Initially this was still powered by the old Aston Martin 4-cylinder, 2-litre engine. For the 1949 Motor Show it was clothed in an attractive roadster body designed by Frank Feeley of Lagonda, a body which seemed to combine some of the points of the Jaguar XK120 and the Sunbeam Talbot 90, so to speak. This roadster entered half-hearted production – some 15 were made – and later became known in some quarters as the DB1, although it was certainly not called that when it appeared. This car

LEFT *Views of a 1957 Aston Martin DB2-4 Mk II, which was first introduced in 1955. This is the coupé version, but convertible and 'notchback' models were also available. About 200 were built before the launching of the Mk III*

3

MODEL
Aston Martin DB2/4

UK price when announced:
£2728 4s 2d

ENGINE
Location: Front, longitudinal
Type: Water-cooled in-line six cylinder. Cast-iron block with removeable liners and cast-iron cylinder head. Four main bearings
Cubic capacity: 2580 cc
Bore × stroke: 78 mm × 90 mm
Compression ratio: 8.16:1
Valve gear: 2 valves per cylinder operated by twin direct-acting overhead camshafts
Fuel supply: 2 SU side-draught carburettors. Twin electric fuel pumps
Ignition: Mechanical by coil and distributor with automatic timing advance/retard
Maximum power: 127 bhp at 5000 rpm
Maximum torque: 178 lb ft at 3000 rpm

TRANSMISSION
Layout: Clutch in unit with engine.
Clutch: Single dry plate Borg & Beck
Gearbox: Four-speed manual synchromesh on top three ratios
Standard ratios:

| 1st 2.92:1 | 3rd 1.33:1 |
| 2nd 1.98:1 | 4th 1.00:1 |

Close ratios:

| 1st 2.92:1 | 3rd 1.26:1 |
| 2nd 1.87:1 | 4th 1.00:1 |

Final drive: Hypoid bevel
Ratio: 3.77:1

SUSPENSION
Front: Independent with trailing links, coil springs and double-acting lever arm shock absorbers
Rear: Live rear axle with coil springs, radius arms and Panhard rod

STEERING
Type: Worm and roller

BRAKES
Type: 12 in (305 mm) dia. drums all round

WHEELS AND TYRES
Type: Dunlop centre-lock wire sheels with 5.75 × 16 in tyres

BODY/CHASSIS
Type: Tubular steel chassis with aluminium panelled coupé body

DIMENSIONS AND WEIGHT
Length: 171.5 in (4355 mm)
Width: 65 in (1651 mm)
Wheelbase: 99 in (2525 mm)
Track – front: 54 in (1372 mm)
 – rear: 54 in (1372 mm)
Weight: 2884 lb (1308 kg)

PERFORMANCE
Maximum speed: 125 mph (201 kph)
Acceleration 0–60 mph: 12.6 seconds
Fuel consumption: 18–22 mpg

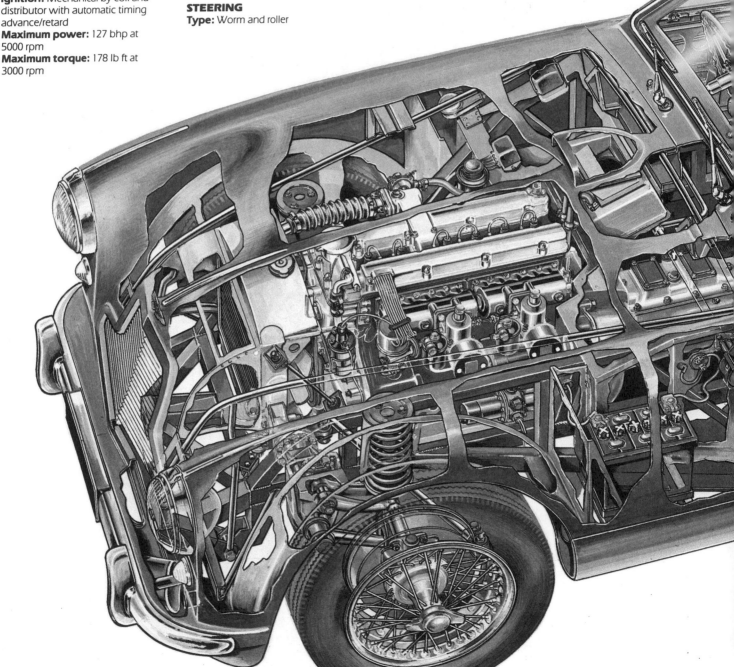

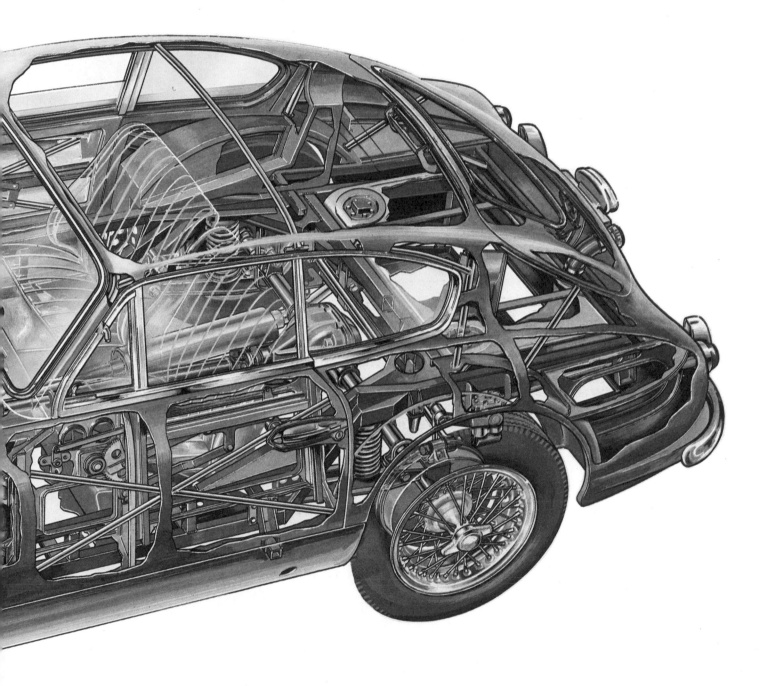

ABOVE The Aston Martin DB2-4, showing its twin-ovehead-camshaft straight six, independent front suspension and live rear axle. The DB2-4 was the first model in the series to offer seating for four, and thus graduated from being a sports car to a high-performance grand tourer, which has been the basis of all subsequent models. The car was an expensive one by the standards of its time, and was also engineered and finished to high standards. As its engine was developed and the performance improved, the DB2-4 naturally evolved into the DB4, introduced in 1959

was not destined to proceed any further, however. Instead, Feeley developed a striking new coupé body which was mated to a shortened version of the original Hill chassis (9 in was cut out of the wheelbase on the recommendation of St John Horsfall whom David Brown had engaged as a consultant). The first four cars were built in 1949, one for David Brown to use on the road and three to enter at Le Mans. Significantly, while two of these cars retained the 2-litre engine, the third race car and the road car were fitted with the 2.6-litre, 6-cylinder engine. They were thus the first 6-cylinder Aston Martins of any kind.

Early in 1950, the car was officially launched as a production model, rather oddly chistened '2½-litre saloon'. The DB2 designation was not long in coming, however, together with the first drophead coupé version announced in the autumn of the same year. Now that the car had arrived the well-heeled motorist could take stock of what it offered. Well-heeled he had to be, for the DB2 was no miraculously priced Jaguar XK120: it listed at £1920 as a coupé ('saloon') and £2040 in drophead form in 1950.

> **'... at the front... the structure had to be quite complicated... '**

The chassis was welded-up conventionally from square-section tube of various sizes, and gained much of its stiffness from its high, ladder-framed sill sections. For the DB2, these were spaced 5 in further apart than in the 'DB1'. A rear extension allowed for the 19-gallon fuel tank to be slung beneath the tail with the spare wheel flat above it; at the front, forward of the solid scuttle, the structure had to be quite complicated in order to accommodate Hill's trailing-arm independent front suspension with its coil springs and anti-roll bar housed within a cross-member. The rear suspension consisted of a live axle, again coil sprung and located by trailing arms and a Panhard rod; the entire suspension was well tried, having been a feature of Hill's earlier Astons. Total suspension travel was 5 in at the front and 7 in at the back, hardly generous by modern standards but enough when combined with stiff springs to achieve a more than acceptable ride/handling compromise in 1950 terms. Since the layout placed the front roll centre at ground level and the rear much higher, just beneath the final-drive centre, the chassis had considerable natural understeer. Steering was by worm and roller

RIGHT *Views of an immaculate DB2-4 Mk III, the version which was launched in 1957. The Mk III's bodywork was restyled, and the grille has the characteristic shape featured on the later DB4/5/6 models. With its 162 bhp 3-litre six the car was capable of 119 mph (191 kph); this example is a regular winner in races and hillclimbs*

with only 2.8 turns of the wheel between extremes of a 35 ft lock, while the brakes in those pre-disc days were massive 12 in drums front and rear. Standard tyre equipment was 6.00–16 in.

It says something for the prejudices of 1950 that there were doubts about the practicality of the body design. Laurence Pomeroy, assessing the DB2 for *Motor*, pointed out that 'the decision to use a full width body of envelope form must immediately raise certain issues in respect of accessibility of the engine and front suspension assemblies . . . .' In this case, he was building up the problem to knock it down, going on to praise Feeley's bold decision to make the bonnet one-piece and to hinge it at the front so that lifting it revealed all. The body itself used alloy panels over an outline frame of Z-section steel with suitable extra strengthening by welded tubes. The windscreeen was two-piece, like most in its time. Pomeroy much admired the body which was stiff and self-supporting in its own right; he pointed expecially to the design of the rear wheel-arch assembly with its transverse bulkhead (it should be said, though, that Pomeroy had been granted the exceptional one-off privilege of a long Continental trip in David Brown's original road-going prototype!). The body was mounted to the chassis by four of the popular Silentbloc bushes.

The body styling was subtle and deceptive. From the side it had a fastback look which would not seem out of place today, except for the lack of any rear spoiler. In a front three-quarter view however the DB2 looks much more conventionally three-box,

> *'...Aston Martin later succumbed to mild American influence ...'*

yet still undeniably handsome. A distinguishing feature of the earliest DB2s was a front grille with vertical bars; Aston Martin later succumbed to mild American influence and changed to horizontal bars, making the car look lower and wider. The body was remarkably compact, with an overall length of 162.5 in for the wheelbase of 99 in. When you allow for those 16 in wheels, that argues very modest overhangs. In fact, while the tail was long enough to be graceful (and never mind what the presence or absence of 19 gallons of rear-cantilevered fuel did to the handling!), the nose was very short indeed when seen in profile. One of the body's drawbacks, certainly to modern eyes, is the lack of any boot lid. There was a small hatch

TOP, MIDDLE & LEFT *Views of a 1952 Aston Martin DB2, the car which, after the tentative manufacture of the 'DB1', began the DB lineage. Its body styling looks less dated than the centrally mounted instruments and the split windscreen* **RIGHT** *A 1961 Aston Martin DB2-4 Mk III, which offered more room and speed*

at the rear whose main purpose was to give access to the spare wheel, but the main luggage space was internal, immediately behind the two seats (extra accommodation was to come later).

The other real point of interest in the DB2 was the Bentley-designed engine. This was not without its odd features, such as a crankshaft assembly complete with its four main bearing housings which was inserted into the block from the rear. However, in most respects it was a classic wet-lined block (made deliberately stiff to compensate for the crankshaft admission tunnel) with modest working dimensions of 78 mm bore by 90 mm stroke to achieve its 2580 cc capacity. Certainly it was notable for its

---

'...There was nothing so uncouth as a red line on the rev counter...'

---

smoothness of operation, while the sohc head gave it efficient breathing – via two 1½ in SU carburettors – to confer a maximum power of 105 bhp at 5000 rpm. A specific power output of 41 bhp/litre may not seem much to us today, but the 'pool' petrol of 1950 forced a compression ratio of 6.5:1.

In the circumstances, it was clearly a good thing that the combined weight of chassis and body was moderate – a little under 2500 lb which was no mean achievement, considering the need to accommodate features like those brake drums. Again, you have to bear in mind the standards of the day when looking at perform .ce figures for the DB2. *The Autocar*'s first road test produced a maximum speed of 110 mph (177 kph) and a 0–60 mph time of 12.4 secs; a typical contemporary big family saloon like the Austin A70 tested by the same magazine in the same year, managed 80 mph and 22.3 secs. In any case, customers could ring the changes to some extent because each was treated as an individual. In its 1950 test, *The Autocar* made the point that higher compression ratios were already available for the engine, which could explain why *The Motor*'s rival test quoted a 7.5:1 compression ratio, 116 bhp at 5500 rpm, a maximum speed of 116 mph (187 kph) and a 0–60 time of 11.2 secs.

The gearbox was a four-speed unit of David Brown manufacture. Again, there was a customer choice: it cost 10 guineas to specify a non-standard set of internal and final-drive ratios. The choice also extended to central floor or steering-column gearchanges (the latter was all the rage at the time, although most surviving DB2s thus equipped have been reconverted since). There was nothing so uncouth as a red line on the rev counter, but the handbook recommended 5000 rpm as a normal limit to allow maximum speeds of roughly 40, 60 and 90 mph (64, 97 and 145 kph) in the lower gears. This again implies that first gear

---

---

was too high to minimise the standing-start time.

The DB2 was a success, even though it was not built in large numbers. In roughly three years of production (mid-1950 to mid-1953) just over 400 were made, of which 50 were the rare drophead version. Three cars a week was a start, but David Brown wanted the car to appeal to a wider audience and the obvious way to do that was to upgrade it from a strict two-seater to an 'occasional' four-seater. There was already a moderate amount of room aft of the existing seats but nothing like enough headroom; there was also the question of where to put the luggage once the main existing stowage had been given over to a back seat.

'...highly practical...one of the earliest true hatchback arrangements...'

The answer was to extend the tail and the roof, adding 7 in to the overall length and giving more of a bulged rear profile which some consider to spoil the original classic DB2 line. It was however a highly practical and still very attractive arrangement, upon which the seal was set with one of the earliest true hatchback arrangements, giving access to the extended rear load platform. Another immediately obvious change was the adoption of a single-piece curved windscreen. 'It must be admitted,' said *The Autocar* test of the DB2–4 in 1953, 'that both headroom and legroom are a little cramped for back seat passengers, particularly if the front seats are set well back'. Even so, the seats were there and they added greatly to the appeal of the car, as did the proper luggage platform which was almost three feet long and wide, and much larger than that if the back seats were neatly folded flat. There was a loss in that the fuel tank had

been squeezed down from 19 to 17 gallons, but against that the longer tail gave near-perfect balance, *The Autocar* quoting 50.4%/49.6% front/rear weight distribution compared with 52/48 for the first DB2.

By the time the DB2-4 had reached production, the dreaded 72-octane pool petrol had gone and premium grades were once more available. The compression ratio of the 2.6-litre engine was therefore raised to 8.2:1 for a power output of 125 bhp at 5000 rpm.

This was just about enough to offset the extra weight of the car (the DB2-4 weighed an extra 150 lb) and *The Autocar* road test figures included a maximum speed of 111 mph (179 kph) and a 0–60 mph time of 12.6 secs. A drophead version continued to be offered but was never overly popular, partly because it now sacrificed much more in the way of accommodation and practicality to the 2+2 hatchback.

Although the road testers were too polite

to say so, it was not really sufficient that Aston Martin performance should have stood still when standards generally were beginning to rise quite quickly. The company was none the less well aware of it, and inside a year the 2.6-litre engine was stretched by the simple expedient of adapting the block to take new liners with an 83 mm bore. This pushed up the capacity to 2922 cc and the power to 140 bhp at 5000 rpm; more important, it resulted in a notable gain in torque output. Less than a year after its 2.6-litre test, *The Autocar* followed up with the 2.9-litre and reported maximum speed up to 119 mph (192 kph), with the 0–60 mph time reduced to 11.1 secs, and all without overall fuel consumption penalty.

The DB2-4 was a big step in the right direction and the two years of 'Mark I' production saw nearly 600 built, including 75 dropheads. Then in 1955 there appeared the Mark II which was something of a cosmetic update, with a restyled tail adding another two inches to the overall length, and a revised bonnet with the side panels now fixed and split from the front-hinged opening section. The interior was also revised, the most notable and convenient change being the switch from an umbrella-handle handbrake under the dash, to a decent floor-mounted type. Also, a third body type was added to the range, a rather ordinary-looking notchback which was built by Tickford.

Perhaps deservedly, the Mark II did not

fare as well as its predecessor, for in two years production ran only to 200 examples of which a mere 40-odd were notchbacks and a further 25 were dropheads. It is also perhaps significant that neither of the British road-test journals of records ever carried a proper Mark II test. Before using this as evidence that the Mark II was a rather awkward interim device, however, you would do well to remember that these were the years of the Suez Crisis, of petrol rationing and the first hint of 'energy crunches' yet to come.

By 1957, Aston Martin was ready with the final incarnation of its original roadster series, the DB2-4 Mark III, which quickly became known more simply as the DB Mark III and thus inevitably suffered confusion with the purely racing DB3. The Mark III was no mere cosmetic update but offered two

---

'…a major redesign of the engine… in the light of racing experience…'

---

important mechanical advances. One was a major redesign of the engine (much of it in the light of racing experience with the DB3) and the other was front disc brakes.

Although the engine retained its working dimensions, its crankcase and crankshaft were new and, in particular, the liners were now top-seated rather than spigotted into an open deck. A revised head and manifold layout helped ensure that, although the standard compression ratio remained at 8.2:1, the power went up to 162 bhp at 5500 rpm. On top of that, owners could specify two more powerful versions with an 8.6:1 compression, the DBD with three SU carburettors and 180 bhp, or the DBB with three Webers and 195 bhp (the standard version of the revised engine was designated DBA).

The front disc brakes answered criticisms which had emerged from otherwise favourable road tests almost from the outset. Servo (hydraulic) assistance was needed to keep pedal pressures within bounds but the be-

haviour in prolonged hard use was much improved; rude comments about increasing pedal travel, noise and judder ceased.

Together with these mechanical improvements, Frank Feeley restyled the body once again, and to much better effect. The tail of the Mark III looked more 'of a piece' with properly integrated light clusters (the Mark II was accused of looking as though Morris Minor clusters had been added as an afterthought) while the nose was beautifully changed in shape to take on the characteristic grille form and overall profile first seen on the DB3S racer, and eventually carried over to the DB4/5/6 series. As for the interior, Aston Martin bowed to the modern trend and shifted the instrument panel from the centre of the dash to a new binnacle in front of the driver.

Beyond doubt, the engine changes restored the performance to respectable levels by 1957 standards. *The Autocar* took the Mark III to a 119 mph (192 kph) maximum but, more importantly, lowered the 0–60 mph time to 9.3 secs. The Aston Martin had once again become a true performance car – and it had brakes to match.

It says something for improved economic circumstances, but also for the esteem in which the handsome new version was held, that the production rate almost tripled once the Mark III had established itself. Again in a two-year production span, from 1957 to 1959, over 550 examples were made, including a handful of notchback coupés and the usual dribble of convertibles.

However successful the Mark III, its days were numbered once the DB4 had been launched in 1958. The new car, bigger, more powerful but also more civilised in its ride and ease of driving, put the old DB into perspective, and in 1959 production of the original series came to an end. It will, however, always retain its classic status partly for the competition successes it enjoyed in the early 1950s when the company was in need of a lift for its image, but mainly as the design which carried a large part of Britain's high-performance reputation through a decade and which was good enough to enable Aston Martin to consolidate and move on to greater things.   JRD

AUDI
quattro

quattro

Audi designer Ferdinand Piech promises that four-wheel drive will become as common as four-wheel brakes. The great quattro has already started the ever growing trend

IT WAS IN MARCH 1980 that Audi revealed their interpretation of a high-performance four-wheel-drive coupé. There, at the Geneva Show ready for the press to drive and the public to view, was a new four-wheel-drive design clothed in two-door bodywork that would serve as the basis for a multiple winner of the World Rally Championship during the 1980s.

More significantly, the quattro (the lower-case q was registered as the company's official trademark in 1984) would make every other motor manufacturer look at four-wheel-drive in a new light. Many of them followed the all-wheel-drive route (albeit using different technical solutions of varying merit), with more new four-wheel-drive cars to be announced in the late '80s.

Audi had studied what had gone before in this field and made unprecedented use of existing parts and previous military four-wheel-drive knowledge, slashing development time and production costs with unmatched ingenuity.

In effect the company's engineers reinvented four-wheel-drive for two primary purposes. The first was to overcome the limited ability of powerful front- or rear-drive cars to cope with the new high-output generation of turbo motors. Secondly, having shown that speed and safety could be incorporated in one practical package, they then had to demonstrate its advantages in the most public manner possible. They chose world championship rallying, and caused the rule book to be rewritten in the process... .

Audi did not, however, invent the first high-performance four-wheel-drive coupé. The prophetic voice had come from Jensen in Britain's Midlands, who between 1966 and '71 made 318 Ferguson Formula (FF) Interceptor V8 coupés, superb machines which only failed to have greater influence on the industry and car-buying public because of their very high price.

During the 1970s, Audi's chief chassis engineer Jorg Bensinger had the occasional task of explaining to outsiders, such as journalists, the advantages and disadvantages of front- and rear-drive systems. He made up a chart which compared the strengths and weaknesses of the popular engine/transmission and drive layouts. It contrasted systems such as Audi's front drive, front engine and gearbox with Porsche's rear-engined 911. Also shown were then conventional cars such as the Ford Escort, with front engine and live-axle rear-drive.

This chart made it obvious that when it came to handling over 200 bhp at the driven wheels, two-wheel-drive systems had severe drawbacks. Former Porsche, BMW and Mercedes employee Bensinger came to the conclusion that the worst snags in such cars were poor traction under full power, constant danger of skidding in bad weather, wildly varied cornering performance when power was abruptly removed or applied in mid-corner, and very rapid tyre wear on all really powerful cars.

All-wheel-drive was the obvious theoretical answer, but when Bensinger was making such comparisons Audi showed no sign

PREVIOUS PAGE *A 1985 Audi quattro*
TOP LEFT *Stig Blomqvist on his way to winning the 1983 RAC Rally*
LEFT *Hannu Mikkola and Arne Hertz during the 1984 RAC Rally*
BELOW *The RAC again, this time in 1982 with Michelle Mounton and Fabrizia Pons*

of having the resources for such a radical solution.

However, in the '70s Audi began to blossom under VW's ownership, and the key ingredients of what would become the quattro started to appear.

For example there was the unique in-line five-cylinder engine, also part of every quattro until the four-cylinder 80q was introduced in Germany last year. That tough engine, with its steel crankshaft, iron block, alloy cylinder head and single-overhead-cam first appeared in the rebodied Audi 100 saloon of 1976. That was a front-wheel-drive saloon with the engine mounted way ahead of the front axle, a layout that was to become an Audi tradition.

Even in 1972 Audi listed an 80 saloon of similar design (but with a four-cylinder engine) and it was this model that literally provided the foundation for the first quattro coupé, for its stretched floorpan was incorporated under both the front-drive Audi

---

'...Audi 200...was the most powerful...saloon in the world...'

Coupé of 1980 and the Geneva Show quattro prototype. The two-wheel-drive coupé was actually announced after the quattro, but VAG in the UK introduced them simultaneously in England in the spring of 1981.

The reason why this first quattro was a turbocharged five-cylinder can be traced to September 1979's top model Audi 200 saloon, a derivative of the 100. This car, capable of over 130 mph (210 kph), was the most powerful front-wheel-drive saloon in the world when it was announced, less than a year before the quattro, for its non-intercooled version of the 2144 cc (79.5 mm × 86.4 mm) five produced 170 bhp. This engine was thus a considerable help in providing a reliable 200 bhp for the following quattro coupé, which featured an intercooler as standard.

Other key items in the transmission and suspension were production parts from

MODEL
Audi quattro (1985)

UK price: £13,928

ENGINE
Location: Front, longitudinal
Type: Water-cooled in-line five cylinder with six main bearings. Cast-iron block and light-alloy head
Cubic capacity: 2144 cc
Bore × stroke: 79.5 mm × 86.4 mm
Compression ratio: 7.0:1
Valve gear: 2 valves per cylinder operated by single belt-driven overhead camshaft and thimble tappets
Fuel supply: Bosch K-Jetronic fuel injection with KKK turbocharger and intercooler
Ignition: Electronic
Maximum power: 200 bhp (DIN) at 5500 rpm
Maximum torque: 211 lb ft (DIN) at 3500 rpm

TRANSMISSION
Layout: Gearbox in unit with engine with integral front differential, lockable inter axle differential and lockable rear differential
Clutch: Single dry plate
Gearbox: Five-speed manual

1st 3.60:1	4th 0.778:1
2nd 2.125:1	5th 0.71:1
3rd 1.458:1	

Final drive: Hypoid bevel
Ratio: 3.889:1 (front and rear)

SUSPENSION
Front: Independent with MacPherson struts, lower wishbones and anti-roll bar
Rear: Independent with MacPherson struts, lower wishbones and anti-roll bar

STEERING
Type: Rack and pinion, servo assisted

BRAKES
Type: Discs front and rear

WHEELS AND TYRES
Type: 15 × 6 inch alloy wheels with 205/60VR × 15 tyres

BODY/CHASSIS
Type: Integral with front auxiliary sub frame. 2-door coupé body

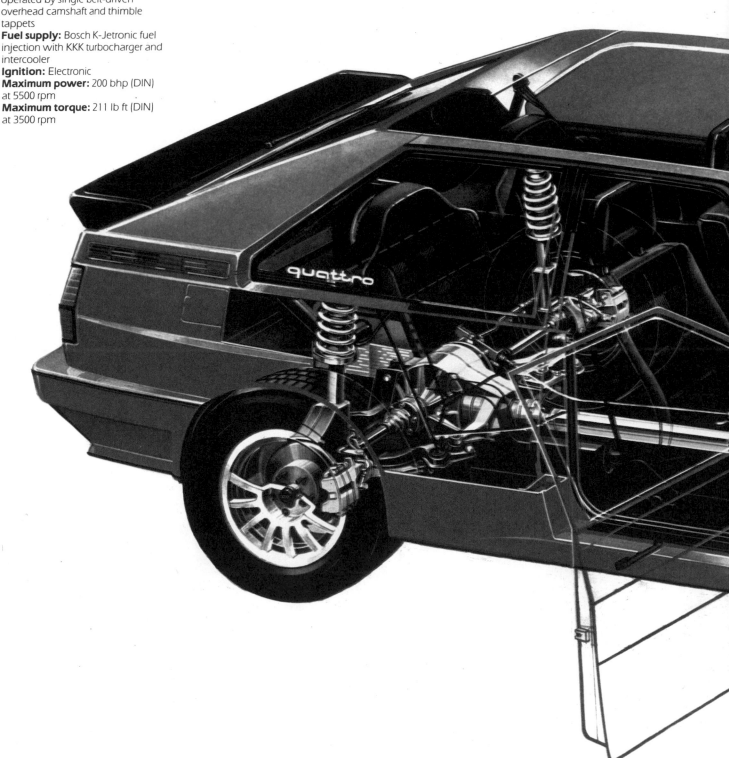

DIMENSIONS AND WEIGHT

Length: 173.39 in (440 cm)
Width: 67.83 in (172 cm)
Wheelbase: 99.37 in (252 cm)
Track – front: 55.94 in (142 cm)
       – rear: 57.13 in (145 cm)
Weight: 2866 lb (1300 kg)

PERFORMANCE

Maximum speed: 132 mph
(212.5 kph)
Acceleration 0–60 mph: 7.8
seconds
Fuel consumption (approx):
21 mpg

The quattro succeeded in starting a trend to four-wheel drive for the road where the Jensen FF of the '60s failed. The permanently engaged four-wheel-drive system is a relatively simple design, inspired by an off-road vehicle, the military VW Iltis. One of its most interesting features is the use of concentric front propeller shafts, the inner one taking the drive back from the central differential to the front differential. That was one way in which Audi managed to achieve a good ground clearance

other models, but where did Audi find the resources to incorporate four-wheel-drive?

Jorg Bensinger recalled the significance of a drab military vehicle called the Iltis that Audi had developed and manufactured for Audi's VW parents to sell for German army use: 'I think it was in 1976 that I realised what was possible with four-wheel-drive for us. We tested the Iltis on the road, and then during the following winter we tested it in Scandinavia. It only had the four-cylinder 1.6-litre engine, no more than 75 bhp, and it was very tall with a short wheelbase. I didn't expect much handling from a machine with the centre of gravity so high in the air, but I was really pleased with its performance on the ice and snow: I became convinced that this could be the future for road cars too.'

Initially Herr Bensinger's inclination was to convert something like the 100 saloon, but Ferdinand Piech, Audi's board member with responsibility for all research and development, had very different ideas. Herr Piech, a significant figure in Porsche's his-

tory and particularly in the development of the 911 road car and 917 flat-12 racer, thought about Bensinger's proposal overnight. Thereafter he became *the* top level quattro loyalist within the Audi company, taking ultimate responsibility for the engineering (but not the detailed execution of the design) both in competition and road car development. It was Dr. Piech who decreed that competition was the only credible way to demonstrate the quattro system's advantages and reliability, and Dr. Piech who realised the advantages of applying the system to a sporting car rather than an everyday saloon. Thus the company could go into production gradually, introducing the system into cheaper and more mass-produced cars if all went well.

Bensinger actually went ahead and issued instructions for the first prototype to be built before official approval was given, and thus had already had some running experience of that A1-coded quattro 80 with the simple Iltis drivetrain (no centre differential was

ABOVE The quattro in full flight during the 1984 San Remo Rally
ABOVE RIGHT The quattro of Mikkola and Hertz in the '83 Safari
RIGHT Walter Roehrl's quattro receives attention during the '85 Monte Carlo
BELOW Roehrl again, winning the '84 Ulster Rally
BELOW LEFT An '85 short-wheelbase quattro Sport which produces 305 bhp at 6500 rpm

installed) when the instruction to proceed with a full-scale programme was issued in September 1977.

Naturally there were development dramas, but usually only when testing to the limit – for example there was a fire in the Sahara desert with a 286 bhp prototype, an engine which nevertheless confirmed its basic bottom-end strength.

Former Mercedes competition and road-car engineer Hans Nedvidek was given the task of designing a suitable transmission system which would also be as light as possible. It was not an easy task, for most modern four wheel-drive systems not only have front and rear differentials, but also a central one that civilises road behaviour by harmonising front and rear wheel speeds after interconnection, and of course this takes up much valuable space. Such differentials are frequently housed in a separate transfer case and need additional propshafts front and rear, and that case will often house

> ‘… a straightforward 50/50 split, achieved with bevel gearing… ’

extra gears to split the power front and rear.

Typical modern systems split roughly a third of the power to the front wheels and two-thirds aft, whereas competition Ferguson systems vary the front/rear power splits between 25/75 for tarmac to a 50/50 balance for the most slippery surfaces. Nedvidek and his team decided on a straight forward 50/50 split, achieved with bevel gearing, but the cleverest feature was to incorporate a hollow shaft within the largely standard Audi 100/200 five-speed gearbox.

Within a length of just over 10 inches (25 cm), Audi included a shaft within a shaft, feeding power from the central differential to the forward diff. Power to the rear was taken simply by propshaft from the rear of the gearbox. Audi were exceptionally fortunate that their standard front-drive layout was a simple longitudinal one, for it made the conversion comparatively easy once they had come up with the hollow transmission

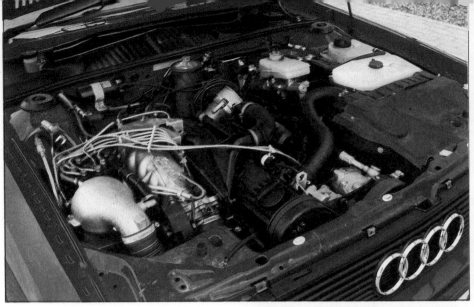

idea for the lower gearbox shaft, which still wore its gear-ratio clusters externally.

As can be imagined, the precision machining needed to achieve the reliable shaft within a shaft was an expensive process, but the weight-saving value could not be ignored. Even today, Audi engineers have some difficulty in convincing the outside world just how expensive that sort of work was in the low-production early days; the quattro's cost was further boosted by the fact that each floorpan had to be individually converted to accomodate the additional rear drive at Baur in Stuttgart. Since then the quattro system has remained fundamentally unchanged, the only significant detail changes concerning the locking centre and rear differentials. These were originally cable-operated from a central transmission tunnel lever set, but vacuum assistance and push-pull knobs and then rotary switchgear, have replaced the original layout, which

> ' *The suspension and braking typified Audi's parts-bin ingenuity…* '

transmitted too much road noise.

The suspension and braking typified Audi's parts-bin ingenuity, for virtually all the components had served in other models. In fact the rear suspension was simply the MacPherson strut/wide-base wishbone system found at the front of many Audis, reversed and with the steering arms replaced by solid transverse links. The struts were taken from the Audi 80/100 series and the driveshafts also came from other models.

Disc brakes were fitted all round, ventilated at the front, and the system was hydraulically powered, like the rack and pinion steering, by a new engine-driven pump. The latter is one of the nicest variable-assistance power steering systems on the market, and its precision and worth can be gauged from the fact that the rally team continued to use it with their 500 bhp cars.

That first quattro coupé used the usual 2144 cc of the largest Audi five-cylinder in association with a KKK-K26 turbocharger

which had a boost pressure maximum of just over 12 psi. Compression within the two-valve per cylinder combustion chambers was the then high figure of 7:1, made possible by an intercooler, transistorised Bosch ignition and the carefully monitored K-Jetronic fuel injection.

The first steel-bodied quattro was no flyweight. The official figure was just over 2800 lb (1270 kg), yet with 200 bhp at 5500 rpm, plus 210.5 lb ft of torque, the distinctive quattro coupé would exceed 135 mph (217 kph), despite its poor aerodynamic qualities when compared to the later Audi 100. According to *Autocar* it could reach 60 mph (97 kph) in 7.1 seconds, and average fuel consumption was 19–21 mpg.

Deliveries of the first quattro commenced in September 1980, but it was March 1981 before they began to arrive in Britain, still in left-hand drive and priced at £14,500 (right-hand-drive models arrived in

1982). In 1980 Audi made less than 300 quattros, but by 1983 they were talking in thousands, for the plan to make four-wheel-drive available downmarket had resulted in the 136 bhp Audi 80 saloon. To get the price well below the equivalent of £10,000 in Germany, the four-door quattro used a straight-forward fuel-injected 2.1-litre five, and after it was shown to the press, in December 1982, sales reached over 5000 in the first year on the German market. With a 136 bhp engine in a body only 200 lb (91 kg) lighter than the original turbo coupé, the 80q's performance was much less exciting, but with a top speed of nearly 120 mph and a 0–60 mph time of under 10 seconds, it competed very well against BMW's 3-series.

The 80q arrived in Britain in the summer

EVOLUTION

Introduced in 1980, the four-wheel-drive Audi quattro coupé was a two-door five-seater based on the modified floorpan of the Audi 80 saloon. The transmission consisted of permanently engaged four-wheel drive with dual-cable operation for the centre and rear differential locks. The quattro was powered by a 2144 cc five-cylinder engine with Bosch K-Jetronic fuel injection and a KKK-K26 turbocharger, with a 12.09 psi wastegate maximum. It produced 200 bhp at 5500 rpm and 210 lb ft of torque at 3500 rpm, and the car was capable of 135 mph (217 kph) and 0–60 mph in 7.3 seconds. The suspension was all independent, with MacPherson struts front and rear

1981 Group 4 quattro coupé announced, for homologation purposes. The engine was available in a variety of tunings, producing up to 320 bhp and 304 lb ft of torque. Its transmission featured a limited-slip differential at the rear, a solid-shaft centre differential and a competition clutch. The bodyshell was much strengthened with an internal roll cage, the rear spoiler was enlarged and wheel arches flared to accommodate wider wheels – which could be specified with 10 in rims. Depending on the gearbox ratios, maximum speed ranged between 108 mph (173 kph) and 158 mph (254 kph), with 0–60 mph times as low as 4.9 seconds. The Group 4 car was up to 200 lb (90 kg) lighter than the standard coupé, depending on modifications.

1983 Audi quattro A1 announced, its engine available in 2145 cc or (with larger bore) 2178 cc forms. Turbo boost maximum was 27 psi, giving the engine a turbo-multiplied capacity of 3048 cc. Maximum power output was 340 bhp at 6000 rpm and 305 lb ft at 3600 rpm. The bodywork was extensively modified to be both lighter and stronger, and a variety of suspension options were available. A typical example had a maximum speed of 115 mph (185 kph) and a 0–60 mph in 4.5 seconds, delivering 5–6 mpg. The price was around £75,000. Also announced that year was the Group B quattro A2, its engine further modified to produce up to 400 bhp at 7000 rpm and 362 lb ft of torque. It had no centre differential and its weight was reduced to between 2200 lb (100 kg) and 2420 lb (1100 kg), the latter version for forest use. In September appeared the Audi quattro Sport, a short-wheelbase model with a 300 bhp/243 lb ft engine, and its transmission included a pneumatic two-stage control to engage either the centre differential lock or the centre plus rear differential locks. It was capable of 155 mph (249 kph) and 0–60 mph in 4.5 seconds. Price was £51,282. That year also saw the debut of the American version of the coupé, less powerful than the European version and a 160 bhp/170 lb ft engine.

1984 The coupé was fitted with an LCD illuminated dashboard and the wheel arches were flared to accommodate wider wheels.

Detail of the '85 quattro
TOP LEFT *The quattro's turbocharged in-line five-cylinder engine produces 200 bhp at 5500 rpm*
LEFT *The interior design is one of the quattro's weakest points*

of '83, right-hand drive and priced at over £11,000, and that year the signs of the quattro's explosive growth became clear, both up and down market.

At the Frankfurt Show Audi displayed a short-wheelbase Sport version of the quattro coupé, designed to defend their honour from 1984 onwards against a new breed of four-wheel-drive rally supercars specially built to depose the quattro. It had won its first rally world title in 1982, when Hannu Mikkola had become champion driver in a 360 bhp quattro.

The Sport quattro's wheelbase was shortened by more than 13.5 in (34.3 cm) and the wheel-arches fitted with bulging light-weight panels. It was powered by a four-valve per cylinder (20-valve) version of the faithful five, topped with a double-overhead-

> *'...a record number of World Championship rally victories...'*

cam cylinder head. In road trim this provided 300 bhp and a maximum speed of over 150 mph (241 kph) for a purchase price of over £50,000. Production was not expected to go much beyond the necessary 220 units for homologation, and all were left-hand drive.

Down-market, the 80 was offered from September 1983 with a 2-litre five, priced at less than £7000 in Germany (and never imported to Britain). This was the slowest quattro made, capable of 114 mph (183 kph) and 0–62 mph in 10.3 seconds, but with the compensation of nearly 40 mpg at a constant 56 mph (90 kph).

The company have continued their policy of offering an alternative quattro version for each mainline Audi, and although not all have been exported, here is a full list of the quattros currently offered in Germany: the 200 bhp/2.1-litre 200 turbo saloon, the 138 bhp/2.2-litre 100 saloon, the 136 bhp/2.2-litre 90 saloon, the 90 bhp/1.8-litre, carburated 80, and the 112 bhp/1.8-litre 80 saloon (the 80s are the only four-cylinder quattros), plus the Avant sporting estate bodies upon 100 and 200 saloon running gear. The Avants have a quattro equivalent for both turbo and non-turbo five-cylinder engines.

Quite a quattro list! Now add in the fact that, struggling or not, Audi gained a record number of World Championship rally victories in 1984, to take both the world marque and driver titles.

The quattro is also assured of a place in motoring history as the car that influenced a wave of similar high-performance cars all over the world, including prestigious performers from Porsche, BMW, Lancia-Ferrari and (possibly) Mercedes. Audi have proved that four-wheel-drive can be combined with performance and economy, and the development story is still unfolding. Perhaps one day 4WD will be universal.   JW

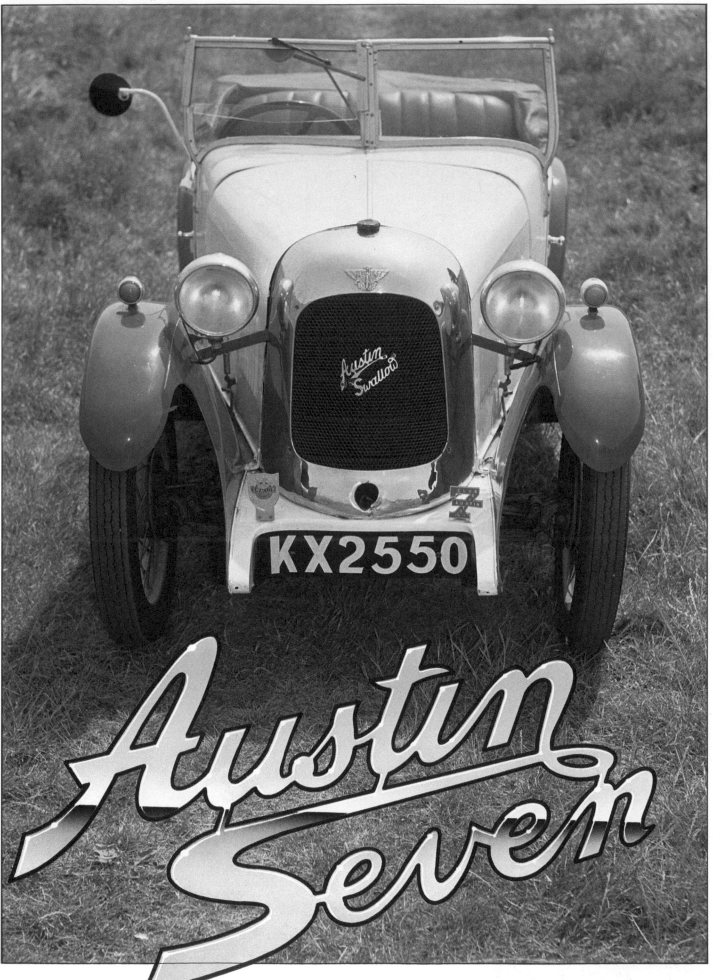

KX2550

Austin Seven

WHEN AUSTIN ANNOUNCED its 696 cc Seven model in July 1922 it was the smallest capacity British made four-cylinder car on the market. It represented a considerable gamble by the Longbridge company which was just emerging from the most crucial financial period in its history and Sir Herbert Austin himself had personally financed the venture in the face of opposition from his co-directors.

In fact the Seven proved an outstanding success; it enjoyed a 17-year production run, from 1922 until 1939, and over 290,000 examples were built. The Seven was the best selling Austin model from 1926 until 1932 and production did not even peak until 1935. It also killed off the flimsy cycle car and provided transport for many families who might otherwise have gone by train.

Although Sir Herbert can be credited with the idea of producing a very small car, the concept of the diminutive four-cylinder engine, which was pivotal to the model's success, came from an 18-year-old draughtsman, Stanley Howard Edge.

Herbert Austin was 38 years old when he left the Wolseley company, where he was general manager, and established the Austin Motor Company in a former printing works at Longbridge, Birmingham in 1905. The coming of war in 1914 transformed the Longbridge works which, by the end of hostilities in 1918, had grown enormously. Sir Herbert, as he had become in 1917, decided to scrap his pre-war range and, like Henry Ford and his Model T, concentrate on just one model. That was the 3.6-litre Twenty, introduced at the end of 1919.

Although 4319 Twenties were built in 1920 demand fell off sharply at the end of the year when the post-war boom suddenly collapsed. Austin's problems were compounded when the so-called Horsepower Tax arrived in 1921 whereby a car's Road Fund Licence was dependent on the RAC horsepower rating. And at £1 per horse power, the Twenty rated at 22.4 hp, which meant the luckless owner would have to pay a £22 yearly tax.

The firm's finances suffered to such an

**'... proved an out-
standing success... over
290,000 were built...'**

extent that, in the April of 1921 (a year of ferocious depression throughout Britain) a receiver was appointed on behalf of the Midland Bank and the Eagle Star Insurance Company, Austin's principal creditors. What was required was a new, smaller car; Sir Herbert realised that with the Twenty he had introduced the wrong model at the wrong time. He took the large car's design and scaled it down to make a 1.6-litre version. Despite the commercial potential of such a model, the receiver would not sanction funds for its development, so Austin was forced to raise funds by selling unwanted

The Austin Seven of 1922 was the first civilised motor car of truly small proportions. It managed to breed contempt and inspire loyalty for nearly two decades

plant and stock. His fortitude was rewarded for after the new Twelve had arrived in 1921 it was soon outselling its larger brother, and remained in production until 1935; it was even produced in taxi form until the outbreak of World War II.

But Sir Herbert wanted another string to his bow. What was required, he felt, was a really small car, rather in the manner of the 8 hp air-cooled two-cylinder Rover, introduced in 1920. Yet although Austin was an accomplished stylist and possessed great drive and determination he was no innovator and was usually content to rely on other manufacturers to provide the inspiration for his designs. He needed someone well acquainted with current design trends who could be used as a foil for his ideas. Fortunately he had found such a person in the Austin drawing office – an 18-year-old draughtsman named Stanley Edge.

Stanley Edge, born in 1903, is a Black Countryman, who hails from Old Hill, Staffordshire. He had been attracted by engineering while at school and asked his father to see if there were any vacancies in the Longbridge drawing office. He did just that and took some examples of Stanley's engineering drawings to the chief draughtsman at the Austin works. This resulted in young Edge getting a job with the firm in August 1917. Soon he began attending the Austin technical college.

At this time aircraft were being produced at Longbridge and Stanley began in the aviation drawing office. But this was no more than a war-time interlude; he was advised to transfer to the car side of the

LEFT *A 1929 Austin Swallow – a conversion available with hood, detachable coupé or hard top*
ABOVE *A 1927 Austin Chummy*

business and this he did by the time the Armistice was signed in November 1918. However, as Stanley used to travel by train line between Old Hill and Longbridge he would arrive at work at 8 am on the only available train, and an hour earlier than the rest of the staff. The office was empty at this time with the exception of Sir Herbert Austin himself and as Edge later remembered: 'we began to discuss design together'.

When Stanley Edge returned from his summer holidays in August 1921, his boss A.J. Hancock wanted to see him 'and when he asked me to sit down I thought I was going to be asked to leave the company'. He asked Edge how he would feel about going to work with Sir Herbert Austin at his home, Lickey Grange. (This was because, although Edge did not know it at the time, Austin had been unable to get any support within the factory for his small car project, so was financing it out of his own pocket).

So, in September 1921, Stanley Edge began work at the Grange; all day Edge worked in the billiards room at the Grange and Austin would arrive in the evening to discuss what he had achieved.

Austin had already done some preliminary work on the design of his baby car. Not surprisingly his first thoughts for a small Austin closely followed the lines of the Tyseley-built air-cooled twin but the Rover was a noisy and crude contraption and Stanley wasted little time in pointing out its deficiencies. It says much for the youngster's direct and informed approach that he was able to get the 55-year-old Austin to abandon the idea of twin and adopt, instead, a small water-cooled four.

Not that Sir Herbert gave up without a fight. For a time the pair wrestled with the pros and cons of a three-cylinder engine while a further excursion into unorthodoxy had a rear-mounted three-cylinder radial engine with the car's wheels set out in a diamond pattern. It was not until the early months of 1922 that these deliberations came to an end for Austin was convinced by Edge that a small four could be produced almost as cheaply as a two-cylinder motor. It

**'The one that caught
Austin's eye was the
668 cc Peugeot'**

would also be far smoother and more refined than the twin.

Edge had compiled a list of 26 small cars, the specifications of which he had culled from the pages of *Motor Trader* magazine. The one that really caught Austin's eye was the 668 cc Peugeot Quadrilette which at the time was the world's smallest production four. Peugeot had established a tradition for building such cars which dated back to 1912 when it introduced its Ettore Bugatti-designed Bébé but the 1920 Quadrilette, with its unusual tandem seating, was even smaller. Austin was sufficiently convinced

MODEL
Austin Seven (1925)

UK price when introduced: £225

ENGINE
Location: Front, longitudinal
Type: Water-cooled in-line four
Cubic capacity: 747.5 cc
Bore × stroke: 56 mm × 76.2 mm
Compression ratio: 4.9:1
Valve gear: Side valves, two per cylinder
Fuel supply: Single Zenith updraft carburettor
Ignition: Magneto
Maximum power: 10.5 bhp at 2400 rpm

TRANSMISSION
Layout: Clutch and gearbox in-unit
Clutch: Single dry plate
Gearbox: Three-speed manual
   1st 3.26:1   3rd 1.0:1
   2nd 1.0:1
Final drive: Spiral bevel
Ratio: 4.9:1

SUSPENSION
Front: Transverse, semi-elliptic leaf springs
Rear: Semi-floating live axle with torque tube. Quarter-elliptic leaf springs.

STEERING
Type: Worm and sector

BRAKES
Type: Drums front and rear, footbrake on rear, handbrake on front

WHEELS AND TYRES
Type: Wire wheels, 700 × 80 tyres

BODY/CHASSIS
Type: U-section steel A-frame chassis with four-seater tourer body

DIMENSIONS AND WEIGHT
Length: 106 in (2692 mm)
Width: 46 in (1168 mm)
Wheelbase: 75 in (1905 mm)
Track – front: 40 in (1016 mm)
Weight: 728 lb (330 kg)

PERFORMANCE
Maximum speed: 35 mph (58 kph)
Fuel consumption: 50 mpg (approx.)

ABOVE Simplicity is the key to the Seven's chassis, although in use the poor suspension location gave rise to some rather quirky handling characteriscics. In sharp corners, for example, the outer rear wheel would move backwards in relation to the chassis and the inner one forwards producing quite violent oversteer which was characteristic of the Seven. Additional axle location was later added to alleviate this problem. Later chassis were given extension pieces to cope with heavier bodywork and indeed many body variations were seen before the demise of the Model.

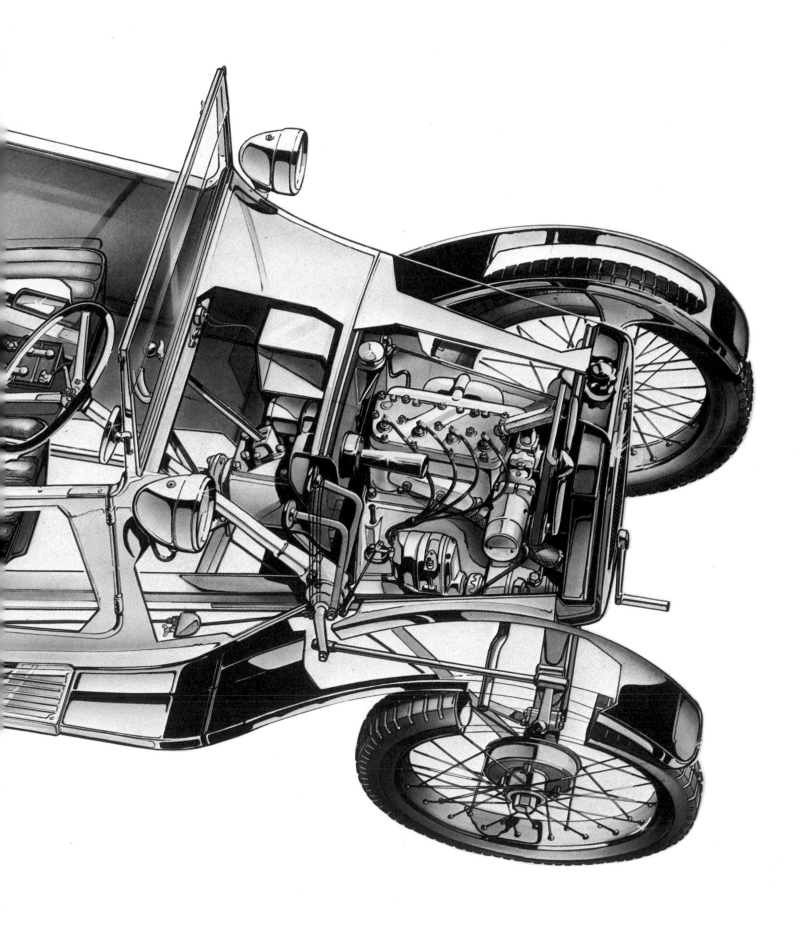

EVOLUTION

The Austin Seven was announced in July 1922 to become the smallest capacity British four-cylinder, with a displacement of just 696 cc

1923 Engine size was increased from 696 cc to 748 cc thanks to an increase in bore size. A fan was added to the engine and an electric starter introduced

1924 The Sports Tourer introduced

1926 The Seven Saloon was introduced

1927 A fabric-bodied version was introduced but only built until 1930

1928 The 'Top Hat' body style was introduced and a nickel-plated radiator replaced the painted type

1929 The lowered Ulster Seven was introduced with optional Cozette supercharger

1930 The brake system became entirely foot operated

1931 Wheelbase and rear track were increased

1933 A four-speed gearbox was introduced and the brakes and tyres uprated. The Opal two-seater was introduced, along with the lowered 65 Seven which had an engine tuned to produce 23 bhp at 4800 rpm

1934 The 65 was renamed the Nippy and the Speedy introduced. Synchromesh appeared on third and fourth gears and the Ruby was introduced along with the Pearl Cabriolet

1936 A central main bearing was added to the 748 cc engine along with a new cylinder head and different spark plugs. Power output was increased to 17 bhp. A twin-cam single seater was introduced for competition. Girling hydraulic brakes replaced the cable variety

1939 The final Austin Seven was built on 17 January

---

for Edge to begin, 'I was the only man on this work and I made out arrangements of detail drawings of everything'. Although the Peugeot had provided the inspiration for the baby Austin for its detail design Edge was inspired by yet another European manufacturer. A keen motor cyclist, he had been much impressed by the four-cylinder Belgian FN and the lower half of the Seven's engine, with its two roller-bearing splash-lubricated crankshaft, were inspired by this motor cycle unit. The remainder of the design followed traditional Austin practice; a side-valve cylinder block, with detachable head, bolted directly on an aluminium crankcase. As designed by Edge, the Seven had a capacity of 696 cc (55 × 77 mm) and a 7.2 hp RAC rating. Edge was also responsible for calculating the ratios in the three-speed gearbox, the clutch dimensions and the transmission specifications. He was not, however, responsible for the rest of the car, as he was first and foremost an engine specialist.

The chassis, steering box and brakes, along with the designs for the coachwork can be regarded as Austin's contribution to the Seven. He adopted an A-frame chassis and it seems likely that the transverse leaf front and quarter-elliptic rear suspension were borrowed from the Peugeot as were the similar wire-spoked wheels. However, the Seven boasted four-wheel brakes, a revolutionary feature for a small car even though they could hardly be regarded as particularly efficient. All the design work was completed by the Easter of 1922 and on the Tuesday after the holiday, Stanley returned to Longbridge carrying the precious drawings of the Seven. A small section of the works was boarded off so the construction of the prototypes could proceed unimpeded. In addition to Stanley there was works superintendent McLellan, along with foreman Alf Depper, four mechanics and an apprentice. The intention was to have three cars completed by Whitsun.

The Midland Motor Cylinder Company

cast the tiny block and Edge can still recall the astonishment of the MMCC men when they first saw the drawings of the tiny block with 3/32 in between the cylinder walls and the eight minute valve chambers. The crankshafts and rods were machined from solid at Longbridge while Stirling Metals produced the aluminium crankcase, Zenith the carburettor and Watford the magneto.

All three cars were ready for a works gathering held at Longbridge at Whitsun. Although the design of the engine and gearbox had been resolved, each of the prototype Sevens had different transmission arrangements. One had an open propeller shaft, the second had the 'shaft contained within a torque tube while the third, which was adopted for production, had a half open shaft and a half closed one. Edge recalls that the example with an open shaft was particularly difficult to drive, 'It hoped like a kangaroo and Sir Herbert shot off like a rocket between the shop buildings'.

Soon afterwards Edge was present when Austin was familiarly addressed by a young man who arrived, unannounced, at the office, challenging Sir Herbert with 'so this is where you hide yourself away'. A rather stilted conversation followed and Edge produced the Seven's drawings, as they were required. The conversation ended with the young man telling Austin. 'My dear sir, the public will just not stand for this'. Austin responded with similar intransigence. 'My dear sir, I am educating the public'. After the visitor's departure, Austin told Edge his identity; he was William (Billy) Rootes, soon to head the country's largest car distributors and to co-found, with his brother Reginald, the Rootes Group in the 1930s.

Details of the new model were unveiled in the motoring press in July 1922. In the first instance it was only available in open form. It was a real four-seater although only children could be carried in the rear, so it was aimed foursquare at the family man and even though its top speed was around the

> **❛ What more could a man of moderate means want for his money? ❜**

38 mph (61 kph) mark, it was a lion-hearted performer. Turning the scales at a mere 6.5 cwt (330 kg), it cost just £165 when it was introduced. On its launch *The Light Car and Cyclecar* commented, 'What more could a man of moderate means want for his money?'.

The public had the first real opportunity of viewing the Austin Seven at the 1922 Motor Show but the model got off to a slow start and only 1936 were built in 1923, the first year of production. By December a number of changes had been made to the original specification. The first came in March when the engine's capacity was increased from 696 cc to 748 cc, achieved by upping the bore size from 55 mm to 56 mm.

This resulted in the engine's RAC rating also increasing, to 7.8 hp. Then, in October, a fan was added to the engine. Originally it had not been included on cost grounds but the little unit overheated somewhat, so it was found necessary to fit one. This required that the position of the water outlet pipe be changed and Stanley Edge, who had by then

> *'... as effective on the race track as it was on the road... '*

returned to his job in the drawing office, accordingly made the alterations. In December another cost-conscious feature was discontinued. This was a mechanical starter positioned on top of the flywheel. The Seven's owner was intended to grasp the T-shaped handle and pull it smartly as if he were starting a motor mower. It was replaced by a conventional electric starter.

Sales for 1924 were better at 4700 and the car also benefited from the fitment of a speedometer. That year an open Sports Tourer was introduced alongside the Chummy although as the two-seater with its distinctive pointed tail merely had standard mechanical parts it was no great performer. The really significant year for the Seven was 1926 when 14,000 left Longbridge making it the best selling Austin and justifying Sir Herbert's faith in the project. In addition the

ABOVE & RIGHT *A 1934 Austin Seven Box Saloon Deluxe – note the forward mounted lamps, deeper wings and plated radiator, developed from the 65 Seven* **FAR RIGHT & BELOW RIGHT** *A 1934 Austin Seven Nippy; the Nippy was introduced in '34 with an engine tuned to give 23 bhp, developed from the 65 Seven*

firm's board of directors had granted him a £2 royalty on each one built which must have given him great cause for satisfaction. A saloon version of the Seven arrived in May of the same year and in 1927 a fashionable fabric variant appeared. It proved popular for a time but was discontinued in 1930; the metal saloon was more enduring. The widedoor, so-called Top Hat arrived in 1928, the same year in which the painted radiator gave way to a nickel-finished one. Coil ignition replaced the magneto for 1929 while in 1930 came a much needed improvement to the braking system. Originally the cable operated brakes were uncoupled with the foot brake operating on the rear wheels and the handbrake responsible for the front ones. This endured until July 1930 when the entire system became foot operated although, it has to be said, it still left much to be desired!

It was in 1930 that the Austin Seven showed that it was just as effective on the race track as it was on the road when an example, driven by *The Autocar's* Sammy Davis and the Earl of March, gained a victory in the 500 Miles race held at Brooklands. This success represented the culmination of

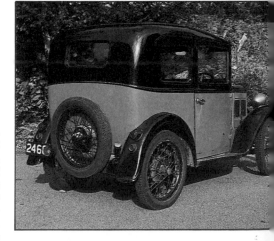

eight years of development with the model. For, back in July 1922 just after Austin had announced the car, an example was placed third in its class in the Shelsley Walsh hill climb. Then, in March 1923 Austin's son-in-law, Arthur Waite won a Brooklands handicap event and the following month took a Seven to Monza, of all places, for the Cyclecar Grand Prix. Again the Seven proved victorious and lapped the Italian circuit at 55.86 mph (89.9 kph). E.C. Gordon England was then approached and began a spectacular racing career at Brooklands with the Seven breaking numerous long distance records. He also maintained the model's 1923 momentum by being placed second in the 1100 cc class in the 200 Miles Race at the same track.

In 1924 the Austin factory introduced its own Sports model which was good for around 50 mph (80 kph) but the same year Gordon England, who also owned a coach-building works, introduced his own Brooklands Super Sports, which was lower than the standard car and capable of 75 mph (120 kph). To prove his point he won the new 750 class in the 1924 200 Miles Race and to show that it was no flash in the pan he repeated the feat in 1925 and 1926. These successes culminated in Austin introducing its own lowered Ulster Seven in 1929 with optional Cozette supercharger.

In truth Austin had the 750 cc class very

much to itself until 1931 but that year MG introduced its 746 cc C-type Midget. Sir Herbert Austin's arch rival, Sir William Morris, had followed in the Seven's wheel tracks and introduced the 847 cc Minor in 1929, although its sophisticated overhead-cam engine was more at home in the M type MG introduced the same year. The smaller

---

*' … managed a class
win in the 1932 British
Empire Trophy race… '*

---

capacity C type was developed specifically for the class which the Sevens had dominated for so long and were immensely successful for the side-valvers were archaic by comparison. They trounced the Austins at the 1931 Double Twelve race; in addition, a continual ding-dong battle for record breaking resulted in the more modern cars from Abingdon having the upper hand, despite Sir Herbert having personally designed the bodywork for a supercharged single seater in 1931.

There was also the Rubber Duck team of Sevens but sadly the cars were plagued with cracked cylinder heads; despite this they managed a class win in the 1932 British Empire Trophy race. The Austin factory was impressed by the performance of an Ulster driven by young Tom Murray Jamieson and

he was hired to sort out the works cars.

Jamieson was, alas, having to make the best of an ageing design although he produced an impressive streamlined single seater in 1935. Whenever Longbridge broke a record, however, MG got it back and Sir Herbert realised that if the Sevens were to make any real impact on the overhead-cam MGs, a completely new design a would be needed. So Jamieson was commissioned to design a new 744cc twin-cam single seater which appeared in 1936, but which falls outside the scope of this article. After some initial teething problems, the new cars found their form but the works MGs had disappeared from the racing circuits because Leonard Lord, Morris's new managing director, had shut down the Abingdon racing department in 1935.

On the road-going Sevens bonnet louvres and trafficators arrived in 1931 and the following year interior accommodation was improved by the Seven's wheelbase being increased by 6 inches (15 cm) from 6 feet 3 inches (190 cm) while the rear track was upped from 3 feet 4 inches (101 cm) to 3 feet 7 inches (109 cm). For 1933 the gearbox received its first major revision since 1922 with the arrival of a crawler cog to make a four speed 'box. At the same time the petrol tank was removed from its traditional position beneath the scuttle, where it supplied the engine by gravity, to the rear. This meant that for the first time the Austin Seven boasted a petrol pump. There were larger

brakes and wider tyres – Sir Herbert's Baby was growing up. Another 1933 arrival was the Opal two seater which, in 1934, was offered in a £100 version. That year the traditional Austin radiator was replaced by a cowl, although the Opal was unique in that it perpetuated the original flat radiator design. Also new for 1933 was the open two-seater

Although the Seven was powered by a diminutive 748 cc engine it was still strong enough to carry a van body, which was introduced in 1923 and continued until the war. Th engine compartment of the first cars was even emptier, without even a cooling fan…which was added later in '23, along with an electric starter

> **❛ …with lowered chassis and engine tuned and refined to give 23 bhp… ❜**

65 Seven with lowered chassis and engine tuned and refined to give 23 bhp at 4800 rpm rather than the standard car's 12 bhp at 2600 rpm. This became the Nippy in 1934, the same year that the similar but more expensive Speedy made its appearance.

The Seven had benefited from synchromesh added to the third and top gears for 1934 and that year came the Ruby which perpetuated the precious stone theme of the Opal. This saloon boasted bumpers, recessed trafficators and the aforementioned cowled radiator. A Pearl Cabriolet arrived at the same time.

It was in 1935, when the Seven was 13 years old, that the model had its best ever production year when 27,280 cars left Longbridge. Then, in June of 1936, the first major revision to the Seven's engine appeared. Although the 748 cc engine remained inviolate, a central main bearing was introduced. Unlike the existing front and rear ones, which were of the roller variety, this was a plain bearing. A new cylinder head was introduced at the same time and 14 mm sparking plugs replaced the 18 mm ones that had been used hitherto. This resulted in output rising from 12 bhp at 3600 rpm to 17 at 3800. At the same time Girling brakes replaced the rather questionable cable-

operated drums that had sufficed until then. On a corporate front this was a big year for Sir Herbert Austin because he was made Baron Austin of Longbridge in Edward VII's one and only birthday honours.

For 1937 the long running Seven was replaced by the 900 cc Big Seven which was to outsell the older car by two to one in 1938. This was the last full year for the Seven but the model lasted into 1939 and the final car was built on 17 January. A van version, which had first appeared back in 1923, lasted about a month and a half longer and was made until 3 March.

Although the Seven had come to the end of the line, its engine continued for another 23 years under the bonnet of the Reliant van and subsequent car until it finally ceased production in 1962. Mention should also be made of the fact that the Seven was built

under licence by the Dixi company in Germany from 1929 until 1932 by which time the firm had been taken over by BMW. Then there was a version by Lucien Rosengart in Paris though, perhaps inevitably, the American Austin Seven, the Bantam, never found its form. In Japan Datsun introduced its version of the design; there were significant mechanical changes although the 748 cc engine was retained.

Also it should not be forgotten that an Austin Seven formed the basis of the first car to be built by William Lyons, a young Blackpool coachbuilder, the stylish Swallow version being built between 1927 and 1932. It was to form the foundation of first the SS and so the Jaguar marque. Post-war, Colin Chapman's first Lotus cars sprang from a much modified Seven. One wonders what Lord Austin would have thought of that?   jw

BMW 328

Its performance was nothing less than breathtaking, yet the pre-war 328 was solidly built and untemperamental. Its 2-litre, six-cylinder engine was a German classic

THERE ARE MANY knowledgeable enthusiasts who would say that if one had to choose one single pre-war car as the most significant in the early development of the modern high-performance sports car, it would have to be the BMW Type 328. Half a century ago, when most German sports cars were uninspired and lacking in performance, the Type 328 made its first appearance at a Nürburgring race meeting, winning its category so convincingly that everybody was highly impressed, and before that first season of competi-

tions ended it was clear that the new model stood head-and-shoulders above the rest.

The 328 was light in weight and good to look at, with lines so far ahead of their time that the car still looked modern a decade later. Its rigid tubular chassis and independent front suspension, allied to rack-and-pinion steering, provided a standard of roadholding and handling that was revolutionary in the middle 1930s, while the six-cylinder engine with its highly unusual valve-gear gave an exceptional power output and a maximum speed of around 100 mph (161 kph).

Until the advent of the Type 328, Bayerische Motoren-Werke had not been greatly admired for their cars. The company had started during World War I as builders of aero engines, and in the early 1920s had earned a fine reputation for their motorcycles, but no cars were produced until in 1928/9 they took over the Dixi factory at Eisenach, where a modified version of the humble Austin Seven was built under licence. For some time the German army had

to do their manoeuvres in these unlikely vehicles, because the Treaty of Versailles forbade their using heavy machinery. There was also a sporting version of the Dixi, not unlike the Austin Seven Ulster model but known as the Wartburg, reviving a name that the Eisenach company had first used at the turn of the century. BMW's experience of the competition world, gained with their motorcycles, helped the little Dixi sports models to win the team prize in the 1929 Austrian Alpine Trial.

In 1932 the BMW company began to move away from their Austin associations with the introduction of the AM-1 or 3/20 model. Its 782 cc engine was related to the Seven unit but had overhead valves, and the chassis was changed completely, being now a central backbone with independent suspension all round by swing axles. This arrangement was not entirely successful, and for the Type 303 of 1933 they reverted to semi-elliptic springs carrying a live axle at the rear. But the chassis frame was now tubular, and there were lower wishbones

The beautifully balanced lines of an immaculately restored BMW 328; its dashboard was extremely informative

instead of swing axles at the front, with a transverse leaf spring.

More significant in BMW's future history was the fact that the Type 303 also had a six-cylinder engine. It was really just the 3/20 engine with two extra cylinders, making the capacity 1173 cc, but this 30 bhp power unit was ideal for Hitler's new autobahns where German drivers were able to maintain a cruising speed of 100 kph (62 mph) for long distances. The Type 303 was also the first BMW with a divided front grille, nicknamed *Nieren* by the Germans (it means 'kidneys') which the shape was thought to resemble!

It was in 1933 that Fritz Fiedler of Horch joined BMW, where he devoted his considerable abilities to developing the six-cylinder cars. His first effort was the Type 315, in which the engine was enlarged to 1490 cc and power went up to 34 bhp, raising the maximum speed to 68 mph (110 kph). An indication of things to come was BMW's entry in the 1934 Monte Carlo Rally with a team of neat, sports two-seaters with three-carburettor, high-compression versions of the Type 315 engine which produced 40 bhp. The type 315/1, as this first true BMW sports model was called, was sold with a guaranteed top speed of 75 mph (120 kph) and made quite an impact on the

LEFT *Like the example on the previous page, this 328 was built in right-hand-drive form for the British market, and sold through Frazer Nash of Kingston upon Thames, Surrey, originally for £695*
RIGHT *A BMW 328 on the open road*

European sporting scene that year, winning the team prize in the Austrian Alpine Trial. In 1935 the Type 315/1 was joined by the near-identical Type 319/1, which had a 1911 cc, 55 bhp engine and was capable of 81 mph (130 kph). Like the 315/1, the 319/1 had disc wheels, but in this case they were of centrelock type.

The Type 319/1 added to the successes of its predecessor in rallies and speed events, attracting the attention of the Aldington brothers at Isleworth. They bought some of the engines to install in their 'chain-gang' Frazer Nashes, and then asked permission to

---

> *'... some were also supplied in chassis form to be bodied in England...'*

---

market the sports BMWs in England. These were built in Germany specially for the British market, and had right-hand drive; some were also supplied in chassis form to be bodied in England and fitted with wire wheels to suit British preferences.

At the Berlin Motor Show in February 1936 it seemed that Fielder and his assistant, Rudolf Schleicher, were moving away from sporting cars, for the new Type 326 had a box-section chassis with completely new suspension and hydraulic brakes. With a 1 mm bore increase the six-cylinder engine was enlarged to 1971 cc and had a power output of 50 bhp at 4500 rpm to propel this

five-seater saloon. Certainly no sports car, it was still the best-selling BMW of its day.

However, when the popular Eifel races were held at the Nürburgring on 14 June 1936, the well-known BMW motorcyclist, Ernst Henne, appeared in a very smart new two-seater powered by the 1971 cc engine, which now had a new type of cylinder head. In this, the first BMW Type 328, Henne ran away with the 2-litre sports car class at an average speed of just over 62 mph (100 kph), finishing more than three minutes ahead of the runner-up.

What Fiedler had done was to design new valve gear for the now familiar six-cylinder BMW engine, achieving a massive power increase to 80 bhp at 5000 rpm. The chain-driven camshaft still occupied the same position, low down on the nearside of the engine, from which it had previously operated in-line valves through pushrods and rockers. Now there were hemispherical combustion chambers in the new alloy head, with inclined valves. The inlets were opened by pushrods and rockers as before, but the exhaust valves now had two sets of pushrods and rockers, one set of pushrods being placed horizontally so that the valves could be located on the other side of the combustion chambers. This arrangement worked well despite its apparent complexity, and provided most of the advantages of overhead camshafts without the need to redesign the whole engine; indeed, with its twin rocker-boxes the Type 328 engine looked very much like a double-overhead-cam unit.

As the inlet ports were paired, and passed

MODEL
BMW 328 (1937)
UK price when announced: £695

ENGINE
Location: Front, longitudinal
Type: Water-cooled in-line six-cylinder with cast-iron block and light-alloy head. Four main bearings
Cubic capacity: 1971 cc
Bore × stroke: 66 mm × 96 mm
Compression ratio: 7.5:1
Valve gear: 2 valves per cylinder operating in hemispherical combustion chambers. Inlet valves operated by pushrods and rockers from single block-mounted camshaft. Exhaust valves operated by horizontal pushrods from inlet side
Fuel supply: 3 Solex downdraught carburettors
Ignition: Mechanical by coil and distributor. Six-volt electrics
Maximum power: 80 bhp at 5000 rpm
Maximum torque: 93 lb ft (approx) at 4000 rpm

TRANSMISSION
Layout: Gearbox and clutch in unit with engine
Clutch: Single dry plate
Gearbox: Four-speed manual with synchromesh on top two gears. Gearboxes were supplied by Hirth or ZF and two sets of ratios were available

1st 3.64:1	3rd 1.487:1
2nd 2.05:1	4th 1.00:1

Final drive: Hypoid bevel
Ratio: 3.90:1

SUSPENSION
Front: Independent with lower wishbones, transverse semi-elliptic leaf spring and lever-arm dampers
Rear: Non independent with live rear axle, semi-elliptic leaf springs and lever arm dampers

STEERING
Type: Rack and pinion

BRAKES
Type: Hydraulically operated drums all round, 11 inches (28 cm) in diameter

WHEELS AND TYRES
Type: Steel disc wheels with peg-drive hubs and 5.25 × 16 in low-pressure tyres

BODY/CHASSIS
Type: Tubular steel chassis with cross members in form of a capital 'A' with the apex to the front. Two-seat, two-door convertible sports body

DIMENSIONS AND WEIGHT
Length: 153.5 in (390 cm)
Width: 61 in (155 cm)
Wheelbase: 93 in (236 cm)
Track – front: 45.5 in (115 cm)
– rear: 48 in (122 cm)
Weight: 1638 lb (743 kg)

PERFORMANCE
Maximum speed: 103 mph (166 kph)
Acceleration 0–60 mph: 9.5 seconds
Fuel consumption (approx): 23 mpg

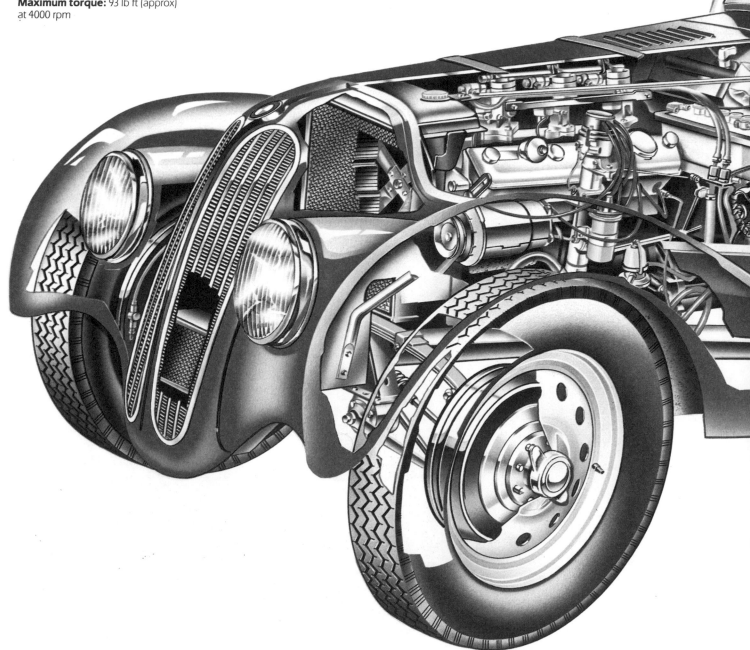

The BMW 328 was one of those rare designs that seemed to be exactly right in every respect, yet there was little completely original in it apart from the stylish semi-streamlined bodywork. Although the front suspension was independent it was a simple system using a transverse semi-elliptic leaf spring. The live axle was also simply located by semi-elliptic leaf springs, but the car still handled extremely well. Its performance matched its handling thanks to the superb straight-six engine which enjoyed the advantages of hemispherical combustion chambers without the need for twin-overhead camshafts. That was made possible by the use of an ingenious cross-over pushrod system (shown right) which was activated by a single block-mounted camshaft

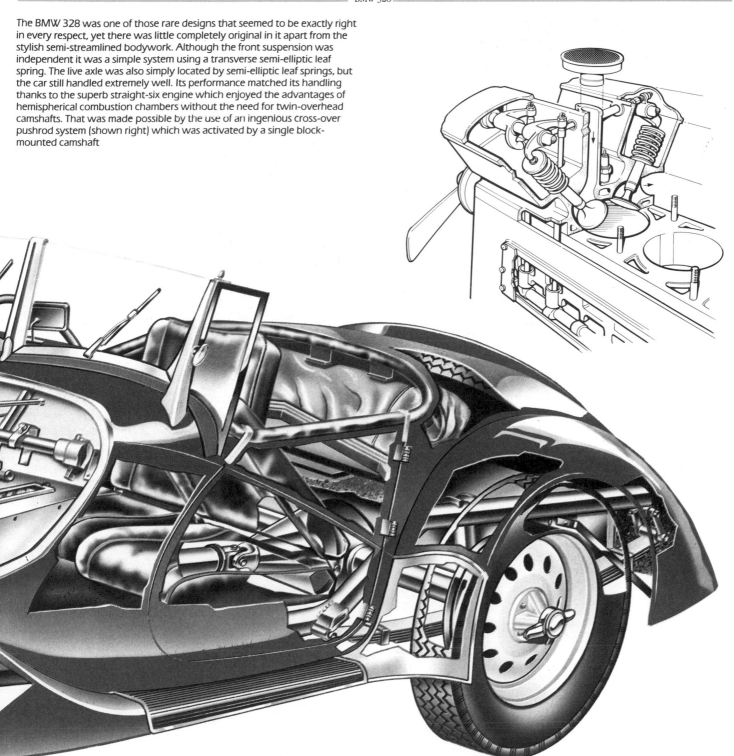

vertically downwards to the combustion chambers, it was convenient to provide the engine with three downdraught Solex carburettors above the cylinder head, although this made the engine rather a lofty affair and a tight fit under the bonnet. Another minor disadvantage was the placing of the sparking plugs symmetrically at the centre of the combustion chambers, making them fairly inaccessible and calling for the use of a special plug spanner.

The crankshaft, running in lead-bronze bearings, had a vibration damper at its forward end and a pulley driving the dynamo and water-pump by vee-belt. A mechanical fuel pump on the nearside was driven from the rear end of the camshaft, which also drove the distributor from a skew gear at its centre, via a long vertical spindle. A single-plate clutch took the drive to a four-speed

> *'... their diameter varied in accordance with the load... '*

gearbox, and thence by open propeller shaft to the spiral-bevel rear axle. An oil-cooler was provided, mounted just ahead of the radiator in two parts to match the two halves of the 'kidney' front grille, and there was a full undertray beneath the car.

The side-members of the chassis were not simple tubes, having been fabricated from sheet steel so that their diameter varied in accordance with the load at each point. A welded box structure carried the transverse leaf spring, lower wishbones and telescopic dampers of the front suspension assembly, with its rack-and-pinion steering, and the

live rear axle was mounted on long semi-elliptic leaf springs. The hydraulic brakes had 11 in (28 cm) drums, and the perforated pressed-steel disc wheels were fitted to peg-drive hubs, with central locking nuts.

At a time when most sports cars still had separate mudguards and headlamps, the Type 328 BMW paved the way for the transition to all-enveloping bodywork: the mudguards merged into the body, with no more than vestigial running-boards, and the headlamps were let into a cowling that united the mudguards with the front grille, while the spare wheel was partially sunk into the shapely tail, where the hood, sidescreens and luggage were stowed out of sight. There was no boot-lid, access to the luggage compartment being made by folding the seat squab forward. The leather bonnet straps – paired and fitted with sprung fasteners – were standard equipment, and the vee-shaped windscreen was split in the middle so that it could be folded down on the scuttle. Even now, half a century later, the Type 328 is so close to modern ideas in body shape that it is difficult to imagine the impact it made when it first appeared, looking almost futuristic among its contemporaries.

There was a three-spoke steering wheel, and instruments included a speedometer, tachometer, oil and water temperature gauges and an oil pressure gauge. The electrical system was 6-volt. The semi-bucket seats were made of leather, and there was a

ABOVE LEFT *The 2-litre, overhead-valve straight-six produced 80 bhp at 5000 rpm*
LEFT *In no way flamboyant in style, the 328 was both smooth and aerodynamic*
BELOW *With the windscreen up, the car's top speed was 100 mph (161 kph); when lowered, it rose to 103 mph (166 kph)*
RIGHT *The smooth rear-wing contours were both functional and attractive*
BELOW *A 328 at the Beaulieu museum*

'one-shot' chassis lubrication system actuated by a separate pedal. One of the weaker points of the Type 328 was the gear-change, for there was synchromesh only on third and top, whilst instead of a proper remote-control there was a rather long gear-lever.

As a sports car it was just a nice, handy size, its overall length being 12 ft 9½ in (390 cm). The wheelbase was 7 ft 10½ in (240 cm) front track 3 ft 9½ in (116 cm) rear track 4 ft (122 cm) exactly. Surprisingly, the ground clearance was almost 8 in (20 cm), which made the Type 328 quite at home on rough surfaces in rallies or trials. As most of

> *' ... it needed little attention to achieve 100 mph ... truly amazing ... '*

the bodywork (apart from the mudguards) was aluminium, the all-up weight was a modest 1830 lb (830 kg), a good figure for a 2-litre car.

Only two cars were built in 1936, and as these were intended to publicise the model in competitions they had lightweight, doorless bodies and one-piece windscreens. Not until February 1937 was the Type 328 available to the public, and these cars, of course, were fully equipped for road use. Soon after, one of the lightweight cars was sent to England, where the sports editor of *Autocar,* S.C.H. Davis, drove it at Brooklands under RAC observation on 15 April, covering 102.2 miles (164 km) in the hour. Running on Discol pump fuel, the BMW maintained a steady 4600 to 4900 rpm and carried a spare wheel, full toolkit and hood in the tail.

Although a standard production Type 328 could scarcely be expected to put more than 100 miles into the hour, it needed little attention to achieve 100 mph, and up to

120 mph (193 kph) was possible with more extensive tuning. To take full advantage of this sort of performance – which was truly amazing for an unsupercharged 2-litre carrying full equipment – the factory made available a wide range of special equipment, including better brakes and dampers, tougher transmission and suspension parts.

Four cars ran at Le Mans in 1937, three of them factory-entered, but one of them, driven by Pat Fairfield, was unfortunately involved in a multiple crash in which he lost his life. Another of the BMWs was badly damaged in the same accident (caused by an inexperienced driver), and the remaining two retired. Four cars were again entered for the RAC Tourist Trophy Race, held that year at Donington for the first time. Dobbs broke a half-shaft as the flag fell, but Fane, always one of the fastest BMW drivers, led the race until he dropped a valve, leaving

Bira to finish· third overall at 68.7 mph (111 kph), with H.J. Aldington in sixth place overall. Bira won the 2-litre class.

Fane was prominent again in the Mille Miglia of 1938, driving the 1000 miles (1609 km) singlehanded in a time of 13 hr 38 min 11 sec to win the unsupercharged 2-litre International class at an average of 74 mph (119 kph), finishing seventh overall. His team-mates came second, third and fourth in the class behind him, Prince Schaumburg-Lippe and Count Lurani being ninth overall, Richter and Werneck 10th and Van der Muhle and Holzclub 11th. The following month saw the Type 328 score another 1–2–3 victory at the Avusrennen in Germany. Soon afterwards the first Antwerp Grand Prix was held in Belgium. Being staged as a sports car event, it too attracted a full entry of BMWs. In this exciting 10-mile (16 km), round-the-houses race the Type 328 achieved a class 1–2–3 once again, this

RIGHT & BELOW *Views of the Frazer Nash BMW Grand Prix Two-Seater, a car of which* The Autocar *said: 'Very nearly unique, it is certainly a most unusual motor car, and sold ready for serious sports car competition work…'.*

second on Index of Performance. Naturally they also won the 2-litre class ahead of Rose and Heinemann (who were seventh overall) and Briem and Scholtz (who were eighth overall), their race average breaking the class record by an easy margin. For the remainder of the season the Type 328 BMWs continued their winning ways to the extent that in Germany, at least, it was rare for anything *but* a Type 328 to be entered for the 2-litre class.

The 1938 Mille Miglia had been the occasion of a disastrous accident when a competing car ran into the crowd, killing nine spectators, and for this reason Mussolini declared that the race was not to be run again. However, the organizers managed to arrange for it to be held – officially as the Coppa Brescia – over a 100-mile (161 km) closed circuit instead of the traditional 1000 miles (1609 km) of open road, the race

---

'The two closed cars proved capable of more than 130 mph...'

---

distance totalling 923 miles (1485 km). Astonishingly, it was held more than seven months after World War II began, on 28 April 1940, for Italy was still a neutral country at that time.

BMW made careful preparations for the race, entering five cars which were extensively lightened and fitted with highly-tuned engines giving 135 bhp at 5500 rpm on a 9.6:1 compression ratio. Three were roadsters, one a coupé built under Fiedler's supervision in Germany, and another coupé was built for BMW by Touring of Milan.

The two closed cars proved capable of more than 130 mph (209 kph), and in the Touring coupé, Huschke von Hanstein (later to become Porsche's racing manager) and Bäumer succeeded in averaging 103.6 mph (167 kph) for the entire race – slightly better than the fastest lap of the pre-race favourite, the Alfa Romeo coupé of Farina and Biondetti! Brudes and Roese came third in one of the open Type 328 cars, and only one of the team, the Lurani/Cortese coupé, had to drop out, having carburettor trouble.

BMW built a total of 461 Type 328 models, including chassis supplied to specialist coachbuilders, but after the war the Eisenach factory was nationalized, and it was not until 1952 that the company were able to build cars again at Munich. A few cars were assembled from parts by the Aldingtons in England, and the classic six-cylinder engine was turned into the Bristol for the post-war cars built by the Bristol Aeroplane Company from 1947. It powered the AFM, the Veritas, the Monopol, Cooper, Frazer Nash, AC Ace, Arnolt and a myriad other high-performance cars in different parts of the world. As the *Autocar* testers said in 1937, 'it has the mark of a racing unit', and gave the impression that it was supercharged, so freely did it increase its revs.

FWMcC

time with Ralph Rouse in the lead at an average of 76.05 mph (122 kph), ahead of Briem and Heinemann, while Prince Schaumburg-Lippe finished fifth in the 2-litre class.

Rouse did it again in the Grand Prix des Frontières at Chimay, winning the 2-litre class ahead of Gubelin's BMW at an average of 72.89 mph, but at Le Mans the team were again out of luck. However, they made up for it in the 24-hour race on the Belgian Spa/Francorchamps road circuit, where Schaumburg-Lippe and Rose shared a Type 328 to win the 2-litre class, followed by Heinemann, Briem and Scholtz – a performance which also gained them the team prize.

In winning the 2-litre class of the French Alpine Rally, Van der Muhle was one of only two competitors to finish the event without losing a single mark. Inevitably, the sports car races accompanying the 1938 German Grand Prix at the Nürburgring saw the Type 328 achieve its usual dominance in the 2-litre class, Greifzu winning from Von Hanstein and Heinemann. It was with understandable confidence that BMW entered four works cars for the RAC Tourist Trophy Race, nominating Dick Seaman (who had won the German Grand Prix for Mercedes-Benz), Prince Bira, Fane and Aldington. There were also two private entrants, the Hon. Peter Aitken and David Murray. But at Donington, as at Le Mans, the BMWs were out of luck, all of the cars giving trouble.

For their third attempt at Le Mans, in 1939, BMW entered three cars, one of which had a most attractive coupé body. It was certainly a case of 'third time lucky'. Prince Schaumburg-Lippe and Wenscher drove the coupé at a tremendous pace to finish fifth overall, averaging a splendid 82.5 mph (133 kph) for the 24 hours and finishing

BUGATTI

They epitomised the excesses and extravagances of the time, and few cars ever attracted as much attention as the legendary Bugatti Royales

THEY CALLED IT A WHIM, but for a whim it was pretty substantial: 14 litres of engine (twice as big as a Rolls), 180 inches (457 cm) of wheelbase (30 inches/76 cm longer than a long-chassis Phantom) and a bonnet of such length that a Mini could be parked on it. Ettore Bugatti called it Royale because it was to sell mainly to crowned heads, and it carried a lifetime guarantee.

Bugatti had dreamed of making such a car even before the Great War, and his wartime designs for aero engines seem to have further stimulated that dream. During the early 1920s, while the Brescia and Type 35 were winning races, *le Patron* designed, built and tested the Royale on all the spikiest roads in the Alps, the Pyrennees and the Massif Central, 'in all weathers, at all altitudes with never a moment's trouble.' He continued: 'The minor roads in the Alps, particularly, were calculated to demonstrate the car's qualities – its flexibility and handiness, its ability to...turn like a bicycle'.

The prototype was shown to the Press in 1926. It was an enormous open touring car painted dark green and lined-out in red, the body of which is said to have come from a Packard in Bugatti's possession; but there was a breaker's yard on the Ile de la Jatte in Paris specialising in used bodywork and it may well have come from there.

Bugatti expected applause and certainly earned it. The greatest compliment, he reckoned, had come from a point-duty policeman in Milan who, staring incredulously at the majestic carriage as it approached, sprang to attention and saluted. Bugatti, delighted, acknowledged this homage by raising his light-brown bowler as he glided

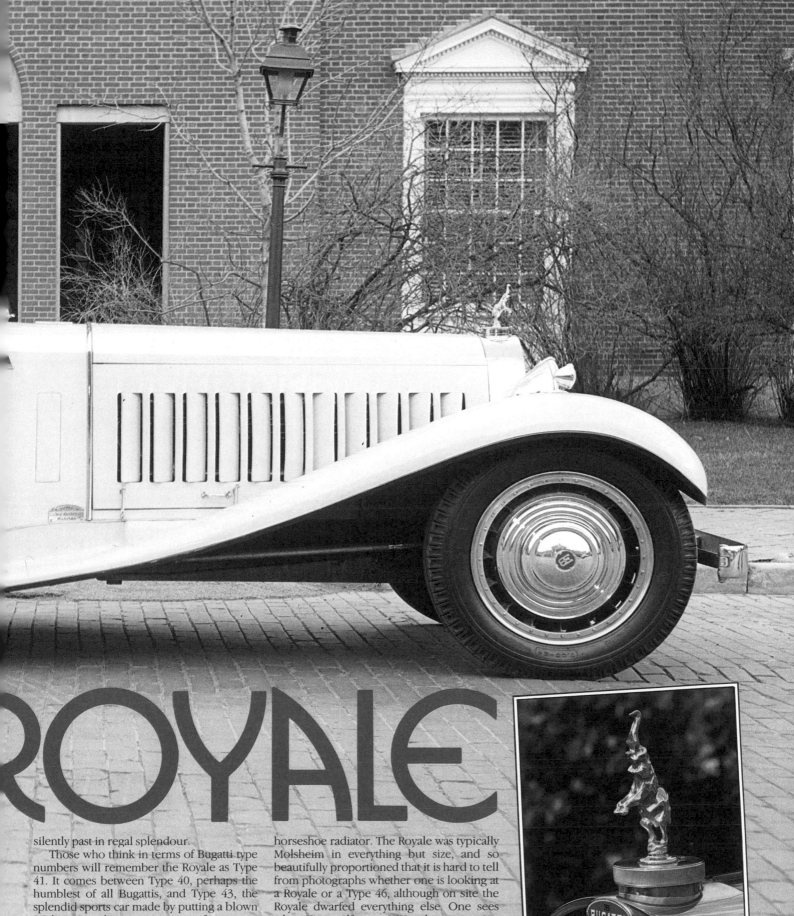

ROYALE

silently past in regal splendour.

Those who think in terms of Bugatti type numbers will remember the Royale as Type 41. It comes between Type 40, perhaps the humblest of all Bugattis, and Type 43, the splendid sports car made by putting a blown 2.3-litre Grand Prix engine into a four-seater for sports car racing. The three models had much in common: a shaft-driven overhead camshaft, three valves per cylinder, non-detachable head, reversed quarter-elliptic rear springing, front springs passing through the axle forging and, of course, the familiar

horseshoe radiator. The Royale was typically Molsheim in everything but size, and so beautifully proportioned that it is hard to tell from photographs whether one is looking at a Royale or a Type 46, although on site the Royale dwarfed everything else. One sees why King Alfonso XIII, that motoring monarch, expressed interest at the Spanish Grand Prix, but he unfortunately lost his throne before a deal could be concluded; let us see what he would have acquired.

The prototype chassis beneath that open tourer was slightly larger both in engine and

ABOVE *The splendid lines of the 1927 Royale cabriolet. The elephant mascot was sculpted by Rembrandt Bugatti*

wheelbase than the six 'production' chassis which followed – 20 mm longer in stroke and 10 inches (25.4 cm) longer in its wheelbase. Later cars had a wheelbase of 14 ft 2 in (432 cm) and an engine bore and stroke of 125 mm by 130 mm, giving a capacity of a mere 12,763 cc. The straight-eight engine weighed 770 lb (349 kg), of which 238 lb came from the cast-iron block and integral head, which was 55 inches (140 cm) long. The two-piece crankshaft, which weighed 220 lb (100 kg), had circular webs and ran in nine white-metal bearings, and was so massive that after the prototype none of the cars had need of a flywheel. The main bearings were carried in the huge cylinder-block casting, and the water jackets were extended downwards to provide water cooling for the mains. Unusually for a Bugatti engine of the period, there was room for water between the bores. There were three valves per cylinder as usual, two inlets and one exhaust, in a flat head; they were pretty massive and the whole engine was lightly stressed, which was just as well because to change a valve meant removing that crankshaft.

The camshaft, like the crank, was made in two pieces, and the shaft drive for it was unorthodox. Mr Charles A. Chayne, a senior engineer at General Motors who rebuilt a Royale engine in 1946, has described it thus: 'At the top of the vertical shaft are two bevel pinions having opposite spiral angles. These mesh with two bevel gears, one of which is fixed to the camshaft. The second gear is concentric with the first, but drives through a friction clutch. As the second pair of gears is one tooth off from an even two-to-one ratio, the friction clutch merely loads these gears so that the thrust on the vertical shaft is balanced by the opposing spiral angles. Just

---

‘The engine had full-pressure lubrication except for the gudgeon pins…’

---

one more example of M. Bugatti's rugged individualism.' The engine had full-pressure lubrication except for the gudgeon pins, which relied on splash. It was a dry-sump system, with two scavenge pumps and a pressure pump circulating oil from a tank on the dashboard holding five gallons (23 litres). There was a single duplex carburettor and ignition was by both magneto and coil, with two plugs per cylinder. From the engine a short shaft and heavy fabric universals took the drive to a normal Bugatti multiple-wet-plate clutch under the driving seat, and from there another shaft connected with a cavernous three-speed gearbox in unit with the back axle. The ratios provided low speed for starting, direct drive in second and a geared-up top. Starter and dynamo were mounted on the clutch housing. Much use was made of roller-bearings in the cable-operated four-wheel brake system, and helical turbine-like spokes for cooling the brake drums were a feature of the vast and decorative cast-aluminium alloy wheels. Various types of tyre were fitted from time to time, but were usually of 39 inches (100 cm).

Before discussing performance, we should look at some of the varied coachwork fitted to the Royale. Obviously the 1926 launch was premature: no doubt Bugatti had his reasons for altering the specification, and he was not ready to accept orders until the smaller car was ready. It was his misfortune that the Wall Street crash and subsequent world slump happened just as he was ready. Ettore Bugatti had been convinced that the Royale would sell itself, and perhaps it would have done had he landed King Alfonso as a customer.

Perhaps, too, he was wrong to retain that open body, for quite suddenly at the end of

ABOVE & BELOW LEFT *When Capt. C. Foster bought his Royale chassis in June 1933, he had it fitted with a saloon body by Park Ward, a replica of the one they had made for his Rolls-Royce*

BELOW RIGHT *The Coupé Napoleon, the last body to be built on the prototype chassis. Note the transparent roof panels*

the 1920s open motoring went out of fashion. The role of the Royale, he now saw, was that of showcar, demonstrator and flagship of the Molsheim fleet. The tourer body was removed and the great man indulged his fancy by building what Regency coachbuilders would have called a chariot and which the French translate as *coupé* because, like a chariot, it comprises the two back seats of a coach with the front part cut off. The first Royale therefore received a closed two-seater body like a brougham – and indeed like the posting chariot in which Napoleon fled from the field of Waterloo. Hence the name (often given to a subsequent Royale body) Coupé Napoleon. The space behind the tiny closed body was filled

in with a free-standing trunk. This car appeared outside the Paris Salon in 1928 and received much attention.

The coupé was not retained long, and was replaced by another Ettore design, again redolent of a carriage. Bugatti had been drawing archaic brougham-like coachwork since 1910 and he saw no reason to abandon this agreeable mixture of straight and curved lines. The 1929 berline, or saloon, might almost have been the coupé re-used with a different back. The same peaked visor recurred, the same curved pillar and 'brougham foot', but the blind quarter panel was replaced by a door, and behind that was a quarter panel featuring a horizontal ellipse.

The next incarnation of the original chas-

ABOVE The Royales were built to impress, which they certainly did (and still do) by virtue of their extravagant dimensions and superb craftsmanship. With a price equal to that of three Rolls-Royces, the Royale was intended only for the most wealthy connoisseurs, and those few who bought them were assured of a mode of transport with few (if any) peers. Some extremely elegant body designs were fitted to the gargantuan chassis, itself necessarily strong to support the length, and weight of the car and cope with the tremendous torque exerted by the 12.7-litre, and in the case of the prototype, 14.7-litre engines. The engine, some 4 ft 8 in (142 cm) long, was lubricated with five gallons (23 litres) of oil, cooled with 15 gallons (68 litres) of water and fed from a petrol tank of 42 gallons (191 litres) capacity. The Royales were originally made with the gearbox in unit with the rear axle, but the example shown has been modified, and an automatic gearbox fitted. Although the Royales failed to secure their intended market at the time, they are today worth a king's ransom, and in the few collections which house them they hold pride of place, virtually priceless

MODEL
Bugatti Royale Type 41 (1930)

ENGINE
Type: Water-cooled in-line straight-eight monobloc. Nine main bearings. Dry sump lubrication
Cubic capacity: 12,763 cc
Bore × stroke: 125 mm × 130 mm

Valve gear: 3 valves per cylinder (2 inlet, 1 exhaust) operated by single gear-driven overhead camshaft
Fuel supply: Single double-choke Shebler carburettor
Ignition: Mechanical by both coil and magneto. 2 spark plugs per cylinder
Maximum power: 275 bhp at 3000 rpm (approx)

TRANSMISSION
Layout: Shaft drive from engine to clutch and from clutch to gearbox in unit with final drive

Clutch: Multi-plate, dry
Type: Three-speed manual
    1st 2.08:1   3rd 0.727.1
    2nd 1.00:1
Final drive: Spiral bevel
Ratio: 3.66:1

SUSPENSION
Front: Non-independent with hollow axle and semi-elliptic leaf springs passing through axle forging. Friction dampers
Rear: Live rear axle with reversed quarter elliptic leaf springs and friction damper

STEERING
Type: Worm and nut. 3½ turns lock to lock

BRAKES
Type: Cable operated drums all round, 18 in (46 cm) diameter

WHEELS AND TYRES
Type: 24 in diameter cast alloy wheels with 6.75 × 36 Rapson tyres

BODY/CHASSIS
Type: Pressed steel channel section chassis with two main longitudinal outer chassis members and cross members. Coupé Napoleon four-door body

DIMENSIONS AND WEIGHT
Wheelbase: 170 in (432.0 cm)
Track – front: 63 in (160 cm)
      – rear: 63 in (160 cm)
Weight: 7000 lb (3175 kg)

PERFORMANCE
Maximum speed: 100 mph (160 kpg) (approx)
Fuel consumption: 6-8 mpg

sis bore coachwork not by the Old Man himself but by the go-ahead firm of Weymann. C.T. Weymann, airman, engineer and go-getter, had patented a form of very light construction in which the body was free to flex, thus abolishing rattles. Instead of being panelled the structure was covered in leather, leathercloth (the so-called 'fabric' body) or, as in this case, with a glossy patent-leather-like skin called *tôle souple*. Weymann was the father of the two-door 'sportsman's coupé' because his lightweight rattle-proof doors, kept in shape by tensioners, could be of almost any width. So the Weymann-bodied Royale was a two-door close-coupled coupé, very light and smart and with a huge trunk on the back. It won numerous *concours d'élégance*, then a very fashionable diversion at seaside resorts like Deauville, often presented by one or both of Ettore Bugatti's daughters, L'Ebé and Lydia. It was a very pretty car but was unfortunately short-lived, being written off in a crash. Yet this ex-Packard, ex-coupé, ex-berline, ex-Weymann chassis (or at least its chassis-number) was to be reincarnated as a master-piece by Jean, as will be seen; but before that could happen Ettore had designed another 1910-derived body for the chassis.

The coachwork with which he presented us he called a double berline, a bizarre and uneasy creation. If the coupé had looked like a travelling chariot, this car looked like a *dormeuse de voyage* (sleeper); it was cer-

tainly double, for it looked as though a coach had telescoped into the back of a chariot. There was a curved brougham pillar to each half, front and back, and to fill the gap between and to allow the windows to drop there was a narrow oblong window in between. The car had a small trunk behind; altogether a strange creation, but practical because beneath all the carriage-oriented presentation the body was in fact a Salamanca cabriolet, a style of great versatility created by the English firm of Barker. By dropping the front windows and rolling back the canopy it became a cabriolet de ville; then the rest of the leather top could be folded, creating pretty much the effect of an open touring car. Useful but unattractive, and one feels that Jean would have disapproved.

The four bodies just discussed followed in rapid succession during 1928 and 1929. In 1930, and as though utterly oblivious of the Slump, Jean celebrated the slough of the Depression by designing perhaps the most elegant town carriage of all time, a coupé de ville. This body, no doubt from its nobility, is often referred to as the Coupé Napoleon although there is nothing Empire about it.

For sheer give-the-cat-another-canary luxury there has never been a car to touch it: the cabin aft of amidships (though well within the wheelbase) and chauffeur and footman in the open air. And because Jean Bugatti was the essence of the young sportsman he combined this extreme formality with slim, swept and sporting mudguards and an inclined spare wheel on the back. Furthermore, in order to lighten what might have seemed an undue acreage of sombre paintwork, he relieved it by means of a shallow depression starting from the bonnet hinge line and running back past the scuttle into the door, a horizontal echo, as it were, of the horseshoe radiator shape. Jean was to use the same device often in future, especially on the Type 55, where it became almost a trademark. Another novelty introduced by Jean on the coupé de ville was the transpa-

rent roof, which quite suppressed any feeling of claustrophobia.

By 1931 the clouds were beginning to lift. The Royale had been on offer for six years with no takers, although by equipping the prototype with so many diverse bodies Bugatti had created an impression of movement – a stage army consisting of one extra and a multiplicity of hats. In 1932, however, the till rang for the first time. Evidently impressed by Jean's coupé de ville, a textile magnate named Armand Esders commissioned an equally splendid folly: not a formal carriage but the ultimate sporting two-seater. The front wings were to be very similar to those of the coupé de ville and were to merge into curved running-boards and continue rearwards in a climbing sweep. There was to be a concealed dickey

---

'.The result was a beautifully balanced drophead cabriolet... '

---

seat for two in the rear decking, complete with disappearing windscreen. The spare wheel was mounted vertically across the tail, but was later inclined. Monsieur Esders saved the designer some work by refusing to have lamps of any kind. He would not, he said, be driving after dark.

Another customer who came forward in 1932 was a Dr A. Joseph Fuchs, who purchased a bare chassis for delivery to the coachbuilding firm of Ludwig Weinberger in Munich, where he lived. The result was a beautifully balanced drophead cabriolet, a style in which German designers excelled at that time. The wing treatment owed something to Jean Bugatti's roadster, but the light-coloured hood, with its landau irons whose slope echoed that of the wings, looked very attractive. There were close-coupled seats for two in the back and a large

ABOVE *The graceful Coupé Napoleon was used by the Bugatti family for many years. Its style was much influenced by that of horse-drawn carriages*
LEFT *Its interior exudes privacy, exclusivity and drawing-room comfort*
BELOW *The last body built at Molsheim was this Berline de Voyage, an inharmonious but versatile creation*

trunk behind. This is the car which Charles Chayne restored, having found it in a junk-yard in New York City, the city where Dr Fuchs had used it for some years until the block was damaged by frost. This car is now in the Ford Museum in Dearborn. The wind-screen and windows are very shallow, in the fashion of the time – one thinks of the Hispano-Suizas and 8-litre Bentleys.

We do have a firm date for the smart owner-driver two-door saloon (a style the French and Americans call coach) which Ettore Bugatti ordered from the Paris coach-builder Kellner, because it was exhibited at the London Motor Show at Olympia in 1932, and won a prize as most costly exhibit. The price would have bought three Rolls-Royces… . Notable for its slim pillars, it remained a favourite with *le Patron* and remained in his stable along with Jean's coupé de ville and double berline.

The last Royale to receive original body-work was purchased new by an English businessman, Captain Cuthbert W. Foster, in June 1933. He sent the chassis to Park, Ward & Co., of London, who built a limousine which was as resoundingly British as Jean's coupé had been French. It is this car, when in the possession of J. Lemon Burton, that the writer has been privileged to try.

Lolling upon the Bedford cord in that stately herse-like interior one felt part Pasha, part corpse. The driver seemed a very long way away, but not so far off as the circus elephant pirouetting on the radiator cap. Symbolically white, this mascot was the gift of sculptor Rembrandt Bugatti to his brother Ettore in 1915. The outside world seemed miles away; and there was very little sound of machinery, but as one looked out at other traffic one recovered a sense of proportion. A Bugatti Royale may be large by car stan-dards, but there are buses and trucks too.

As soon as I was ensconced in the driver's seat I realised that there has never been a finer bonnet to look down; the forward visibility is good. There are sound practical reasons for having the gear-lever and hand

TOP LEFT The 12.7-litre straight-eight virtually fills the engine compartment
ABOVE The interior of a Royale was not particularly spacious. Note the large steering wheel, necessary for leverage with the large and distant front wheels
RIGHT & BELOW This Kellner-bodied two-door owner-driver saloon was exhibited in 1932, but, unsold for many years, stayed in Bugatti's private collection

some 1820 rpm at 60 mph (96 kph) in second gear, slightly more than the 1700 rpm quoted as being the maximum-power speed of the engine. None of those on board – Lemon Burton, Cecil Clutton and the writer – felt disposed to believe publicity stories of 'zero to 90 mph in second gear', but all agreed that the car's direct drive was a very practical gear for a three-ton (3048 kg) vehicle. Overdrive was usable when the road was clear, its 2.66:1 ratio giving 43 mph (69 kph) at 1000 rpm and a majestic 70–75 mph (113–121 kph) at peak revs, about right, then, for a ceremonial carriage.

The main question was how well would the Gold Bug handle? The answer came through within the first few yards: the steering was pure Bugatti, typically smooth and precise, although fairly low-geared at 3½ turns from lock to lock. It could hardly have been otherwise with Ettore's own favourite toy: there were three Royales at the family chateau when he died.

> **'... a magnificent folly, but far from a waste of time '**

One other Royale body remains to be described. The Armand Esdars two-seater came on the market in 1938, when Jack Lemon Burton considered buying and importing it to England despite a British tax rating of 78 hp, but the Munich crisis put him off. The car changed hands in France, the two-seater body was removed (and eventually destroyed by bombing during the war) and a new coupé de ville body commissioned from Binder, the Paris coachbuilder. It looked superficially like Jean Bugatti's masterpiece but lacked its slim elegance.

The Royales were a magnificent folly but far from a waste of time. They brought wonderful publicity and they gave both Ettore and Jean a chance to develop coachbuilding ideas. From the Type 41 evolved the Type 46 in 1929, a scaled-down Royale with a mere 5.3 litres of engine which, probably to Ettore's relief, siphoned off most the Royale clientele. At that time of crisis Bugatti found a new market for his great lazy 14.75-litre engine – not in boats, as its marine configuration might sugggest, but on the railways. The French national network at that time was developing streamlined railcars and Bugatti secured contracts for engines and rolling-stock which kept his factory going for more than 20 years. Powered by either two or four Type 41 engines, Bugatti *autorails* were fast, comfortable and quiet, the latter quality attributable to a layer of rubber between the wheel and its steel rim. The first car entered service in 1933 and was not withdrawn until 1954. Normally they cruised at 70 mph (113 kph), but one day Jean Bugatti startled the railways by covering 70 kilometres (43 miles) at more than 120 mph (196 kph): an excellent performance for these Royale engines   DBT

brake central, in the American fashion, but it nevertheless seemed rather atypical of Bugattis. The wood-rimmed steel-spoked wheel however, was perfectly Molsheim in feel and appearance, and it was a good idea to put a finger-tip horn push behind each spoke. The central boss was originally occupied by a beautiful built-in stopwatch.

Jack Lemon Burton then explained the gear positions, which are the same as those of a P3 Monoposto Alfa: a dog-leg change, forward right for first and forward left for second. After moving off in first one changes immediately into second, which gives direct drive and is used most of the time. Bugatti sources and also Charles Chayne, who took the trouble to measure, give the axle ratio as 3.66:1. Chayne used special tractor tyres on the car, and Lemon Burton fitted tyres from a couple of field-guns (retired), 7.50 × 24s, the nearest available size to the original Rapson balloons. These 39-inch (99 cm) tyres give approximately 520 revs per mile (318 turns per km), which means that the engine, with it 3.66:1 axle, would be doing

CADILL

AC V16

CADILLAC V16

LEFT AND BELOW *The Maharaja of Tikari's 1931 V16 Phaeton. The 'goddess and drape' mascot was introduced during the '30s, with several variations*

Designed to reinstate Cadillac at the top, the V16 proved a grand finale to the Roaring Twenties. Unrivalled in engineering refinement and luxury, it appeared just as the Depression began to winnow the American motor industry

AT A RECENT CONCOURS in Detroit, the proud owner of a quartet of V16 Cadillacs was asked the obvious question: 'Why do you need *four* V16 Cadillacs?' He thought for a moment, then responded: 'You can never have too many V16 Cadillacs . . .'.

That, I suppose, is a remark that Ernest Seaholm and Owen Nacker, creators of the world's first and most successful V16 car, would have been proud of, for the V16 was intended as the ultimate extravagance, a supreme gesture that placed its owner above the common ruck of motoring.

To find the reason why such an extravagance was launched just as the Depression was gathering momentum, you have to look back to 1925, when Cadillac, top of the American luxury car league, was rudely swept aside by Packard, thus diminishing General Motors' pride in having overtaken Ford in terms of sales. Although General Motors was 21 years old when the V16 was launched, the start of the corporation's irresistible rise began in 1923, when Alfred P. Sloan was appointed President, and began to rearrange the corporate structure.

As conceived by Sloan, the product spread of General Motors was such that it could provide cradle-to-grave transport for Everyman, catering for his economic and social progression from Chevrolet through Pontiac, Oldsmobile, Buick, and LaSalle to Cadillac, each marque a clearly-defined step and status symbol.

Imagine, then, the displeasure that Sloan must have felt when Cadillac suddenly lost leadership of the luxury car class to Packard, who moved ahead in terms of sales by a ratio of over two to one in the mid-1920s.

Plans were laid as early as 1926 for a grand gesture that would reassert Cadillac's place at the top of the league. Packard had established an image as a company who could achieve the ultimate in engineering with its Twin Six, the world's first series-production V12 car, of which over

MODEL:
Cadillac Series 452 V16 (1930)

UK price when announced:
£1500 (chassis only)

ENGINE
Location: Front longitudinal
Type: 45 degree V16
Cubic capacity: 7412 cc
Bore x stroke: 76.2 x 101.6 mm
Compression ratio: 5.5:1
Valve Gear: 2 in-line valves per
cylinder, operated by single block-
mounted camshaft
Fuel supply: updraught Cadillac
carburettor to each bank, fed by
vacuum pump
Ignition: dual 6V coils, mounted in
radiator header to stabilise
temperature
Maximum power: 165 bhp at 3400
rpm

TRANSMISSION
Layout: Unit gearbox, torque tube
final drive
Clutch: Double dry plate
Gearbox: Three-speed
synchromesh in unit with engine
   1st. 3.47.1   3rd: 1:1
   2nd: 1.48:1
Final drive: Hypoid bevel
Ratio: 3.47 (to 1/6/30), 4.07, 4.39,
4.75:1

SUSPENSION
Front: Non independent with
semi-elliptic leaf springs and
hydraulic dampers
Rear: Non independent with live
rear axle, semi-elliptic leaf springs
and hydraulic dampers

STEERING
Type: worm and sector

BRAKES
Type: Mechanical vacuum-servo,
footbrake, internal-expanding on
front, external contracting on rear;
handbrake internal expanding on
rear

WHEELS AND TYRES
Type: Wire wheels, 7.50/19 tyres

BODY/CHASSIS
Type: 15 body styles available;
pressed steel channel section frame
with wide top flange

DIMENSIONS AND WEIGHT
Wheelbase: 148 in (3759 mm)
Weight: 6200 lb (2812 kg)

PERFORMANCE
Maximum speed: 84-100 mph
(135-160 kph)
Acceleration: 10-60 mph: 21.1
seconds
Fuel Consumption: 10 mpg

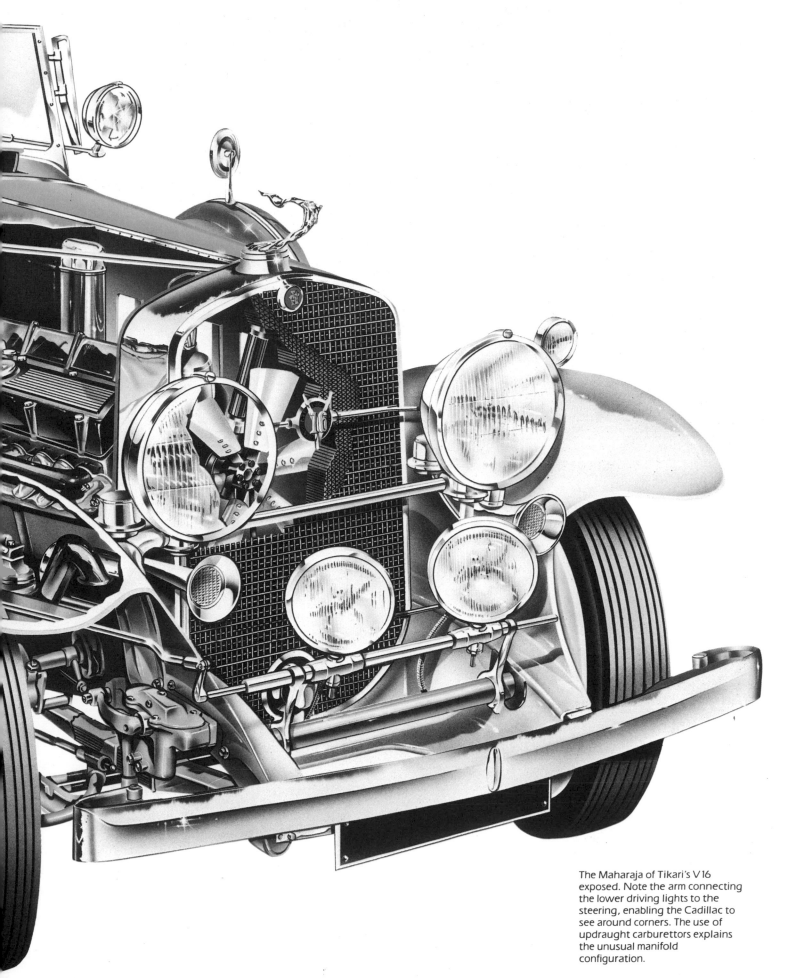

The Maharaja of Tikari's V16 exposed. Note the arm connecting the lower driving lights to the steering, enabling the Cadillac to see around corners. The use of updraught carburettors explains the unusual manifold configuration.

35,000 were built between 1915-22.

The success of that car partly dictated the way that Cadillac had to go. The new Cadillac had to be faster, more powerful and more refined than anything else on the market. The answer was to enlarge the power unit of the existing Cadillac V8, but this would not do, for a bigger V8 would lose something in terms of smoothness, could have thermodynamic problems and most certainly would possess torque characteristics that would necessitate the development of a new, stronger transmission.

That, for several reasons, was not desirable. Cadillac's existing transmission was generally quite satisfactory, the company was working with Earl A. Thompson to adapt his new Syncro-mesh mechanism to their gearbox and the extra development cost, plus the possible reliability problems that could follow, dictated that the new engine, despite extra power, should possess similar torque characteristics to the V8 and thus share a common driveline.

That meant extra cylinders to even out the torque – but there were strong reasons against a V12, not the least of which was that Packard had been first in the field with an excellent product, and however good were such a unit developed by Cadillac,

there would always be comparisons and charges of plagiarism.

So the die was cast; sixteen cylinders it had to be, a configuration not previously seen in any motorcar, and rarely found even in non-automotive installations like racing motorboats. Even there, the few 16-cylinder powerplants had been composed of two V8 engines, not conceived as a hexadecimal whole.

The V16 project coincided with the arrival at Cadillac of a new engine designer, Owen Nacker, who had previously worked as a consultant with Alanson P. Brush. Though Brush's products had not been renowned for their refinement, Nacker was an exceptionally gifted engineer whose first project at Cadillac had been to develop the 341 Series V8 engine – which initially appeared in the first-ever LaSalle in 1927 – and who then turned his attention to the development of the new V16.

The entire project was the responsibility of Chief Engineer Ernest Seaholm, and the degree of secrecy in which it was developed was quite remarkable. Most of the lower-echelon engineers and outside suppliers – the principal sources of leaks – were convinced that Cadillac was developing a new commercial vehicle, since the

blueprints were mostly marked 'Bus' or 'Coach'.

Body styling too was carried on inhouse, as Fleetwood was part of the General Motors organisation.

The launch of the V16 consequently took the press and industry by surprise. The statement by *The Autocar* on the Cadillac's Olympia Motor Show debut, that 'something of a sensation should be caused by the appearance of the sixteen-cylinder Cadillac, showing in practice a type of engine of which more will be heard in the United States in the future', was a masterpiece of understatement. Cadillac was less modest; an early advertisement for the V16 proclaims it merely as 'the very finest of its kind . . . a mechanical masterpiece . . . there is no power plant in any motor car so

A 1931 Fleetwood Sports Phaeton built for the Maharaja of Tikari – hence the right-hand drive. The lower lights swivel with the front wheels and passengers could monitor progress via the supplementary speedo and clock

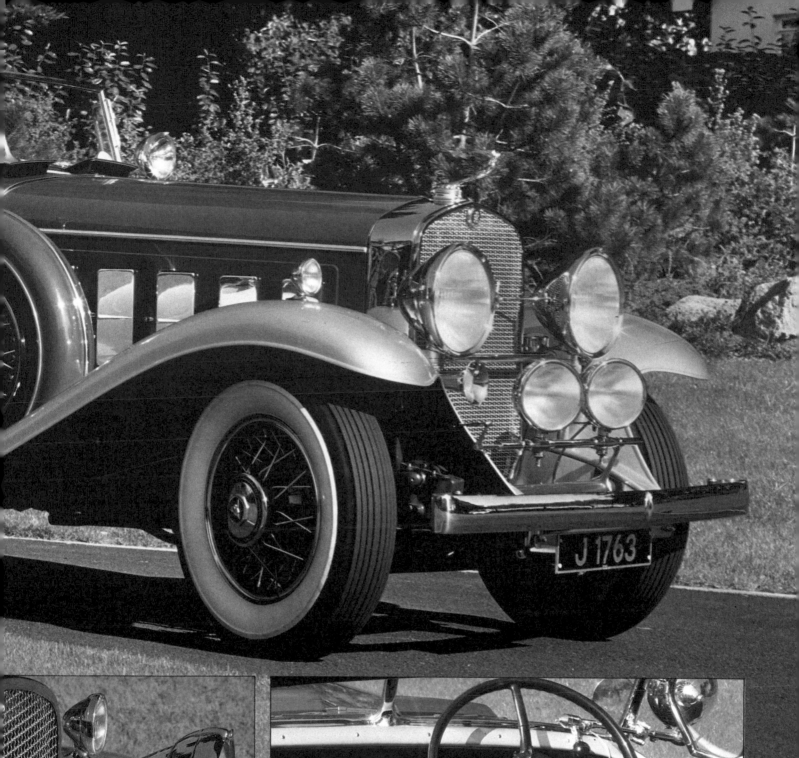

smooth, so quiet, so flexible – or so generally satisfactory – as Cadillac's 16-cylinder engine . . .'

This remarkable smoothness was almost certainly the result of 'automatic adjustment of rocker clearance which requires no attention and ensures silent running'. The Cadillac V16 had conventional pushrod overhead valves, but instead of the hydraulic tappets which are commonly used nowadays, the rockers were pivoted on snail-cam eccentrics with an hydraulic plunger pushing at one end. Thus the centre around which the rocker pivoted was varied by the hydraulic plunger until

> **'… even Rolls-Royce could not match this level of refinement '**

all the clearance had been taken up at either end. While it wasn't a new idea – it went back to Amédé Bollée *fils,* who patented the idea in April 1910 – the V16 Cadillac was the first production car to use the principle, and it brought an unprecedented degree of refinement to the Cadillac's manner of going.

In 1962, *Motor Sport* tested a 30-year-old Cadillac V16 and remarked that: 'Extreme silence and flexibility is the beauty of this monster from Detroit . . . engine, transmission and back axle are well-nigh inaudible.'

According to Cadillac experts the only sound audible when the engine is ticking over should be the spark at the contact points, augmented when the engine is running at cruising speed by the hiss of the air intake and the sound of the fan blades. Even Rolls-Royce could not match this level of refinement, and it's worth noting that when their Phantom III was launched a few years later, the engine was equipped with

hydraulic tappets . . .

Cadillac however, were particularly interested in Rolls-Royce's renowned riding qualities. Cadillac head, Lawrence Fisher (one of the seven body-builder brothers) had engaged Maurice Olley, who had been working at Rolls-Royce of America at Springfield and had done much work on suspension design, to improve the ride of Cadillacs. Olley brought in Rolls-Royce techniques, such as swinging a car from overhead pivots to determine its moment of inertia, and set up a 'bump rig' – a crude form of rolling road – for the dynamic testing of suspension and ride on a static, and hence more observable, car.

Thus in 1931 came Cadillac's 'K' test vehicle, a seven-passenger limousine equipped with weights which could be moved to vary the moment of inertia and front and rear suspension deflection while the car was in motion. Using this rig Olley was able to show that for a really flat ride

the front spring rate had to be slower than the rear; he then began to investigate the use of independent front suspension to reduce the frustrating front-wheel shimmy and brake wind-up, as well as to secure accurate steering geometry. A Dubonnet system was tried, and then Olley developed a system with unequal-length wishbones and coil springs. This had the advantage that the wheelbase remained constant throughout the suspension travel. This SLA independent front suspension was adopted on 1934 Cadillac V16s.

Also praiseworthy was the braking on the Cadillac V16 which, after some problems with brake fade on early V16s, was the subject of a $200,000 investment which produced fully-machined cast molybdenum iron drums ground to an accuracy of 0.007 in for concentricity. In conjunction with cast aluminium brake shoes which expanded as they heated to counteract brake fade, these modifications gave im-

LEFT *Elegance personified in the form of a 1931 V16 convertible*
ABOVE *The 1932 V16 featured a modified chassis, restyled body and choice of two wheelbases. 296 were built*

pressive braking characteristics, particularly with Cadillac's vacuum servo system. Any shortcomings by modern standards can be attributed to the problems inherent in overcoming the inertia of a fast-moving car weighing some two and three-quarter tons (2800 kg) . . .

Though the Cadillac V16 was aimed at a small and exclusive market, sales got off to a good start. The V16 was introduced at the National Automobile Show in January 1930, and by April that year the thousandth car was being shipped; three months later, the 2000th left the factory, and sales volume was reported as having reached $13.5 million. It was a false dawn: some idea of the way that the Depression affected sales can

be gained from the fact that the first six months of V16 Cadillac production represented 52 per cent of all the overhead valve V16s built over the model's seven year life, nearly 46 per cent of total Cadillac V16 output. Only 500 V16s were sold in the latter half of 1930, and in 1931 sales totalled 750, despite big discounts by dealers.

Since the entire market was 42 per cent down that year, the 70 per cent drop in V16 Cadillac sales is perhaps not so startling; production, however, was just 346 cars, since many of the 1931 sales were of cars left over from the year before. That represented a collapse of over 87 per cent in terms of cars actually built: and worse was to come . . . In 1933, Cadillac announced that it would build just 400 V16s – one for each of that legendary top echelon of American society, the Four Hundred? – and in the event made a mere 126. From then on, an average of 50 V16s a year was built until production ceased in 1937.

EVOLUTION

Series 452 V16 introduced in January 1930. High-speed axle dropped 1 June. Annual production: 1826 cars.

1931 Series 452A introduced. Annual production: 1424 cars.

1932 Series 452B introduced in January with restyled bodies, triple-silent gearbox, mechanical fuel pump, air-cooled generator, controlled free-wheeling and vacuum clutch, modified chassis, ride control, 7.50/18 wheels and choice of 143 in (363 cm) and 149 in (378 cm) wheelbases. Annual production: 296 cars

1933 Series 452C introduced in January with modified axle ratios and 7.50/17 wheels. Annual production: 125 cars

1934 Series 452D introduced in January with 185 bhp power output, dual X-braced chassis, open propeller shaft, independent front suspension, 154 in (391 cm) wheelbase. Annual production: 56 cars

1935 Series 60 452D introduced in January. Similar to 1934. Annual production: 50 cars

1936 Series 90. Similar to 1935 but with modifications to bodywork. Annual production: 52 cars

1937 Series 90 continues with hydraulic brakes added. Last season for overhead valve V16. Annual production: 49 cars

1938 Series 90 with 135 degree side-valve 7023 cc V16 engine introduced. Dual downdraught carburettors, single-plate clutch, helical gearing, hypoid final drive, 141 in (358 cm) wheelbase. Annual production: 311 cars

1939 Series 90 continues. Annual production: 136 cars

1940 Series 90 production ends. Annual production: 61 cars. Total V16 production amounted to 4386 cars

To some extent, Cadillac had diluted the potential of the V16 in August 1930 with the announcement that they were to build a V12 of their own, This was a derivative of the V16, but using the biggest of the V8 chassis, and with a bore of 79.4 mm against the 76.2 mm of the V16.

Another factor in the V12's favour – which must have weighed heavy in post-Wall Street Crash America – was that it cost considerably less than the V16. At the launch in late 1930, the V12 models cost between $3795 and $4895; the comparable V16s were priced between $5350 and $9200. Since the V12 was mechanically similar to the V16, and offered almost equal levels of refinement, it's small wonder that right from the start it outsold the V16. By 1937 ten V12s were being sold for every V16.

Nevertheless, the V16 did stimulate Cadillac's rivals into action: Packard retaliated with a new-generation Twin-Six with sleek styling and hydraulic valve lifters, but sold only 549 of them between June 1931 and January 1933 (in the same period

'… only two other firms dared to compete… Both failed… '

Cadillac sold some 7700 of its V12). Lincoln launched its KB V12 in 1932, but again sales were nowhere as good as those of the V12 Cadillac; V12s also came from two declining giants, Pierce-Arrow and Franklin, but only two other firms dared to compete by producing V16 cars. Both failed.

In January 1931 Marmon unveiled a 'car of exceptional interest', an overhead valve 200 bhp V16 with an aluminium-alloy engine which had pressed-in steel cylinder liners. The Marmon was certainly an impressive car, but lacked the ultimate panache of the Cadillac. Few were built.

Then there was the Peerless V16, last-ditch stand of a company which had formerly been one of the greatest American luxury-car makers. It appeared during 1930, and matched the Cadillac V16 in terms of performance, for its 7.6-litre power unit developed 173 bhp. Despite this, the Peerless failed to pass the prototype stage, and production ceased in 1931.

So, in comparison with its rivals the Cadillac V16 was not as unsuccessful as it first appeared, and proved that Cadillac was again a serious contender in the luxury car field.

Of all the early Cadillac V16 models, none achieved greater fame than the 1930 'Madame X' series, which acquired its name as the result of a visit to the cinema by Harley Earl in 1929. He saw a much-acclaimed talking picture in Detroit in which the central character, was 'Madame X … different, mysterious, exciting and, above all … intriguing'.

At the time, the GM Art and Color Studios was working on a new body style with

slender pillars and a pronounced windshield rake; it had, thought Earl, the same characteristics as 'Madame X'.

No expense was spared, and some of the early Madame X Cadillacs had stainless-steel coach striping sweated to the bodywork instead of the traditional painted stripes; gold-faced instruments and stainless-steel wire wheels were also featured.

Individual variants were not only legion but rare. For instance, even in 1931, only two right-hand-drive V16s were built, while in the 1934-37 period, the most built with one body style in one year was 24. The majority of body styles were built in ones and twos, and some were truly extravagant, like the one-of-a-kind 1934 Convertible Victoria Coupé which still exists in Chicago. As close-coupled as a coupé riding on a massive 154 inch (391 cm) wheelbase (the longest used by any major American manufacturer), the car has pontoon wings (the rear wheels fully faired in) and a projecting boot; horizontal louvres in the bonnet sides are echoed by louvres on the front

TOP *A 1935 V16 in California*
ABOVE RIGHT *The superb 1931 V16. Bore was 3 in and stroke 4 in to give a displacement of 452 cu in (6½ litres) and 165 bhp*
RIGHT *By 1937 coachwork had given way to pressed steel*

wings for aesthetic reasons.

In 1937 Cadillac announced, not unexpectedly, that the V16 was to cease production; what was unexpected was that its replacement was to be a new V16. As much as any ultimate extravagance could be, the new engine was more in tune with the austere climate of the late 1930s. Its specification had been simplified so that it needed only half as many parts, resulting in a 250 lb weight reduction, yet it was as powerful and smoother than the original V16. It was more compact, yet had nine main bearings against the 1930 V16's five; its cylinders were splayed at 135 degrees for superior balance, yet it took up only about two-thirds of the volume.

And, intriguingly, this new V16 flew in

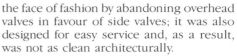

the face of fashion by abandoning overhead valves in favour of side valves; it was also designed for easy service and, as a result, was not as clean architecturally.

Nonetheless, the 1938 V16 found few customers – just 508 of them in its three-year production life but a distinct improvement over the 50-a-year of its predecessor.

Progress in engine design and installation had rendered the concept of a super-smooth sixteen an anachronism. The V8 Cadillacs of the late 1930s were both smooth and flexible, and developed almost as much power as the V16 (135-140 bhp against 185), yet cost from only $2290 in comparison to a starting price of $5140 for the V16. Since they were also available with as wide and elegant a range of coachwork, what logical choice could anyone have made but the V8? As the late Michael Sedg-

---

' the 1930 V16 established Cadillac in the front rank of constructors... '

wick pointed out: 'in the era of alligator hoods, only those who worked on the engine got a clear view of it ...'

The motorist of the late 1930s was also less interested in mechanical specifications than his predecessor of a decade before, and the concept of paying more than twice as much for eight more cylinders, when the car performed just as well with the V8 power unit, made it generally redundant. The 1930 V16 had set a fashion and established Cadillac in the front rank of constructors; a decade later, the V8 had become perfectly adequate.

Moreover, hadn't Cadillac proved its worth by riding out the Depression, where so many of the other luxury car manufacturers had foundered?   DBW

CHEVROLE

America's sports car started life as a glassfibre-bodied six-cylinder convertible in 1953 and grew in stature to become the powerful Sting Ray muscle car of the '60s and then the high-tech sports car of the '80s

A NAVAL ESCORT as fast as it was uncomfortable – it was truly a stroke of genius to choose the name Corvette for 'America's sports car' in 1953.

It can be argued that the Corvette was GM's riposte to the post-war British invasion of MGs and Jaguars – perhaps, but if you produce the number the General does, the number of sports cars imported then would hardly have raised a corporate eyebrow. No, it wasn't the numbers (how could it be with the production capacity of the British car industry?) but the inspiration that counted.

By the middle of this century Harley Earl had risen to be chief of GM's Art and Colour studio in Detroit, and that made him as important then in North America as Giugiaro is today in the whole world. His admiration for the Jaguar XK120 led him to father a truly American answer, aided and abetted by a figure destined to be just as influential, Ed Cole – the force behind the later '57 Chevy. In 1953 Cole had not long been Chief Engineer at Chevrolet and his burning desire was to improve Chevrolet's staid and rather boring image. That, coupled to Earl's vision, was bound to produce something special. Vision and enthusiasm, however, were not enough to sway one of the most conservative of car companies to produce something speculative and radically different just on a whim; the Corvette would have

to earn its corn as a mobile test bed. It was to be the first mass-production glassfibre car and a relatively risk-free way for the GM hierarchy to evaluate glassfibre for sedan use without committing themselves to 'real' mass production. Although glassfibre didn't take over, the Corvette has continued its test bed role throughout its life, with the current car pioneering the use of lightweight mono-filament transvere leaf springs fore and aft.

Naturally enough, for a low-volume and somewhat speculative mobile test rig GM were not generous in allocating funds, and the first car was largely an amalgam of available production parts, such as Chevy's venerable and stolid 235 cu in (3.8-litre) straight six, suitably modified with solid lifters and different cam timing to produce 150 bhp at 4500 rpm. It was mated to that most sporting of transmissions, the Powerglide two-speed automatic, and drove the rear wheels via a leaf-sprung axle, all mounted on a solid box section X-braced frame.

Although the first cars were anything but elegant compared to the Jaguar (or much

The second generation Corvettes were introduced in 1956 with a 210 bhp 4.3-litre V8 and three-speed manual transmission at a base price of just $3149. It was one of the most elegant of 1950s American cars

T Corvette

else come to that), with their deep slab sides making them look more like freighters that the weapon the name evoked, when the Corvette was introduced at 'Motorama' (GM's travelling extravaganza) public reaction was wildly enthusiastic. That response was enough to put the car into production, briefly on a very small six-car line in Flint, Michigan, before being transferred to St Louis where the car was built for many years until the 1981 move to its present home in Bowling Green, Kentucky.

Unfortunately the American public did not put its money where its mouth was, and by the end of 1954 a mere 3600 of the year's models had been sold, leaving another 1500 homeless. The answer came in 1955, and it wasn't the extra 30 cubic inches but the fact that the new 265 cu in engine was Chevrolet's latest V8, lighter (by 30 lb/14 kg) and more powerful (by 45 bhp) than the archaic six. Nevertheless the damage had already been done for the first generation Corvettes, and it was not until 1956 when the ugly duckling turned, as they are all supposed to, into an elegant swan, that the Corvette took hold of the American imagination.

The combination of V8 power, a manual transmission (albeit only a three-speed) and a body that was exactly right worked wonders, and sales proved it, with 3388 sold in 1956, compared with just 674 in 1955. By

that time the Belgian engineer Zora Arkus-Duntov's influence was beginning to be felt. Up went the compression ratio and the power, to 9.25:1 and 225 bhp respectively. With 270 lb ft of torque at 3600 rpm and a virtually even weight distribution the '56 car was very rapid indeed. It had finally turned into a genuine sports car capable of 7.5-second times to 60 mph (96 kph) and a top speed of 120 mph (193 kph), and measured by the all-important American yardstick, it could cover the standing quarter mile in 14.2 seconds with a terminal speed of 93 mph (150 kph). Performance improved

This 1967 Sting Ray Coupé represents the end of an era, dating from the last year of Sting Ray production. The first Sting Ray Coupés of 1963 featured a split rear screen but that was soon discarded in favour of the wide screen (ABOVE), much to the designer Bill Mitchell's disgust. Mitchell felt the split screen was an essential feature of the whole design. The coupé proved popular, immediately accounting for 50 per cent of Corvette production ABOVE LEFT *Sting Rays were well equipped inside with a plethora of instruments to supplement the large speedo and tach*

even further when the Borg-Warner four-speed transmission became available in 1957.

The second generation Corvette lasted for seven years before the starkly different Sting Ray appeared in 1963, yet during that time it epitomised the traditional open sports car. It was not exactly sophisticated but was strong, looked simply terrific and was *very* fast.

Under that elegant glassfibre, the quality of which had improved dramatically since the first cars, tradition reigned. The stout box frame soldiered on, carrying the live

as well as it went, and by that time it certainly *would* go… That V8 had gradually been getting bigger and bigger, and by '59 it had been bored out to displace 283 cu in (4.6 litres) with power to match its greater size. Rather neatly, the short-stroke V8 (3.87 in × 3 in/98.3 mm × 76.2 mm) gave one horse-power for each cubic inch of displacement, with the 283 bhp (SAE gross) being deli-vered at 4800 rpm. Admittedly that was with the high-performance Rochester-built GM fuel injection, which unfortunately proved to be every bit as troublesome to GM as Lucas fuel injection had on the Triumphs of the late '60s. When it worked properly, however, the results were spectacular and it would power the '57 Corvette to 60 mph in just 5.5 seconds; it was hardly surprising that at the end of the standing quarter mile the car would be touching 100 mph (161 kph).

Such impressive power and speed should obviously be raced, and the second generation 'Vettes were quite successful in the SCCA Class B Production class in 1958 and '59. Sadly for sports-car development in the United States, however, the National Safety Council managed to convince the Auto Manufacturers' Association (AMA) that direct involvement in racing was tantamount to endorsing death on the roads, and in June 1957 the infamous AMA ban on factory in-volvement came to pass. The AMA edict did

was replaced by a rear end with strong overtones of the Sting Ray to come in 1963.

Bill Mitchell had become Chief of GM Design in 1961 and his ideas spelt the end for the '50s styles. To his credit however, Mitchell did not stop developing the second generation cars until his favoured form appeared in '63, and some critics consider the 1962 models to be among the best. By that time the Corvette sported a 327 cu in (5.3-litre) V8 producing 360 bhp and a top speed approaching 150 mph (242 kph). In retrospect perhaps Mitchell was right; that sort of power deserved to be housed in something more up to date than an obsoles-cent braced frame with semi-elliptic rear leaf springs and a live axle. Sales figures for 1963 seemed to prove the point; the new car, the Sting Ray, prompted a 50 per cent rise in sales, with half of the 21,000 sold being the new hardtop Coupé.

What was so modern about the Sting Ray? In the early '60s there was a clear world-wide trend towards rear-mounted engines, a fashion that inspired cars as disparate as the Porsche 911 and the Hillman Imp, the Renault Dauphine and the Chevrolet Cor-vair, and thus Zora Arkus-Duntov was strong-ly tempted to follow with the Corvette. In the end the Corvette tradition won, and the front V8 remained in a car strongly modelled on one of the fragile fruits of Chevrolet's racing

> *the mechanical changes were far less radical than the styling*

Corvette programme. Duntov's stillborn Sebring SS of 1957, with its magnesium body, steel space frame and de Dion rear axle, had been remodelled by Mitchell to form the Stringray racing car, successfully campaigned by Dick Thompson in SCCA C-Class Sports during 1959 and 1960. In 1962 Mitchell turned the car into his person-al road car, which exists in a pristine silver to this day, and it illustrates just how much it influenced his design of the third generation cars, although they, naturally, did not feature the racing style hump behind the driver's seat…

The looks may have been similar but there was no chance of the alloy bodywork or spaceframe chassis being put into pro-duction, and the mechanical changes were far less radical than the styling. The major difference lay with the rear suspension. It wasn't the racer's de Dion arrangement but a rather odd device using something almost as traditional as a live axle, a transverse semi-elliptic leaf spring, which gave the Corvette independent suspension for the first time. The differential was bolted to two of the cross members in the new upswept ladder perimeter frame with the spring bolted to the diff carrier. Transverse location for the wheels was provided by two lower tubular radius arms and double-jointed drive shafts, while longitudinal location came via two trailing arms.

rear axle on leaf springs, although Duntov had revised the spring mountings to give more precise handling. The front suspen-sion was a wishbone and coil spring arrangement with positive recirculating ball steering (with just three turns lock to lock).

By 1959 Chevrolet were starting to cater for serious drivers by offering a perform-ance suspension option, consisting of a front anti-roll bar and uprated springs and dam-pers all round, complemented by quicker steering and a limited slip differential. That, allied to a wide track and a 52:48 front/rear weight ratio meant a Corvette that handled

not slow down the NASCAR stockers all that much, and somewhere deep in the bowels of Ford and GM racing parts continued to be built and delivered to favoured teams. The Grossman/Fitch Corvette that finished an extremely commendable 8th at Le Mans in 1960 did not exceed 150 mph (242 kph) down the Mulsanne straight with a stock engine…

Nevertheless, at the beginning of the '60s the Corvette was hardly the child of the race track. It had grown bigger and started to sprout too much extraneous chrome until finally, in 1961, that graceful rounded tail

RIGHT The 1984 Corvette is notable for its use of plastic monofilament transverse leaf springs for both front and rear suspension and for its superbly forged aluminium alloy suspension arms

BOTTOM RIGHT The '84 Corvette has moved away from the traditional ladder frame to the perimeter steel chassis built of galvanised high strength steel. The subframes front and rear are in aluminised steel

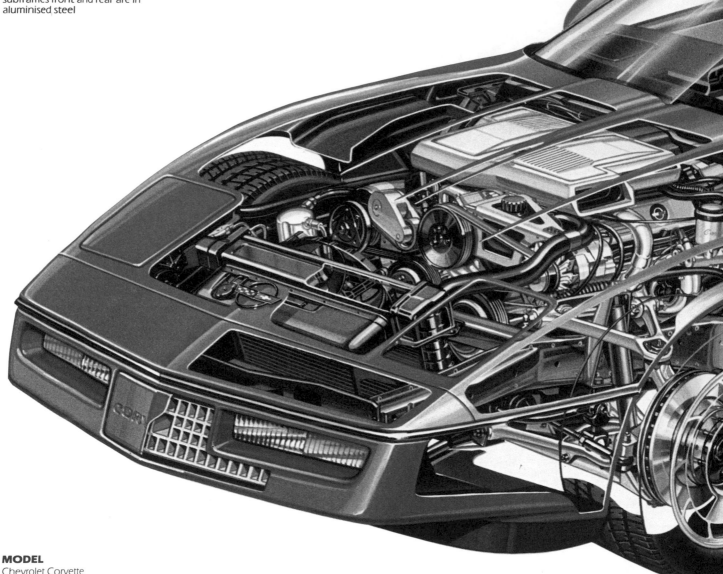

MODEL
Chevrolet Corvette
UK price (1984): £28,600

ENGINE
Location: Front, longitudinal
Type: Water cooled V8 with cast iron block and heads
Cubic capacity: 5736 cc
Bore × stroke: 101.6 mm × 88.4 mm
Valve gear: 2 valves per cylinder in line operated via single block-mounted camshaft, pushrods and hydraulic tappets
Fuel supply: 'Cross Fire' throttle body fuel injection
Ignition: Delco Remy high energy electronic with engine management control
Maximum power: 205 bhp at 4200 rpm (SAE net)
Maximum torque: 290 lb ft at 2800 rpm (SAE net)

TRANSMISSION
Layout: Clutch and gearbox in unit with engine
Clutch: Single dry plate
Gearbox: Four-speed manual with computer-controlled overdrive on top three ratios or Turbo-Hydramatic four-speed automatic with following ratios

1st 3.060:1	3rd 1.00:1
2nd 1.630:1	4th 0.70:1

Final drive: Hypoid bevel with limited slip differential
Ratio: 2.730:1

SUSPENSION
Front: Independent with wishbones, anti-roll bar and transverse monofilament plastic leaf spring
Rear: Independent with five links – upper and lower control arms per side with lateral Panhard rod, transverse monofilament leaf spring

STEERING
Type: Rack and pinion, servo assisted with 2.36 turns lock to lock

BRAKES
Type: Discs front and rear with 329.9 sq in (2128 sq cm) swept area

WHEELS AND TYRES
Type: Alloy 16 in × 8 in with Goodyear 225/50VR16 radial tyres

BODY/CHASSIS
Type: High-strength steel perimeter frame with glassfibre and SMC 2-door, 2-seat coupè body

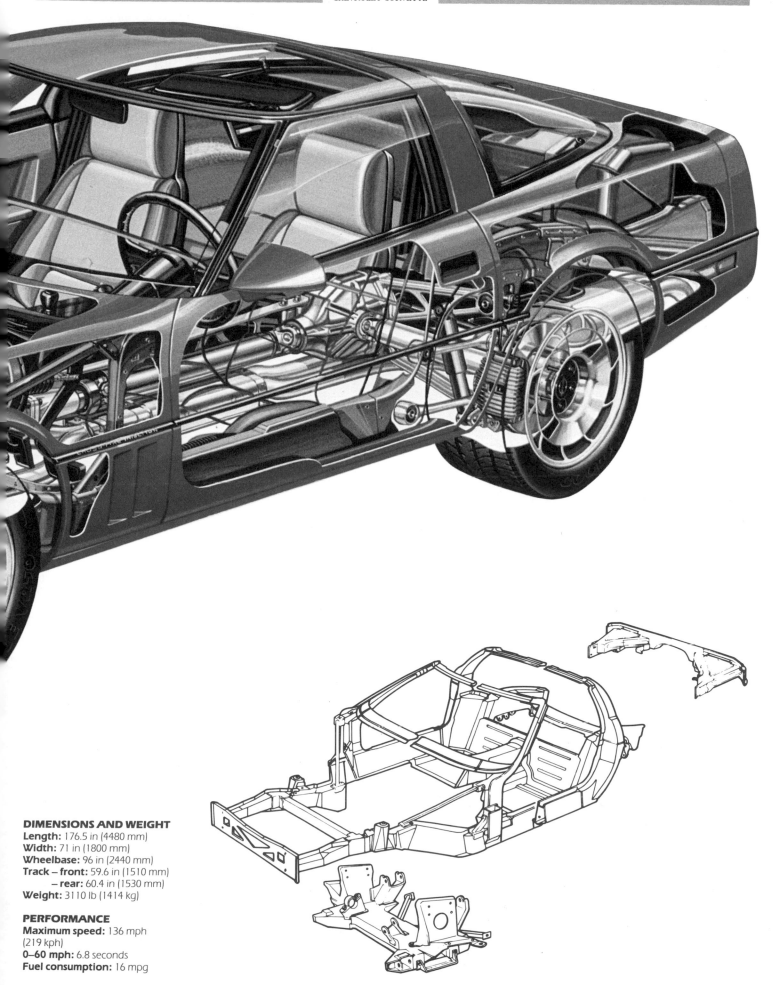

DIMENSIONS AND WEIGHT
Length: 176.5 in (4480 mm)
Width: 71 in (1800 mm)
Wheelbase: 96 in (2440 mm)
Track – front: 59.6 in (1510 mm)
     – rear: 60.4 in (1530 mm)
Weight: 3110 lb (1414 kg)

PERFORMANCE
Maximum speed: 136 mph
(219 kph)
0–60 mph: 6.8 seconds
Fuel consumption: 16 mpg

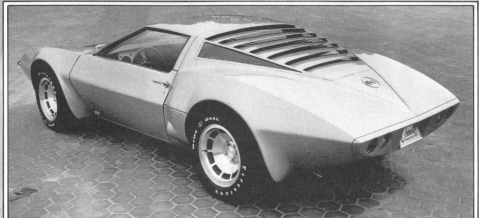

ABOVE LEFT *The original Sting Ray, transformed into Bill Mitchell's road car*
LEFT *Many Corvette prototypes never made it into production, including this 1970 V8 mid-engined example*
ABOVE AND BELOW *A fourth generation Corvette of 1976 vintage. By 1976 the 5.7-litre V8 produced just 185 bhp*

That transverse spring had no intrinsic merit other than it saved space – there was simply no room for coils in the new design – but that hardly seemed to matter, for the new rear proved a great success, putting an immediate end to two of the earlier car's faults – terminal oversteer and axle tramp.

In the 1960s there really was no substitute for cubic inches, and when the Corvette entered the horsepower battle it did so in full, with the 427 cu in (7-litre) engine. With solid valve lifters and an 11:1 compression ratio, that engine didn't need fuel injection to impress; with a four barrel Holley carburettor it produced 425 bhp at 5600 rpm and a massive 465 lb ft of torque.

That spells performance in anyone's language and Corvette customers could choose exactly how much of it they wanted; usually there were four engine options, and in 1966, for example, the range was wide, from the mundane base 300 bhp 327 cu in (5.3-litre) V8 to the top performance 427 cu in (7-litre) V8. If one chose the 427 with the 4.11:1 final drive then the car would break the 5-second barrier to 60 mph and still reach 140 mph (225 kph) while with a more conservative rear end 160 mph (257 kph) was theoretically possible. That extra power was cheap too; in 1966 the 427 engine was a $312 option.

A huge V8 is guaranteed to make your progress rapid but it's a lot of metal to stop, and for years that was the Corvette's main problem. By the early '60s the Corvette's massive alloy drum brakes had been given special sintered iron linings, but even they could not cope, as the racers discovered. The solution, long overdue, appeared in 1965 with disc brakes – 10 years after Jaguar's D-type proved their effectiveness. Strangely, when *Autocar* tested a Sting Ray in 1963 they did not find the drum brakes a problem, declaring that they were 'light in operation, very powerful at all speeds and free from fade…', although they did lock prematurely. Otherwise they quibbled at the car's lack of refinement compared to high-performance European GTs. On a more positive note they liked the gear lever's action ('smooth, short and extremely light') and were surprised by the comfort above 50 mph (80 kph) despite the hard spring and damper settings that made the rear step out of line through bumpy corners.

Overall the tone was grudging, even though the test car out accelerated the E-type, Jensen CV-8 and Maserati Sebring which they compared it to, both to 60 mph and over the standing quarter (which the Corvette managed in just 13.5 seconds).

When the American magazine *Sports Car Graphic* tried a '65 427 with disc brakes they were far less stilted: 'We didn't even bother to take it to Riverside or Willow Springs for acceleration runs…all you need is a two-block-long straight. From a 70 mph cruising speed you can accelerate to…140 mph in roughly a mile. Sixty to 100 mph in top gear takes a mere 7.2 seconds. Tell us you'd like a hotter performing road machine than this and we'll call you some kinda nut!' Like *Autocar* they noted the initial understeer which turned into slight oversteer with the power on. 'The limit is reached with the rear end breaking loose all of a sudden and, even though it takes quick reflexes, a slight twitch of the wheel and an instant lift with the accelerator foot will bring it back under control. But you have to be going gawdawful fast to reach the limit – very near competitive racing speeds.'

Even more exciting were Arkus-Duntov's Grand Sports, built to rival Carroll Shelby's AC Cobras in SCCA Production racing. The original plan was to build 125 for homologation and to take the car to Le Mans in 1963. Duntov was confident that his twin-plug per cylinder, fuel-injected experimental alloy 550 bhp 377 cu in (6.1-litre) V8 would push the Corvette to 180 mph (290 kph) along the long Mulsanne straight. GM spoiled the fun, forcing Chevrolet to veto the project, citing the old AMA ban. That also meant an end to the 125 production run, but the Grand Sport did have its moment of glory when three of them went to the Nassau Speed Week in the Bahamas in 1963 and proved themselves dramatically quicker than a host of Cobras. Perhaps the oddest thing about the Sting Rays was that they lasted only five years before the fourth generation cars took over, and yet those cars were around until 1983, when, by common consent, it was hardly a classic. The exaggerated coke-bottle styling, with the wasp waist and long front and rear overhangs, was certainly not as striking as the original Sting Ray's, the car was never as fast, and to top it all, was more cramped.

Part of the explanation for its over-long

> *the 'new' Corvette… was aimed at a significantly more wealthy clientele*

life lies in the troubles the American auto industry had to face through the '70s, with oil crises and the increasing tide of Japanese competition. A new Corvette was hardly a priority, and despite the numerous cosmetic styling updates the basic design stagnated as proposed replacements fell by the wayside. The Astro Vette was no great loss but the Asto II of 1968 showed what the Corvette should have looked like in that era. In the late '70s, the Aerovette very nearly did make it into production for 1980. Its transverse V8 was mid-mounted with a complicated drive arrangement involving chain drive to the differential. Before the energy crisis finally killed off GM's interest in the Wankel engine the Aerovette became a test bed for both two and four rotor rotaries before reverting to the 400 cu in (6.5-litre) V8. It was in V8 form that it would have entered production had not three of the Corvette's most influential figures, Ed Cole, then GM President, Bill Mitchell and Zora Arkus-Duntov, retired at the same time.

By the time the 'new' Corvette finally did appear in 1983 it was long overdue and marked a dramatic shift in policy. The first Corvette's base price was $3513, and that level was maintained through the years, to the $7600 of the '76 model and the $16,300 of 1981, as inflation took its toll. The '84 model was aimed at a significantly more wealthy clientele, with a base price nearer $30,000.

What could possibly make a Corvette worth so much? After all it was still only a front-engined, rear-drive V8.

The '84 Corvette was a quantum leap forward in design, handling… and price. At one stage the car cost £28,000 in the UK (partly due to a weak pound it's true). Enormous care was taken to make the under-bonnet area as attractive as possible with careful colour matching of all leads, pipes and wires. One of the most attractive features of the new 'Vette was its electronic dashboard – it changed from metric to imperial at the flick of a switch

That, claim the Chevrolet engineers, was a deliberate policy, a reaffirmation of the American way… The engine itself is certainly nothing special; even with throttle-body fuel injection (known as 'cross-fire injection' at GM) its 350 cu in (5.7 litres) delivers only 205 bhp at 4300 rpm, but, as Aston Martin or Rolls-Royce would put it, the power output is 'adequate'. This Corvette has been built for handling rather than outright performance, the goal being to equal the best of the Europeans, like the Porsche 928.

Naturally, with that level of ambition some new suspension was called for, and the rear has been remodelled with two short trailing links per side with an extra control arm to enable toe in and out to be set precisely. The transverse plastic leaf spring introduced in 1981 was retained; Chevrolet have been so pleased with its performance that they decided on a similar system at the

moulded on the company's FI rain tyres. The massive 'gatorback' 255/50VR16s are unidirectional and thus can only be used on one side of the car. Allied to those stiff damper settings they mean that 1 g cornering is almost within reach.

European GTs are meant to be nimble, so very 'quick', precise steering was regarded as essential, and the '84 Corvette has the most precise rack and pinion system ever seen on an American production car. Basically the Corvette engineers, under chief engineer David McLellan, had free rein, and the end result is a car with superb reactions and response on the race track, where its prodigious grip and massive disc brakes come into their own. McLellan claims that 'With its totally new suspension configuration, this car will be at home and respected on the interstate, the autobahn, or any highway in the world.' That may have been the intention but the reality turned out to be rather different. On the ordinary road the unfortunate '84 Corvette driver finds that refinement has fled, to leave him fighting a heavy and wilful car that seems to have a mind of its own, with steering that's really too sharp and a tendency to follow every

> *'the car has... too many rough edges to make it one of the world's great GTs '*

crack and undulation in the road.

It's a major mystery why the Corvette is not tuned to the road, and equally puzzling is the car's weight. The new car is significantly smaller than its predecessor in every dimension except width, its perimeter chassis uses lightweight high-strength steel, the bonnet is in SMC (sheet moulding composite), the springs are in plastic and the drive shafts, propeller shaft and even the radiator fins are in aluminium. The net result is...a car weighing nearly 3200 lb (1451 kg).

As it stands at present the car has rather too many rough edges to make it one of the world's great GTs, which, after all, is what is claimed for it. The manual gearbox, for example, is clearly inferior to that used years ago and praised in road test after road test; the present GM four-speed has a truly truck-like action almost requiring two hands to change gear. When queried about it a GM engineer argued that easy-shifting gearchanges just couldn't handle the power... It is rather more sophisticated than a straight four-speed in that it's blessed (if that's the right word) by a computer controlled overdrive (0.67:1) operating on the top three ratios, linked to the engine management system which tells it when to engage overdrive for optimum fuel economy. That change is automatic unless the car is under hard acceleration. In principle it's a good idea but it has proved to be nothing but trouble.

Nevertheless, despite the problems with transmission and normal road handling the Corvette will prove a worthy successor to the '60s Sting Rays. KB

front, working with short double wishbones and an anti-roll bar. All the suspension arms are beautifully forged in aluminium, a material also used for the propeller and drive shafts and the central chassis beam connecting differential to gearbox.

One of the most time-honoured ways to achieve reasonable handling characteristics is to stiffen the suspension to the point where the wheels can hardly move out of their ideal plane, and if you choose to use ultra-low profile 50-section tyres as GM have, it becomes even more critical to keep the contact patch flat on the road. The Corvette's ride has become, to put it mildly, firm, or if you choose the Z51 performance suspension option, damn near solid.

An even easier route to a handling heaven is through modern tyre technology and Chevrolet commissioned Goodyear to build Eagle GTs specificaly for the Corvette,

CORD

The Cord of 1935 was regarded as one of the finest examples of styling of all time, yet its futuristic body shielded a host of obscure problems

'THE NEW CORD proves that it *is* possible to build a radically different motor-car which is still in absolute harmony with the highest standards of beauty and good taste.'

That was how advertisements of 1936 promoted the 'new, original and ornamental design for an automobile' which had been patented by Gordon Miller Beuhrig in May 1934 and which later went into production as the Cord 810. In fact the car should have

been a baby Duesenberg.

In 1933 Errett Lobban Cord's Auburn-Cord-Duesenberg Corporation was laying plans for future models, and because of the decline in sales of luxury cars during the Depression and the fact that those who could still afford them wanted less outwardly ostentatious means of transportation, it was determined that work should start on a lower-priced Duesenberg line.

810/812

Buehrig, chief body designer of the Duesenberg Corporation, saw this as the opportunity to translate into a production car a design concept he had entered for a contest organised by Harley Earl of General Motors. His design had run completely counter to accepted standards of car design, for instead of a radiator shell there were horizontal louvres round the bonnet, and when not in use the headlamps retracted into the front pontoon-type wings; on this early design study the twin coolant surface radiators were mounted in the airstream between wings and bonnet.

A prototype body was built and fitted to an experimental Auburn chassis early in 1934, and Buehrig then applied for a patent. He was, however, now working for Auburn, having been transferred in an emergency move to restyle the Models 850 and 652 Auburns for 1935, the 1934 models having proved a dismal failure.

After creating the classic Model 851 and 852 Auburns, Buehrig returned to his baby Duesenberg project, which had been put on ice in the interim. He discovered that the car would now be a Cord, a spiritual successor to the grandiose L-29 Cord of 1929–32, and like its predecessor it would be front-wheel-driven. He started work on a quarter-scale model of the revised project, and it was

> *'... the board was persuaded to give the project the go-ahead...'*

completed by the late summer, when Buehrig took a brief honeymoon.

On his return he found that the baby Duesenberg project had been shelved once again; the Auburn-Cord-Duesenberg management was instead attempting to promote a stop-gap project using components from the Auburn V12. The design staff responded to this suggestion by producing a stupendously ugly mock-up, and the ill-considered idea was quickly dropped. Nevertheless, time and money were rapidly running out, and Auburn president Roy Faulkner believed that the decision should be taken to resume the front-wheel-drive Cord project. He persuaded Buehrig and his assistant Dale Cosper to prepare a presentation in a day so that it could be laid before the Auburn-Cord-Duesenberg board of directors at their imminent meeting in Chicago, when a decision would be made.

Faulkner made the presentation and the board was persuaded to give the project the go-ahead. Only four months remained before the first show opened, and for the car to be eligible as a production model in the eyes of the Automobile Manufacturers' Asso-

ciation, a minimum figure of 100 cars had to be built. To meet this almost impossible deadline within the desperately tight financial constraints of the Auburn-Cord-Duesenberg group, certain short-cuts had to be taken; dies, for instance, were only made for right-front and left-rear doors, for the doors were symmetrical apart for the cutouts for the rear wheelarches, which were removed afterwards by an extra cutter die. Again, the Auburn-Cord-Duesenberg corporation did not possess a large enough press to stamp out the roofs of closed models in one go, so this panel was welded together from smaller pieces.

The interior door handles were bought cheaply at a bankruptcy sale and fitted with showy plastic knobs to make them look expensive; instruments were acquired cheaply, too, and mounted in an engine-turned aircraft-type control panel designed by Buehrig.

Those retractable headlamps were another economy turned to good effect, for they were actually landing lights from Stinson aircraft (Stinson was yet another Cord group company, as was Lycoming, who built the Cord's V8 power unit), though the fact that they had to be cranked up and down manually can hardly have endeared them to Cord owners. By fully utilising such economies the necessary 100 Cords were built in time for the New York Show, although these

lacked the complex front-wheel-drive transmission, in which the gears were selected electro-pneumatically by a miniature lever moving in a gate on the steering column.

With its unusual styling, the new Cord proved an instant sales success. Many orders were taken at the show with promises of delivery by Christmas, but the inevitable problems with the transmission retarded the development programme, and all that those hopeful customers received for Christmas was a tiny scale model Cord mounted on a block of marble.

Perhaps surprisingly, unlike its contemporary, the Chrysler Airflow, the Cord didn't frighten customers away with its avant garde styling; instead, it proved embarrassingly attractive. Even those two hard-boiled critics, Montague Tombs and Freddie Gordon Crosby of *The Autocar* felt that 'The radiator must be subordinated to the design of the whole job, and the design of the whole must first be practical, and it is not practical unless the forward vision is unimpeded, which means a lower scuttle and bonnet and a sloping front… Just about this time the Cord projected itself into range of the companionate vision, and was instantly met, not with contumely, but with a real appreciation of a fine piece of bold and original designing work

OPENING PAGE *A 1937 Cord Beverly Sedan* **LEFT** *The Cord 812 chassis provided the base for this 1938 Phantom Corsair* **RIGHT** *A 1936 Cord 810 Westchester Sedan, named after the exclusive New York town to give an idea of the car's status value* **BELOW** *A 1937 supercharged 812 Phaeton*

…the writer and the illustrator fell to unalloyed appreciation of original work, not forgetting the clever details of the trapdoors for lamps in the streamline wings and the manner in which the bottom edges of the wings are not left straight down, but are neatly curled inwards.'

'… the advantages of front-wheel drive were exploited to the full…'

There were other clever design details, the petrol tank filler was concealed under a faired-in hinged flap, the hood was completely hidden when folded down, and the advantages of front-wheel-drive were exploited to the full in providing a 'step-down' entrance and a flat, uncluttered floor. The

twin tail lights were faired into the 'fastback' tail and the door hinges were completely concealed. Tenite plastic was extensively used for trim hardware, and there was a choice of interior colour and trim designed to complement the external finish.

Buehrig's design for the Cord was so far ahead of its contemporaries that it was subsequently honoured by the Museum of Modern Art in New York as one of the 10 finest examples of industrial styling of all time, the only car to be so recognised.

When *The Autocar* tested a production 810 saloon in 1936, priced then in Britain at £880 (including tax), their report was highly favourable. They wrote: 'An unusual performance is automatically expected from so unusual a car, and one is not disappointed, for this Cord is really fast and the acceleration is very good indeed…'. At Brooklands the testers managed 0-60 mph in 20.1 seconds and achieved a top speed of

MODEL
Cord 810 (1936)
UK price when announced: £895
(phaeton)

ENGINE
Location: Front, longitudinal
Type: Water-cooled 90deg V8 built
by Lycoming
Cubic capacity: 4729 cc
Bore × stroke: 88.9 mm ×
92.25 mm
Compression ratio: 6.5:1
Valve Gear: L-head side-valves,
operated by cam and roller
mechanism
Fuel supply: 1 in duplex
downdraught carburettor
Ignition: Single breaker Autolite
Maximum power: 125 bhp at
3500 rpm

TRANSMISSION
Layout: Front-wheel drive
Clutch: Semi-automatic single dry
plate
Gearbox: Electro-vacuum finger-
tip controlled four-speed
  1st 2.11:1 3rd 0.90:1
  2nd 1.36:1 4th 0.64:1
Final drive: Spiral bevel
Ratio: 4.3:1

SUSPENSION
Front: Independent, with trailing
arms, semi-elliptic leaf springs and
friction dampers
Rear: Non-independent, with
tubular dead axle, semi-elliptic leaf
springs and friction dampers

STEERING
Type: Gemmer centre-point

BRAKES
Type: Hydraulic 12" drums all
round

WHEELS AND TYRES
Type: 6.50 × 16 disc wheels with
six-ply tyres

BODY/CHASSIS
Type: Steel boxed channel chassis
with separate four-door sedan body

DIMENSIONS AND WEIGHT
Length: 189 in (4800 mm)
Width: 77 in (1956 mm)
Wheelbase: 125 in (3175 mm)
Track – front: 56 in (1422 mm)
 – rear: 61 in (1549 mm)
Weight: 3650 lb (1656 kg)

PERFORMANCE
Maximum speed: 93 mph
(150 kph)
Acceleration 0–60 mph: 20.1
seconds
Fuel Consumption (approx):
18 mpg

BELOW A 1936 Cord 810 Beverly
Sedan. The Cord was an advanced
front-wheel-drive design and was
all the more impressive given the
extremely short time allowed for its
design and the limited resources.
The doors, for example, were made
symmetrical to save on tooling; dies
were needed only for one front and
the opposite rear door

92.8 mph (149.3 kph). 'Exceptional average times are possible,' they continued, 'for this car has no speed that can be called a cruising rate, and is virtually as happy at 80 mph as at 60 mph where conditions allow. Certainly it is as fast as most people ever wish to use or our roads permit.'

The gearbox on this car was trouble-free and simple to operate: 'A pause is necessary, with release of the throttle pedal momentarily, to secure engagement of each gear, the action usually being devoid of any noise provided it is not hurried, or at the most there is a mild "clonk".' The finger-tip control was so positioned that once accustomed to it, the driver did not need to look at it to select gears.

The writers found the engine extremely smooth and quiet, 'free from thrash or thump when being accelerated, likewise from mechanical fuss or carburettor intake roar. High praise can be given to the Cord for the manner in which it is able to propel itself slow or fast without giving the occupants any real impression of the speed at which they are travelling. This results from the qualities of the engine…and the high gear ratios that are used. The top gear of 2¾ to 1 is among the very highest ratios employed on production cars of recent years; very few cars have had such a ratio…the performance is astonishingly effortless'.

> *'…the target had been for 1000 cars a month…'*

Whilst the styling and performance of the Cord were collecting plaudits, its mechanics were still causing problems. That front-wheel-drive transmission, with its electric preselection of the gears by a tiny gearlever moving in a miniature gate on the steering column, was an attractive concept that failed to live quite up to its promise. It was beset by a host of obscure problems. Even when properly adjusted, there was sometimes a timelag between operating the clutch pedal and the engagement of the pre-selected ratio by a complex arrangement of electromagnets and vacuum-actuated diaphragms. It was clever but over-ambitious.

The transmission was only part of the Cord's mechanical problems, however, for early examples of the 4.7-litre V8 Cord FB engine, specially built for the car by Lycoming of Williamsport, Pennsylvania (yet another member of the Auburn-Cord-Duesenberg group), had restricted water passages in the aluminium cylinder heads, which frequently overheated and cracked.

The Cord power unit was, otherwise, a carefully-designed three-bearing V8 with main bearing inserts, poured connecting rod bearings and a counterbalanced crank. Valves were set horizontally between the blocks, and operated by cam-and-roller mechanism. Domed aluminium pistons were used. The rest of the car was just as

carefully designed. The front suspension featured a novel arrangement of trailing arms sprung by a transverse semi-elliptic leaf spring while the rear was taken care of by a light 'dead' axle and two longitudinal semi-elliptics. All told that meant a reduction in unwanted unsprung weight of around 40 per cent compared to a conventional rear-drive car and the trailing-arm front suspension had the advantage of keeping the wheels vertical, eliminating the camber changes found with other independent systems. That was a very important considera-

tion with front-wheel drive.

All the mechanical failings of the Cord had a debilitating effect on the proposed rhythm of production: the target had been for 1000 cars a month, while in reality the Cord factory could only manage to build 1174 cars in the first 12 months.

It seems likely, too, that E.L. Cord had lost interest in the project; during 1936 he unloaded the greater part of his holdings in the Auburn-Cord-Duesenberg corporation for $4 million and the next year was to be found in Nevada pursuing a new-found interest in

ABOVE *The elegant lines of a 1937 Cord 812 Phaeton*
LEFT *Auburn Automobile Company president Roy Faulkner (centre) with the first supercharged Cord 812 outside the factory, a car built for the New York Salon*
RIGHT *A 1936 Cord 810 Phaeton*

radio and television. In his absence the Auburn-Cord-Duesenberg management decided to apply the same tactics that they had used to boost flagging sales of Auburns and Duesenbergs during the Depression: fit the car with a supercharger and outside exhaust pipes....

The result was the Cord 812, introduced for 1937 with an improved Lycoming FC engine. A Schwitzer-Cummins centrifugal supercharger was fitted, driven at six times crankshaft speed by a ring gear in the centre of the camshaft; at high loads the friction drive to the impeller was designed to slip to relieve torque loads on the blower drive gearing. The faster, more flamboyant 812 could be distinguished by twin flexible exhaust pipes protruding from either side of the bonnet which then vanished into the pontoon wings to merge into a single tailpipe.

As originally produced, the 812 engine developed 170 bhp at 3500 rpm; on later models the boost pressure was increased, lifting peak output to some 195 bhp at 4200 rpm. It was claimed that a well-tuned Cord 812 was capable of developing more than 200 bhp, while the Bonneville record breaker Ab 'Mormon Meteor' Jenkins said that during AAA observed test runs on the Utah salt flats his car was developing

225 bhp. Jenkins recorded a top speed of 121 mph with a stock Cord sedan but couldn't maintain it because the standard tyres threw their treads.

The Autocar testers were extremely impressed with the supercharged 812 when they drove a Westchester-bodied sedan, priced then at £1025 (including tax): '...there is no question that a terrific performance is given... Fine and easy though the performance of the unsupercharged car proved to be last year, this present machine unquestionably excels it... Yet in no sense

have the softness, quietness and smoothness of an excellent type of eight-cylinder engine been impaired...the general effect is of an exceedingly quiet, easy running machine. It is superlatively good in these respects at medium and high speeds, even to as much as a genuine 80 mph, wafting along with hardly a suggestion of mechanism working. The speeds shown by the speedometer seem quite unbelievable...the acceleration of this machine is tremendous...'. They reported that only by careful listening would one detect the sound of the supercharger.

ABOVE, RIGHT, BELOW RIGHT *A 1937 Cord 810 Beverly Sedan. Note how far back in the car the engine is mounted, contributing to the car's good weight distribution. The instrumentation was almost excessive. The flexible exterior chrome exhaust pipes were a hallmark of many 1930's American cars*

The acceleration was certainly much improved, and in trials at Brooklands the 812 travelled from rest to 50, 60 and 70 mph (80, 96 and 113 kph) in 10.5, 13.2 and 19.6 seconds respectively, reaching a top speed of over 102 mph (164 kph). On this car the testers noticed some of those transmission-selection defects: 'A "plonk" sound frequently accompanies the actual engagement of a gear, but this is not serious, and occasionally a gear is missed and does not engage instantly. First and second make no more than a subdued note, while third and top are to all intents and purposes quite dead.' More than that they did not say, but motoring journalists were more forgiving in those days. The third and fourth gears were widely spaced ratios, giving respectively 19 mph (30.6 kph) and 28.2 mph (45 kph) per 1000 rpm. The latter, they wrote, 'is a sort of super top, intended to be the fast cruising gear, though it can be kept engaged for considerable periods of time…'.

The ride and handling of the 812 and 810, were praised, the cars being found comfortable, stable and easy to take through corners at speed. 'It can be cornered fast confidently, and does not seem to mind whether bends or even sharper turns are taken with the engine pulling or on the overrun, though for a quick corner there is something to be said for keeping the engine on the drive. Generally, however, one is very apt to forget that

front wheel drive is utilised…it introduces no disadvantage or special difficulty. Tyre "scream" can be produced on a very fast corner, in which case there may also be some tendency to sideways motion of the body, but the car basically feels steady even then.'

With the introduction of the remarkable 812, Cord also attempted to woo the luxury market with a 'Custom Series' of two new long wheelbase models. These had longer, higher bodies with greater head and leg room than the standard Westchester and Beverly sedans, and attempted to conceal their larger overall dimensions with a taller 'coffin nose' incorporating eight horizontal louvres instead of seven. Unfortunately, the general effect was slightly overblown, though nowhere near as unsightly as the one-off long-wheelbase six-light limousine

EVOLUTION

Cord 810 introduced at the 1935 New York Motor Show, but the first 100 prototypes were not fitted with front-wheel drive. The unusual and attractive appearance attracted many orders, but development problems with the transmission and engine delayed the commencement of production.

1936 Production began of 810, available in Westchester and Beverly sedan form (identical but for upholstery) and four-seat Phaeton and two-seat Sportsman convertibles. The 810 was powered by a 4.7-litre Lycoming V8 driving the front wheels through a four-speed transmission with Cotal finger-tip electro-mechanical selector

1937 Production began of Cord 812, similar to 810 series but with Schwitzer-Cummins supercharger fitted to the Lycoming V8, which raised output to 195 bhp. Production also began of Custom Series Cords, with larger, longer bodies, intended for the top end of the market

1938 Production ended when the receiver sold off the Auburn-Cord-Duesenberg group. In all, 2320 Cord 810 and 812s were produced. The body dies were sold to Hupmobile who switched to rear drive, producing the unsuccessful Skylark.

which had louvres in the bonnet and looked ridiculously high and narrow!

The Custom Series cars were well-equipped; the Custom Beverly had normal pleated upholstery, plus an integral luggage boot, while the Custom Berline was designed for the chauffeur-driven end of the market. Therefore it had a wind-down glass division between front and rear compartments, and the rear seat passengers had built-in vanity case, smoker's companion, additional radio loudspeakers and an electric telephone for communicating with the chauffeur. Not surprisingly the Custom Series accounted for only a small part of total Cord 810/812 production, which reached 2320 units before the receiver was called in.

Just before the end, the LeBaron coach-building company produced some conventionally-styled design studies on the front-wheel-drive chassis: these had radiator grilles, side-hinged bonnets and running boards, but all they did was to prove just what a skilful design job Gordon Buehrig had performed with the coffin nose design.

In 1938 the receiver sold off the remains of the Auburn-Cord-Duesenberg group for what he could get – sadly it was to one Dallas

> **'The Cord dies were eventually thrown out as scrap... '**

E. Winslow of Detroit, who was not interested in reviving car production.

The body dies for the 810/812 Cords were sold to Hupmobile, another once-great company in financial straits. They adapted the bodies to fit their normal rear-wheel drive chassis and had the cars built as the 'Hupmobile Skylark' by Graham, who were by this time renting a large part of the Hupmobile factory. Graham, in return, were permitted to fit their own power units into the same chassis/body combination, and sell the result as the 'Graham Hollywood'. Neither car proved a success, and production of both Skylarks and Hollywoods petered out in 1940-41. It was predictable, said Buehrig, for the Cord body dies hadn't been designed for mass production (in that case, were those early production targets of 1000 Cords a month realistic or just wishful thinking from the start?).

The Cord dies were eventually thrown out as scrap, but by some devious route found their way to Japan – this was still before Pearl Harbor – where they were bought by Nissan, which couldn't bring itself to put the hammer to the old Cord dies. So there they remained, crated in a warehouse at least until the 1960s.

Although some attempts were made to revive the marque they never amounted to very much and as for the famous Errett Loban Cord he died in January 1974, having long severed all connection with the car that bore his name
DBW

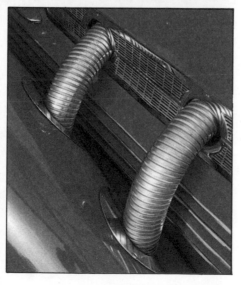

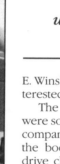

Ferrari 250

The 250 series, with its extended range of body styles and models, contains some of the greatest Ferraris ever

THE EARLY FERRARIS were all identified by a number which represented the capacity of a single engine cylinder, and thus the 250 was by definition a V12 with a nominal capacity of 3 litres. Until the development of the V6 Dino engines, Ferrari power units, with the exception of the Grand Prix racing in-line fours, all used the classic 60-degree V12 layout – which perfectly balances all the principal unequal forces.

In the 1950s there were two such engines in production at Maranello – if production is the right word for a process which involved such small numbers and so much skilful assembly by hand. For want of any better description, they tend to be known as the 'short' and the 'long' V12s. The short engine,

LEFT & BELOW *A splendid 250GT Lusso Berlinetta, a model launched in 1962*

designed by Gioacchino Colombo, was a little jewel and the first Ferrari power unit of all; it had started life with a capacity of only 1.5 litres in the original Tipo 125 sports car of 1947. The long engine, physically much bigger, was the work of Aurelio Lampredi, and began life in 1951 as a 4.5-litre GP power unit aimed at wresting supremacy from the Alfa Romeo Alfettas (which, of course, it did).

When it came to a 3-litre engine, the choice lay between these two, because the short engine could be opened up all the way to 3-litre capacity while the long one could be sleeved down. It really depended upon the design priorities: the bigger engine promised greater reserves of strength and reliability, but inevitably it was much heavier and needed to be installed in bigger chassis.

It is hardly surprising, given the way in

MODEL
Ferrari 250 GTO (1962)

ENGINE
Location: Front, longitudinal
Type: Water-cooled, 60-degree V12, all alloy, with seven-bearing crankshaft
Cubic capacity: 2953 cc
Bore × stroke: 73 mm × 58.8 mm
Compression ratio: 9.6:1
Valve gear: Two valves per cylinder operated by single overhead camshafts
Fuel supply: Six Weber twin-choke 38 DCN carburettors
Ignition: Mechanical, with twin Marelli distributors
Maximum power: 295 bhp at 7500 rpm
Maximum torque: 203 lb ft at 5500 rpm

TRANSMISSION
Layout: Clutch and gearbox in unit with engine
Clutch: Fitchel & Sachs, single dry plate
Gearbox: Five-speed manual with Porsche-patented synchromesh

1st	3.11:1	3rd	1.50:1
2nd	2.05:1	4th	1.21:1
		5th	1.03:1

Final drive: Limited-slip differential
Ratio: 4.85:1, 4.57:1, 4.25:1, 4.0:1, 3.89:1, 3.77:1, 3.66:1, 3.55:1

SUSPENSION
Front: Independent, with double wishbones, coil springs and telescopic dampers
Rear: Non-independent, with rigid axle and semi-elliptic leaf springs

STEERING
Type: ZF worm and sector

BRAKES
Type: Dunlop discs all round

WHEELS AND TYRES
Type: Rudge hubs (42 mm) with 15 in (38 cm) Borrani wire-spoke wheels with Dunlop racing tyres, 600 × 15 RW3711 front and 700 × 15 RW3808 rear

BODY/CHASSIS
Type: Two-door, two-seat aluminium sports coupé built over tubular steel spaceframe

DIMENSIONS AND WEIGHT
Length: 175 in (4445 mm)
Width: 63 in (1600 mm)
Wheelbase: 102 in (2590 mm)
Track – front: 53 in (1354 mm)
    – rear: 53.3 in (1349 mm)
Weight: 2800 lb (1270 kg)

PERFORMANCE
Maximum speed: 165 mph (266 kph)
Acceleration 0-60 mph: 6 seconds
Fuel consumption: 19 mpg

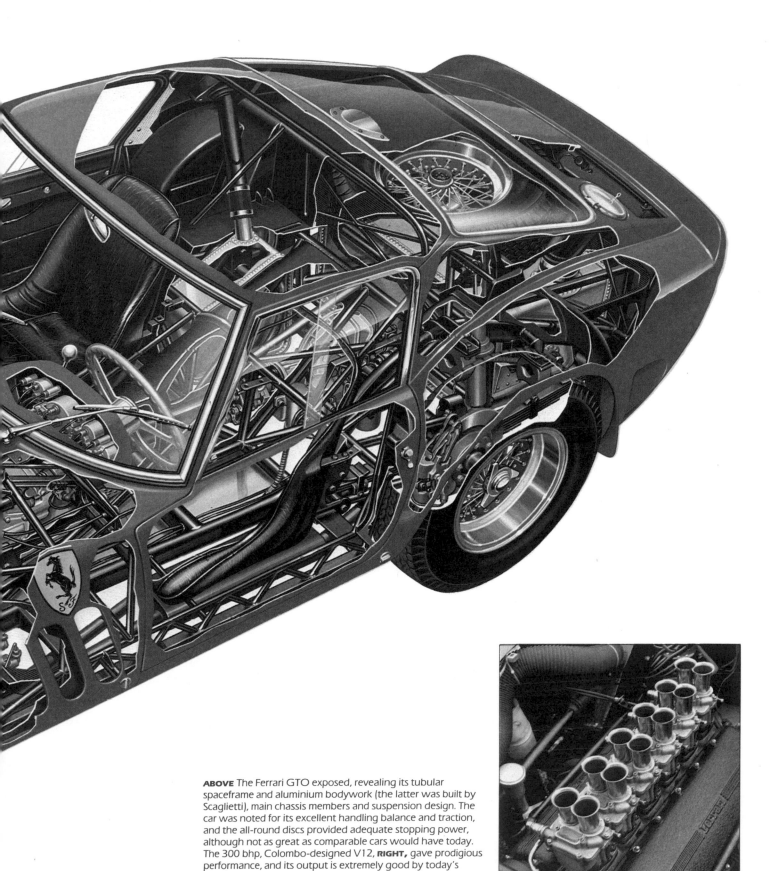

ABOVE The Ferrari GTO exposed, revealing its tubular spaceframe and aluminium bodywork (the latter was built by Scaglietti), main chassis members and suspension design. The car was noted for its excellent handling balance and traction, and the all-round discs provided adequate stopping power, although not as great as comparable cars would have today. The 300 bhp, Colombo-designed V12, **RIGHT,** gave prodigious performance, and its output is extremely good by today's standards. It was also a very noisy engine, sometimes deafening in the cockpit, and some drivers who use GTOs today wear earplugs for long journeys. Built by a company from which practically every model has become a classic, the GTO was a masterpiece of engineering and styling

which Ferrari's product planning was carried out in the 1950s – which is to say that broadly speaking, there wasn't any – that the 250 emerged by confused stages and with versions of both the available engines before finally settling, many years later, into the configuration which was to gain status as perhaps the most desirable of all Ferraris – the 250GTO. One of the seeds was sown in 1952 with the appearance of the 250 Sport, in which the short engine for the first time reached 3-litre capacity with a bore of 73 mm and stroke of 58.8 mm, giving an actual capacity of 2953 cc. The real point of interest here was that this engine replaced the long engine which had hitherto been used in Ferrari's larger sports models, the 340 America and Mexico.

Such was the improvement in handling achieved by the adoption of the smaller, lighter engine that the 250 Sport won the 1952 Mille Miglia, with Bracco defeating the might of the Mercedes 300 SLs. Eventually,

---

'... in this form was reputed to deliver 200 bhp at 6000 rpm...'

---

this line of development led through the 250 Mille Miglia and thence to the deservedly famous 250 Testa Rossa. Yet the definitive Ferrari 250, the road-going GT car which first appeared in 1953, began life with a shrunken version of the long engine!

In essence, the original 250 Europa was seen as a version of the 375 America. While the more powerful car's 4.5-litre engine achieved its actual 4522 cc capacity with a bore of 84 mm and stroke of 68 mm, the 250 saw it sleeved down to the square dimensions of 68 mm × 68 mm, giving 2963 cc. The engine in this form was reputed to deliver 200 bhp at 6000 rpm, though this looks suspiciously simple arithmetic when you realise that the 4.5-litre 375 – half as much engine again – was rated at 300 bhp! Whatever the truth of the case, it didn't

matter much because the 250 Europa was a fairly awful car. It had perforce to use the America chassis, a huge device with a 115 in (292 cm) wheelbase and 54 in (137 cm) track, with suspension of rather doubtful merit (by Ferrari standards), consisting of front double wishbones with a single transverse leaf spring, and a live rear axle with simple leaf-spring location.

It is perhaps as well that this first 'production' 250 ran to no more than 20 examples, including the one seen on the stand at the 1953 Paris Salon where the model was announced. Probably the lesson of the 250 Sport was already being taken aboard, for by the following year the so-called Second Series 250 Europa had already appeared. This used the short engine first seen in the 250 Sport and was in effect a wholly new car, sitting on a much shorter wheelbase of 102 in (260 cm) and looking infinitely more handsome in its Pininfarina bodywork. The entirely different character of the engine can be seen in its power output of 220 bhp at 7000 rpm, achieved when breathing through three Weber 36 DCZ twin-choke carburettors – a choke for each pair of cylinders, in effect. As in the former engine, there was a single chain-driven camshaft for each cylinder bank, operating the opposed valves

by rockers. Drive was taken through a four-speed gearbox, and the chassis too was much improved, with coil springs in place of the front transverse leaf and a rear Watt linkage to relieve the leaf springs there of the strain of locating the axle in the side-to-side sense. Since it was still only the mid-1950s, the brakes were of course drums all round, a major shortcoming in a car capable of excellent performance. In those days, even more than now, press road-tests of Ferraris were very hard to arrange, and one can best judge the potential of the 250 by dividing its 220 bhp output by its kerb weight of just over a ton (1016 kg).

The new, much improved 250 Europa officially lasted little longer than its clumsy predecessor. Perhaps 35 had been made when, in 1955, there came a shift of designation to 250GT. To some extent this reflected the needs of the moment: the Le Mans disaster of that year caused a welcome switch of emphasis away from long-distance racing with thinly-disguised GP cars and back to something like genuine road-going machinery. This pitched the Ferrari 250 against the Mercedes 300SL (and the Jaguar C-type) and it was understandable that Ferrari wished to emphasise the civilised GT nature of his car.

of the weight-saving came from a new light-alloy body by Scaglietti; power output was eased up to 260 bhp, still at 7000 rpm. These cars, the 250 Berlinettas, were remarkable not only for what they achieved, but for the handicaps under which they did so: for they retained four-speed gearboxes and drum brakes as well as the live rear axle.

It was clear, though, that steady development of the existing car would not keep the Ferrari flag flying for ever, even in the Tour de France. Something altogether lighter and more nimble was needed: something which would, however, still be identified as a 250GT. There would be every justification,

> *' What was done...*
> *was to chop a lump out*
> *of the wheelbase... '*

for the main mechanical elements would be retained. What was done, quite logically, was to chop a lump out of the wheelbase – easily enough done with a simple tubular chassis frame – and commission new bodies for the result. One body (built by Scaglietti again, to a Pininfarina design) would serve for the new line of Berlinettas, while Pininfarina himself (again) would come up with an equivalent road-going car.

The actual choice of wheelbase was equally logical. If the original was 102 in, the shortened version would be 94.4 in (240 cm) which was quite sufficient to allow the design of a snug two-seat coupé – or even a generous one, given the greater front and rear overhangs permissible in a road car – while making the 250 substantially lighter

ABOVE LEFT & ABOVE *A 1962 GTO, and* **TOP & LEFT,** *another '62 GTO, but with three side louvres instead of two; the former was a feature on later cars. Introduced by Ferrari at a press conference on 24 February 1962, only 39 were built during the next two years. The GTO was very successful in racing and is today one of the most valuable and sought-after classics in the world*

Whatever the reason, the 250GT became outstandingly successful for Ferrari, in competition and in production terms. It stayed in production until 1964, when it was replaced by the 275, and even that was little more than a bigger-engined 250 with the vital modification of independent rear suspension. However, in the years on either side of 1960, the 250's handling was quite good enough with its well-located live rear axle.

What did happen through those years was that in true Ferrari fashion the basic 250GT was refined, chopped about, fitted with different bodies and generally treated in a way that could only have happened at Maranello.

The 250GT was quickly launched into racing: indeed, it had already collected its first victory by the time it made its official debut at the Brussels Motor Show early in 1956. From then on it was never really bettered in 3-litre GT racing until the 1960s appearance of the new generation of mid-engined racing cars. In particular it made a habit of winning the then-prestigious Tour de France; its nine wins in a row in this event speak volumes for the effort Ferrari was prepared to put into its development, for its rivals certainly did not stand still.

Those early race-winners retained the standard 260 cm wheelbase but were (naturally) substantially tuned and lightened. Much

and quickening its steering response. The results of these labours emerged in 1959 and met with deserved acclaim. It was not just that the car was lighter and more nimble, or even that the Berlinetta at least looked very pretty: at last the 250GT had been given Dunlop disc brakes, and this was enough to sharpen their competitive edge – being worth a good deal more, in terms of lap times, than the further engine tuning which lifted power output to 280 bhp.

If the short-wheelbase Berlinetta was almost an instant classic – and there are Ferrari enthusiasts who today rate it the best of the entire breed – the Pininfarina road cars were less of a success. There were two, a coupé and (for the first time) a convertible Cabriolet whose body was certainly not stiff enough: despite their use of chassis frames, Ferraris also depended on the extra torsion-

> *'… entirely capable of being driven legally… if not… easily… on the road'*

al stiffness contributed by the body. The earliest road-going cars were also hampered by retaining drum brakes.

However, these cars were relatively short-lived, for the development bandwagon was really rolling and Ferrari had plans to split the 250 line far more positively between racing and road-going cars (it is worth noting, in passing, that while the Berlinettas were the 'racing' as distinct from 'road-going' models, they were in keeping with the spirit of their age and were entirely capable of being driven legally, if not always easily or quietly, on the road). The results of these further deliberations emerged in 1962 with the 250GTO and the 250GT Lusso.

The GTO designation resulted from one of the more famous linguistic accidents. Ferrari needed his new lightweight coupé to be homologated for GT racing: in Italian, 'omologato'. Thus the car was named the GT

TOP LEFT & LEFT *A 1963 Ferrari 250 LMB: in fact most LM models had 3.3-litre V12s and should have been called 275 LMs*
TOP & ABOVE *The 250 Testa Rossa had a 300 hp V12 and was successful in the World Sports Car Championship*
BELOW *A 250 GT Pininfarina Cabriolet,*
BOTTOM RIGHT *A 250GT Pininfarina Coupé*

the stability. Bizzarrini used the University of Pisa's wind tunnel, plus a good deal of cut-and-try track testing, to achieve a shape which says much for the innate Italian ability to make cars look good even when working within this kind of technical constraint. Even so, the final touch remained to be added as an afterthought: having solved the problem of front-end lift, Bizzarrini discovered at a very late stage that the back was going light instead, and the final solution was to add two rear spoilers. The first, easily visible above the Kamm-type tail panel, became a kind of GTO trademark. The second, beneath the fuel tank, was equally valuable but much less obvious. The production GTO bodies were yet again built by Scaglietti.

It was Scaglietti also who built the corresponding road-going car, the Berlinetta Lusso. This was an extremely beautiful machine, but with none of the hard-won aerodynamic refinement of the GTO. In some ways it resembled a stretched version of the Alfa Romeo GTV of the same period, but was none the worse for that; its real drawback lay in the shape of the elegant but high-set nose which must have been worth a substantial amount of Cd all by itself. Against that, it is probably one of the easiest of the classic V12s to see out of, with extremely slim pillars all round and none of the blinkered tightness of modern exotics.

The GTO engine was itself an interesting unit, since in effect it was the famous Testa

Omologato, or just plain GTO.

Unlike any previous Ferrari, the GTO was not styled as such. Bizzarrini, then Ferrari's chief development engineer, had realised the need for proper aerodynamic research – since even GT races were already being fought out at speeds above 150 mph (241 kph) on the longer straights. It was already accepted that the existing Berlinetta body had a nose shape that caused both drag and front-end lift at high speed, and these faults needed urgent rectification, as did the narrow rear track which did nothing to assist

EVOLUTION

First tested in 1952, the Vignale-bodied prototype 250 Sport was the earliest Ferrari fitted with a 3-litre version of Colombo's V12. also shown that year was the 250 MM, based on the Sport. In all, 17 Pininfarina coupés, 13 Vignale spyders and one coupé were built

1953 The road-going version of the Sport was introduced, the 250 Europa, fitted with a 3-litre, sleeved-down version of Lampredi's 4.5-litre V12. Approximately 20 were built

1954 The Second Series 250 GT Europa was announced, fitted with the short Colombo engine and with a shorter wheelbase; styled by Pininfarina, about 32 were made

1956 The 250 GT Boano 'low-roof' coupé was announced, of which 70–80 were made, along with the 250 GT long-wheelbase Tour de France Berlinetta Coupé, of which 74 were made over the next three years

1957 The 250 GT Pininfarina Cabriolet was launched at the Paris Salon; in all about 45 were built. The 250 GT 'high-roof' Ellena coupé was introduced (of which 50 were made), as was the sports-racing 250 Testa Rossa, designed for the 1958 World Sports Car Championship. This it won, as well as in 1960 and '61. In all, 34 were built. Also introduced was the long-wheelbase, Pininfarina-styled 250 GT California Spyder, 46 were made

1958 The 250 GT Pininfarina Coupé was launched, a highly successful model of which 350 were built

1959 The short-wheelbase GT Berlinetta was launched for racing. 162 were made

1960 The short-wheelbase 250 GT California Spyder was launched. 55 were built

1962 The 250 GT 2 + 2 was introduced, styled by Pininfarina; about 900 were made. Also offered was the 250 GT Berlinetta Lusso, styled by Pininfarina, of which 400 were made, and the 250 GTO of which 39 were built

LEFT & BELOW *Views of a 250GT 2+2 (GTE), designed for the family man and styled by Pininfarina. It was first seen as a course car at Le Mans in 1960*

Rossa racing engine but without the red cam-covers which gave it its name. This retained the familiar short 3-litre engine dimensions but was revised in many respects. Most important was the change in breathing arrangements, the siamesed inlet ports of the standard 250 V12 being replaced by six separate inlet ports per head (and by six Weber 38 DCN carburettors to feed them!). This was not as simple an exercise as it sounds, since the existing spark-plug positions could no longer be used and the plugs had to be switched to the other side of the heads. The whole bottom end of the engine was also stiffened through the adoption of

---

' … the theoretical maximum speed … worked out at 180 mph … '

---

seven main bearings for the crankshaft instead of the previous five.

In this form, the GTO engine delivered a genuine 295 bhp at 7500 rpm. At this point the power curve was still climbing, but that was the maximum officially stressed speed of the engine. It is possible that drivers brave enough to go past the red line may have seen the 310 bhp sometimes claimed for the unit…for a while! The drive was taken through another innovation, a proper five-speed gearbox (later road-going 250s had offered an overdrive, but never a genuine five-speed box) driving through a ZF limited-slip differential. As befitted the car's competition status, various final-drive ratios were available ranging from a 'sprint' 4.85:1 to a 'Le Mans' 3.55:1. With the latter ratio and standard tyres, the theoretical maximum speed at the red line in fifth gear worked out at 180 mph (290 kph), though it seems unlikely that the GTO would ever have exceeded 165 mph (266 kph) in practice. Acceleration depends even more on the final-drive ratio fitted, but the GTO's ratio of torque to weight suggests that it should have bettered 6 seconds to 60 mph (97 kph) without too much trouble.

There was just one problem with the 250 GTO. Although it was Omologated on the understanding that the requisite number would be produced, they never were. The most authoritative record suggests that 40 GTOs were built in total, and three of those certainly didn't count because they were powered by vastly stretched 4-litre engines. The FIA countenanced this failure but made sure it wasn't repeated when Ferrari presented his planned GTO replacement, the mid-engined 250LM. It was three years before the necessary papers were issued – and in just about that time, the 250 GTO itself had made the transition from front-running GT racer to sought-after classic. JD

Ferrari
Dino

The mid-engined 206
and 246GT Ferrari Dinos were not
only a break with front-engined Ferrari tradition
and breathtakingly beautiful but a tribute to Enzo's only son

ONE OF THE MOST sought-after of all Maranello-built cars did not, strictly speaking, carry the Ferrari label at all. At the time the Dino was conceived in the mid-1960s Ferrari's reputation was that of a V12 builder and nothing else, yet the factory – with the considerable assistance of Scaglietti's coach-building works – produced, between 1967 and 1974, well over 4000 examples of a relatively small and light V6-engined car, a model which has come to be regarded as one of the most beautiful post-war coupés.

The origins of the Dino are linked to some grievous Ferrari domestic history. Enzo Ferrari had but one son, baptised Alfredo but who was almost always the affectionate 'Dino' to those who knew him. Dino showed every sign of becoming as gifted an engineer as his father, and after his graduation he joined the Maranello works and took a special interest in the engine and cars then being planned, in the early 1950s,

for an assault on Formula Two racing. Then he contracted leukaemia and in 1956 he died, aged just 24.

It was Enzo Ferrari's decision to name the whole series of smaller racing engines after his son. The original unit was designed

---

❛…a V6 – in effect, half of one of the much-admired Ferrari V12s…❜

---

by Vittorio Jano, who elected to meet the need for a 1.5-litre engine by making a V6 – in effect, half of one of the much-admired Ferrari V12s and with the advantage of compactness. In the event things did not transpire quite like that because Jano was worried about the amount of space available inside the vee of the engine to accommodate

adequate breathing arrangements between the twin overhead camshafts. In order to gain space he opened the vee angle from the theoretically ideal 60 degrees to 65 and restored equally spaced firing intervals by juggling with the crankpin angles.

This was the start of an engine series which was developed through all the vicissitudes of racing and hillclimbing for 10 years. In some versions its vee-angle was reduced to 60 degrees, while in others it was extended to 120. Whatever the changes, it remained a V6, and it was there in 1965 when Ferrari decided he needed to widen his market, if only to generate enough profit to keep all his racing programmes in operation. There was also the new and real threat of the Porsche 911 to meet, since the then-new car from Stuttgart added beauty to the promise of formidable performance.

By stages a road car was devised. The bodyshell was designed by Pininfarina, who

MODEL
Ferrari Dino 246 GT (1971)

ENGINE
Location: Mid, transverse
Type: Water-cooled 65-degree V6 with cast-iron block and alloy heads
Cubic capacity: 2418 cc
Bore × stroke: 92.5 mm × 60 mm
Compression ratio: 9.0:1
Valve gear: 2 46-degree inclined valves per cylinder operated by twin gear- and chain-driven overhead camshafts per cylinder bank
Fuel supply: 3 Weber 40 DCF twin-choke downdraught carburettors
Ignition: Marelli transistorised
Maximum power: 195 bhp (DIN) at 7600 rpm
Maximum torque: 166 lb ft (DIN) at 5500 rpm

TRANSMISSION
Layout: Gearbox mounted beneath engine
Clutch: Single dry plate
Gearbox: Five-speed manual synchromesh

1st 3.07:1	4th 1.25:1
2nd 2.12:1	5th 0.86:1
3rd 1.52:1	

Final drive: Helical
Ratio: 3.62:1

SUSPENSION
Front: Independent with unequal length wishbones, coil springs and dampers and anti-roll bar
Rear: Independent by unequal length wishbones, coil springs and dampers and anti-roll bar

STEERING
Type: Rack and pinion. 3.2 turns lock to lock

BRAKES
Type: Discs all round. 10.6 in (27 cm) diameter front, 10 in (25.4 cm) diameter rear. Vacuum servo-assisted.

WHEELS AND TYRES
Type: Light alloy wheels with Michelin 205/70VR14 tyres

BODY/CHASSIS
Type: Multitubular steel frame with square-section tubing and steel coupé body

DIMENSIONS AND WEIGHT
Length: 171 in (434.3 cm)
Width: 67 in (170.2 cm)
Wheelbase: 93.5 in (237.5 cm)
Track – front: 57 in (144.8 cm)
        – rear: 57.25 in (145.4 cm)
Weight: 2770 lb (1256 kg)

PERFORMANCE
Maximum speed: 151 mph (243 kph)
Acceleration 0–60 mph: 6.8 seconds
Fuel consumption: 16–20 mpg

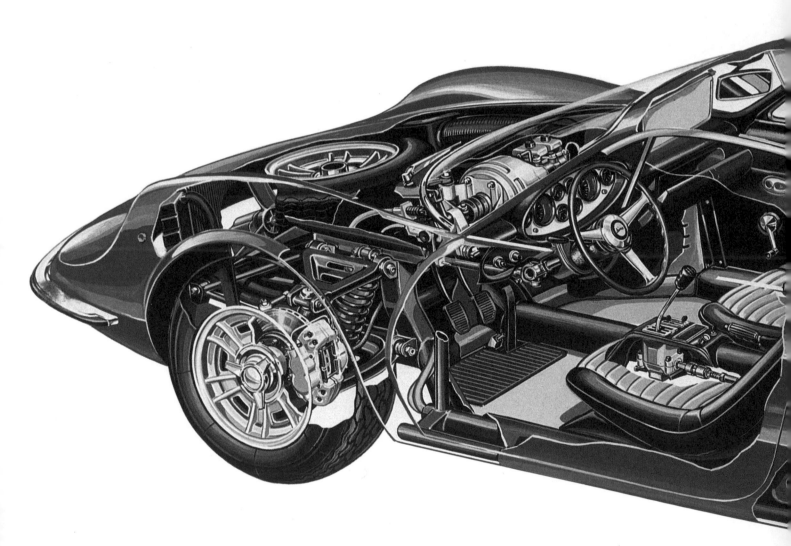

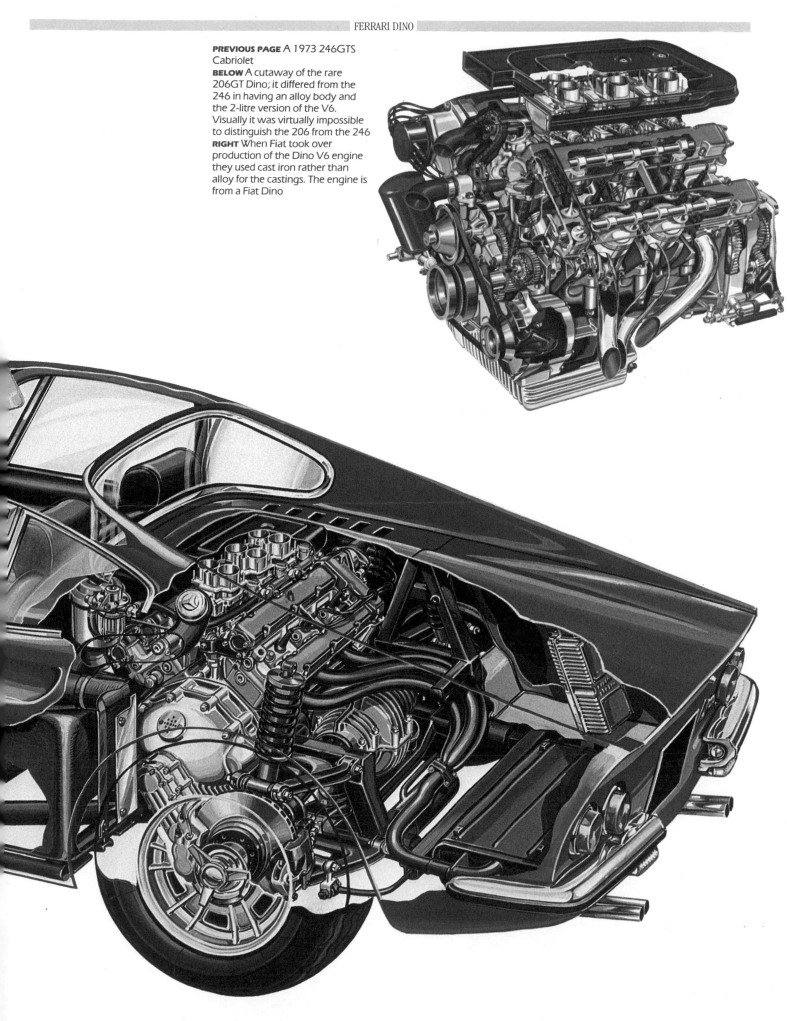

PREVIOUS PAGE A 1973 246GTS
Cabriolet
BELOW A cutaway of the rare
206GT Dino; it differed from the
246 in having an alloy body and
the 2-litre version of the V6.
Visually it was virtually impossible
to distinguish the 206 from the 246
RIGHT When Fiat took over
production of the Dino V6 engine
they used cast iron rather than
alloy for the castings. The engine is
from a Fiat Dino

drew much of his inspiration for it from the sports-racing and hillclimbing bodies made for Ferrari by Piero Drogo of Modena. It was designed to fit over a multi-tube chassis which carried the V6 engine installed transversely, immediately ahead of the rear wheels. Thus, among other things, the road-going Dino was a mid-engined car at a time when all the 'proper' V12 Ferraris were front-engined: the Dino's big brother was indeed the magnificent Daytona.

In the established Italian manner Pininfarina softened up the market by exhibiting one-off prototypes at the major motor shows. His first effort, seen at Paris in 1965, was virtually right first time. By the time of the 1966 Turin show he had reacted to initial opinion: the entire body had been raised slightly, which also gave the car some much-needed headroom, and the headlamps had been transferred from a completely stream-lined (and illegally low) plastic fairing in the extreme nose to recessed fittings in the front wings. Farina also tidied up the big airs-coops in the rear wings which fed air to the carburettors and rear brakes and complied with the factory's chosen engine installation, for the Paris show car had had its power unit

LEFT, BELOW AND RIGHT *A 1974 246GT with engine and interior detail. Engine accessibility is not the car's strong suit but the instruments are plentiful*

installed in-line rather than across.

Before then the road-going engine had also undergone a major redesign. The engineer, Franco Rocchi, had adapted it to be more suitable for production needs, and fixed its capacity at the desired 2 litres. The original 65-degree angle between cylinder banks was retained so that three Weber 40DCOE carburettors could be installed without compromising the inlet manifold passages. Inevitably, the engine had dimensions well over-square with a bore of 85 mm

> *'...producing its claimed 180 bhp at no less than 8000 rpm...'*

and a stroke of only 57 mm to give an actual swept volume of 1987 cc. Such figures made it no surprise that the Dino V6 was a high-revving unit, producing its claimed 180 bhp at no less than 8000 rpm. Ferrari was extremely reticent about quoting a torque figure, but working back from known figures for the later, larger version of the engine, it was probably about 140 lb ft, with a peak that could hardly have been less than 6000 rpm. The twin overhead camshafts per bank were driven in true Ferrari tradition by gears from the crankshaft to an intermediate

sprocket and thence by short chains. The valves opposed each other in a 46-degree vee and were operated directly through bucket tappets.

The five-speed, all-indirect gearbox was mounted beneath the engine, with spur gear drive aft to a limited-slip differential. A single very complex alloy casting served as engine sump, gearbox lower casing and final drive housing.

Suspension design allowed little compromise, since the Dino used double wishbones at both ends. The front upper and lower assemblies were of very nearly equal length, with the very short concentric coil spring/damper units squeezed between them. The steering geometry included a very large positive offset. At the rear the lower wishbone was considerably longer than the upper, and the spring/damper unit (with notably longer stroke) had to act on the upper member to leave the way clear for the drive shaft. Any possible shaft-locking problems were overcome in advance with the use of constant-velocity joints at each end.

For the first time in a production Ferrari, rack and pinion steering was adopted, a decision no doubt made easier by the light load on the front wheels. The latter were alloy of course, and shod with 185–14 in tyres. The relatively large wheel size left room for massive brakes, and 10.6-inch diameter discs were used front and rear, more than sufficient for a car whose kerb weight was under 2000 lb (907 kg). The spare wheel was housed in the car's sloping nose where, in company with such items as the washer bottle and the master cylinder, it left scant

room for any luggage. The luggage locker was actually housed at the extreme rear of the body, behind the engine compartment, and whilst not exactly large, any contents, as some early testers pointed out, were kept nice and warm by the exhaust system.

In this form the Dino entered production in 1967, but at an extremely cautious rate. Enzo was certainly worried about whether the world's enthusiasts would accept the idea of a 'poor man's' Ferrari, although at the advertised price indigence in this context was strictly relative. It may have been that this worry, just as much as the desire to make the car into a mobile monument for his son, led Enzo to insist that the Dino was a marque in its own right.

The late 1960s were a fraught and complicated time for Ferrari. Fiat effectively bailed Maranello out of financial trouble, and one of the results was that Fiat inherited the Dino V6 technology and set about rationalising it, not least for use in two of their own sporting models – the Fiat Dino Coupé (Bertone-styled) and the Fiat Dino

Spider (by Pininfarina, but by no means with the flair and assurance which marked Ferrari's 'real' Dino 206GT). For this purpose Fiat put the V6 into production at its own Turin works, using castings from Fiat foundries, some of which bore the Fiat imprint even in the Ferrari-built cars!

In order to provide Fiat's models with the

> *'... by changing the camshaft profiles, peak torque was boosted...'*

torque and reliability which the company felt was needed, substantial changes were made. The 2-litre engine was opened out to 2418 cc by the process of boring to 92.5 mm and lengthening the stroke to 60 mm. This actually made the bore/stroke ratio even greater than before (increasing it from 1.49 to 1.54) but by retaining the same carburettors and changing the camshaft profiles

the peak torque was boosted to 166 lb ft at 'only' 5500 rpm, while the power output showed a modest rise to 195 bhp at 7600 rpm.

From the purist's point of view, the worst thing abut Fiat's rationalisation of the V6 was their changing the cylinder block material from light alloy to cast iron. This had many advantages – of cost, block rigidity and even noise level – but it made the engine substantially heavier. On the other hand, since the unit now offered a little more power and substantially more torque the changes might be said to have paid for themselves.

Meanwhile, back at Maranello, the ultra-slow pace of early 206GT production was about to quicken. It is worth noting that to

powerful but heavier engine there was another change to the 246GT which offended the purist. The 206 body had been of aluminium panels, hand-shaped in the Scaglietti works and applied to the chassis tubing but although the 246 shell was fabricated in exactly the same way it was made in sheet steel. The result yet again was a weight penalty with the 246GT, even by Ferrari's figures, scaling nearly 450 lb (203 kg) more at the kerb than its predecessor, bringing the power/weight ratio back to close to where it had started.

That was not quite as bad as it seemed because in the process of transition the Dino had gown substantially. In the kind of move which one only dares undertake in a car blessed with a fairly simple steel-tube

> ‘The Dino production process was complex to say the least...’

ABOVE AND LEFT *Pininfarina presented this be-spoilered Dino at the Frankfurt Show in 1967. Public reaction was mixed*
BELOW *A 1966 prototype. It had a longer nose than the production car*
BELOW RIGHT *The first prototype, shown at the Paris Salon in 1965, had a full-width transparent nose section*

underline the Dino's nominal independence from Ferraris proper, its designation was based on a new system. Whilst the V12 cars had always been numbered for the cubic capacity of a single cylinder (thus for instance any 250 had a 3-litre engine) the Dino was numbered for its total engine capacity and the number of its cylinders. During two

years of production only 150 206GTs had been wheeled out of the factory (according to Maranello, although researchers who have investigated engine numbers are convinced there must have been more). Now the picture was about to alter with the appearance of the 246GT.

The change was needed not only to bring Ferrari practice closer to Fiat's, but because the acknowledged rival, the Porsche 911 (which had already been in production for four years!), was rapidly growing up. Stuttgart was offering bigger engines with more torque, simultaneously achieving better performance and handling. To maintain its challenge the Dino had to be developed.

Apart from the adoption of the more

skeleton under a hand-crafted body, the 246GT gained 2.3 inches (5.8 cm) in its wheelbase and 3.7 inches (9 cm) overall, while its height went up by a further three inches (7.6 cm) to silence complaints from Ferrari's taller customers! It is a tribute to the skill with which the operation was carried out that short of parking the two models side by side the only way most people can tell the 206 from the 246 is by differences in the wheels – the knock-on type on the 206 – and the fuel filler cap, which on the 206 is a protruding chromed device rather than the flush-fitting flap of the later model.

The Dino production process was complex to say the least, and hardly aided the car's resistance to corrosion (Dinos have a

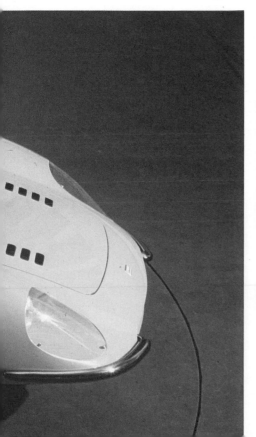

fairly evil reputation in this respect). The entire chassis/body assembly was made by Scaglietti in Modena, shipped down the road to Ferrari for engine, transmission and suspension installation, and then taken back to Scaglietti for equipping, trimming and finishing. Regardless of the complications the production really got under way when the 246GT replaced its smaller brother, and in the six years from 1969 to 1974 the factory built 2700 of these classic little coupés.

> **' The GTS proved popular and Pininfarina was... proud of it... '**

As late as 1972 the coupé was joined by a sister GTS cabriolet, its roof cut away and replaced by a stiff, removeable Targa panel. The GTS proved popular and Pininfarina was supposed to have been especially proud of it; the conversion was no great technical problem because the Dino body was essentially unstressed, the loads being taken by the tubing beneath. In only two years of production alongside the coupé nearly 1200 GTS cabriolets were made.

The rarity of the 206GT and the extreme reluctance of the factory during the mid-1960s to provide cars for road tests meant

that no authoritative performance figures for the model were ever published. *Motor* had better luck with the 246GT and established a maximum speed of 148 mph (238 kph) and a 0–60 mph (96 kph) time of 7.1 seconds. These are near-supercar figures and may have eased the pain of near-supercar fuel consumption, measured by the magazine at 16.1 mpg. The 246GT had a capacity of 14.5 gallons (66 litres) in its twin tanks.

The real joy of the Dino is that it goes and handles as well as it looks. Partly by virtue of its greater weight the 246GT was given wider tyres of 205–14 section, which if anything improved the ultimate roadholding without a deleterious effect on the delicacy and precision of the steering. Certainly the

ABOVE, LEFT AND BELOW *A 1973 GTS Cabriolet. The GTS was introduced in 1972 and 1200 were built between '72 and '74* **RIGHT** *A Dino 246 GTS in its element, alone on the open road*

feel of the steering belied its moderate gearing, for over three turns of the wheel are required lock to lock, and the car has a poor 36-foot (11 m) turning circle.

The gearbox is an acknowledged delight (except in old cars with ultra-worn syn-chromesh on second gear) and the gear ratios are well chosen for quick road driving even though second presents professional road testers with a familiar nightmare, falling fractionally short of 60 mph at the 7800 rpm red line. By Italian standards the driving position is well suited to tall, long-legged drivers, but the Dino is, of course, strictly a two-seater. The low-speed ride is usually criticised: given the angles of damper in-stallation, it is not surprising that they suffer from 'stiction', or binding, at town speeds, but the Dino smooths out beautifully when driven with the appropriate verve.

Naturally, the 246GT has its drawbacks. The engine noise is a matter of taste: a beautiful sound to many enthusiasts' ears but probably too much of it in the long term. Although the driving position is well laid out for the most part the two main instruments are always half-hidden by the steering wheel rim, especially for tall drivers. Rear visibility is extremely poor and the headlights are in no sense matched to the car's performance. The heating and ventilation system is a joke. Owners admit to such faults, as well as to long-term rust problems and the notorious reputation of Italian electrics – British-market Dinos had electrically-operated win-dows as standard equipment – yet they insist that the pleasure of driving a 206/246GT ranks ahead even of looking at it parked in your driveway. In every sense the car rates as a classic, possessing in nimbleness what it might have lost in outright performance when compared with the mighty V12s.

There was a real sadness when produc-tion of the 246GT ended in 1974. The car

> *'... The Dino has justly earned its reputation amongst the classics...'*

was replaced by a new Dino, the 308GT, a 2+2 more in line with the tastes of the market, and powered by a bigger V8 engine. It says something for the reputation gained by the 246GT/GTS during its relatively short production life that its replacement carried the Ferrari badge. The Dino concept was no longer something to be treated with caution, at half an arm's length. Later still there emerged the 308GTB, which, returning to the design ideas and concepts of the 246GTB, proved that the Dino had justly earned its reputation amongst the Ferrari classics. JRD

EVOLUTION

1965 Prototype shown at Paris Show with longitudinally-mounted V6

1966 Second prototype introduced at Turin Show. It was higher than the first car and featured revised headlight design and smaller side airscoops

1968 Dino 206GT entered production with 2-litre V6 mounted transversely

1969 Dino 246GT replaces 206GT. The car was introduced at the German Show and featured a larger version of the V6 with bore and stroke increased to give 2.4 litres. The block was now in cast iron and produced by Fiat. The 246GT was longer overall and in the wheelbase than the 206GT.

1972 GTS Cabriolet introduced with Targa top

1974 Dino production ceased. Total production was 2700 coupés and nearly 1200 cabriolets

FORD M

It was America's first muscle car, and the Mustang's sales grew as rapidly as did the options list and power output. Today's models are different, with brains as well as brawn

'DESIGNED TO BE DESIGNED BY YOU' went the advertising slogan in the '60s and '70s, and for once the advertising did not lie. Anyone could, and many did, design into the simple pony car exactly what they wanted; Ford deliberately made the option list so long that you needed a computer to keep track of it. As the publicists claimed, the Mustang was a state of mind....

Bottom of the range when the cars were introduced in 1964 was the cheap and cheerful 170 cu in (2.8-litre) straight-six with a three-speed manual. With just 101 bhp and soft suspension it hardly represented a performance breakthrough. What it did represent was a new image; the (relatively) small nimble 'personal' car was a reaction to the chromed opulence of the '50s, and the products of the post-war baby boom bought it in huge numbers. Ford's vice-president Lee Iacocca saw them coming – his salesman's intuition told him that a car which looked sporty, could carry four people and cost (just) under $2500 would have a huge market. The Mustang was so exactly right for the times it sold 22,000 on the day it was introduced and 417,000 in its first year of production, prompting the opposition to rush out their own personal-size performance cars. The Mustang was responsible for the Camaro and Firebird from General Motors and the underrated Javelin from American Motors, while even Chrysler tried to fight back with the Barracuda before bringing out the fearsome Charger.

Like the Corvette, the history of the Mustang from the mid-'60s to the mid-'80s reflects the state of the American motor industry. Brash enthusiasm characterised the early models and that rapidly began to focus on the serious pursuit of pure power until the second generation Mustang II appeared in 1974, by which time things were getting gloomy for Detroit and Dearborn. Ford's

USTANG

Mustang II was gloomy too, a quantum leap backwards compared to the European and the increasing Japanese competition. So mediocre was it in fact that it's safe virtually to ignore the whole range and the early examples of the third generation too. It was really only in 1983-4 that the Mustang regained some appeal.

In the early '60s, although those who knew their way around the option list could order themselves a genuine high-performance muscle car, Ford decided that some racing exposure would do wonders for sales and who better to coordinate the effort than Carroll Shelby, whose Ford-engined Cobras were almost unbeatable?

The Shelby programme got underway as early as late 1964 and the Mustang he chose

The '85 Mustang GT convertible is powered by a 5-litre V8 producing 210 bhp and is capable of 0–60 mph in 7 seconds

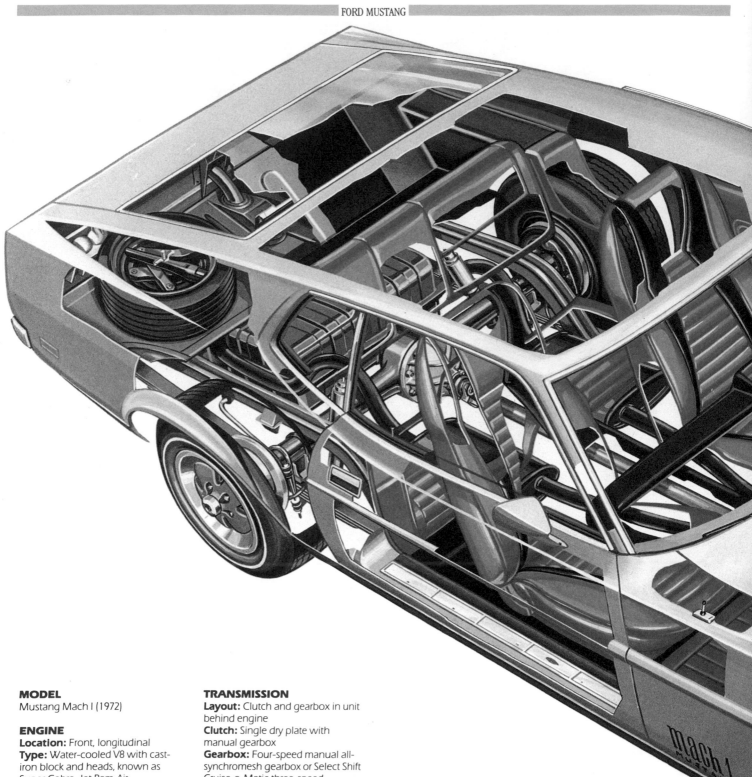

MODEL
Mustang Mach I (1972)

ENGINE
Location: Front, longitudinal
Type: Water-cooled V8 with cast-iron block and heads, known as Super Cobra-Jet Ram-Air
Cubic capacity: 7030 cc (429 cu in)
Bore × stroke: 110.7 mm × 91.2 mm
Compression ratio: 11.3:1
Valve gear: 2 valves per cylinder operated by single camshaft mounted in centre of vee, pushrods, rockers and solid tappets
Fuel supply: Single Holley 9510 D00F downdraught 4-barrel carburettor
Ignition: Mechanical with coil and distributor
Maximum power: 375 bhp (SAE gross) at 5600 rpm
Maximum torque: 450 lb ft at 5600 rpm

TRANSMISSION
Layout: Clutch and gearbox in unit behind engine
Clutch: Single dry plate with manual gearbox
Gearbox: Four-speed manual all-synchromesh gearbox or Select Shift Cruise-o-Matic three-speed automatic with torque convertor (automatic ratios in brackets)

1st	2.32:1	3rd	1.29:1
	(2.46:1)		(1.00:1)
2nd	1.69:1	4th	1.00:1
	(1.46:1)		

Final drive: Hypoid bevel
Ratio: 3.50:1

SUSPENSION
Front: Independent with wishbones, lower trailing links, coil springs, telescopic dampers and anti-roll bar
Rear: Live axle with semi-elliptic leaf springs and inclined telescopic dampers one each side of axle

STEERING
Type: Recirculating ball

BRAKES
Type: Discs front and drums rear, with 282.8 sq in (1824 sq cm) rubbed area

WHEELS AND TYRES
Type: Steel wheels 14 in × 6 in with E-200 Firestone crossply tyres

BODY/CHASSIS
Type: Integral steel chassis with two-door coupé body

DIMENSIONS AND WEIGHT
Length: 185.9 in (4722 mm)
Width: 74.1 in (1882 mm)
Wheelbase: 109.0 in (2768 mm)
Track – front: 61.5 in (1562 mm)
    – rear: 61.0 in (1549 mm)
Weight: 3220 lb (1460 kg)

PERFORMANCE
Maximum speed: 130 mph (209 kph)
Acceleration 0–60 mph: 5.7 seconds
Fuel consumption: 14 mpg

ABOVE Although it shares the same front-engine, live-rear-axle layout as the muscle-car era Mach I shown in the main cutaway, the 1984 SVO Mustang is a far more advanced machine, boasting electronic fuel injection and engine management to complement the intercooled turbocharged engine. The SVO's coil-sprung rear axle is rather better located than the simple cart-sprung affair of the Mach I, using a variety of links and gas-filled Koni dampers to improve its handling

to rework was the aggressive-looking fast-back rather than the ordinary hardtop or the convertible. Shelby had to abide by SCCA (Sports Car Club of America) rules, which specified that either the engine or the suspension had to stay essentially standard. Believing, like a good Texan, that power was the answer, Shelby chose to retain, more or less, the standard suspension and rework the engine.

The standard suspension was exactly what you would expect of the times – dou-

> '*The standard chassis... an ideal platform on which to build a performance car*'

ble wishbones at the front with the coils mounted above the top wishbone, an anti-roll bar and a live rear axle located by semi-elliptic leaf springs. That all stayed put but the standard anti-roll bar was discarded in favour of a thicker one, the bottom wishbones were lowered and the standard dampers thrown away in favour of vastly superior Konis. Top-mounted traction bars were

tang had the largest engine available, the 289 cu in (4.7-litre) V8 mated to the four-speed manual. Like every other contemporary American V8 it was a cast-iron pushrod engine, which sounds mundane in the extreme but Ford's advanced thin-wall casting techniques meant a relatively light engine to go with the compact layout. With suitably modified valve timing Shelby raised the output of Ford's High-Performance short-stroke (4 in × 2.87 in/101.6 mm × 72.9 mm) V8 from 271 bhp at 6000 rpm to over 340 bhp. That was measured in SAE gross terms of course and in race trim but it was enough to give the Shelby Mustang the 350 GT designation even though the road-going cars produced just over 300 bhp....

Shelby's revisions were so successful that his Mustangs took the SCCA B-Production class national title in '65, '66 and '67, beating mostly Corvettes and the odd hybrid like the V8 Sunbeam Tiger.

In 1964 *Motor* tested the car on which the GT-350 was based, the High Performance 289, and found it capable of a maximum 128.5 mph (206.8 kph). Only its low gearing held it back as that top speed needed nearer 7000 rpm than 6000 rpm, but that same low gearing meant excellent acceleration which

installed at the rear to help control the axle with its rather crude limited-slip differential, and quicker steering was installed to help keep it all on the road or track. Stopping was improved too with larger front discs although the rear had to soldier on with drums.

Shelby was lucky in one respect. The standard chassis, described by *Motor* as a 'welded punt frame with high torsional rigidity', was indeed very stiff and an ideal platform on which to build a performance car. Some of that torsional rigidity was accidental; in the '60s there was no computer-aided design and as Ford had very little experience of building small cars they erred on the side of caution, knowing that some heavy and powerful engines would find their way into the new car.

Naturally Shelby's building-block Mus-

saw the car leap to 60 mph (97 kph) in 7.6 seconds, to 90 mph (145 kph) in 15.9 seconds and cover the standing quarter mile in 15.2 seconds. With less wheelspin the figures would have been a great deal more impressive!

Strangely, given the popular prejudices about American cars, *Motor* liked the gearchange and the suspension, even finding the powerful synchromesh gearbox '...delightful to use though it requires a fair amount of energy as the light flywheel dictates a quick change.' The suspension was found to be '...quite firm without having the rigidity associated with some British sports cars.... It strikes a pleasant balance between firm handling and good ride over indifferent surfaces, at the same time keeping roll down to a comfortable minimum.'

On the other hand the brakes (which

ABOVE *The classic shape of the early Mustang; this is a 1966 289*
LEFT *The interior from the '66 289*
FAR LEFT *By 1968 the Mustang had already grown to house increasingly large and powerful engines. This is a 1968 GT*
BELOW LEFT *The original Mustang I resembled the production Mustangs very little. Ford vice-presidents H. C. Misch (left) and Gene Bordinat admire the car*

were drums all round as optional front discs did not become available until the next year) were found to be 'quite inadequate' and the handling as tricky as they expected in the wet. Even so the appeal of a V8 with 312 lb ft of torque was revealed in their nicely understated conclusion: 'Perhaps the greatest safety point of the Mustang is the ease with which a skilful driver can accelerate out of trouble.'

Americans, of course, were not prone to understatement and Dan Gurney let his enthusiasm get the better of him to the extent of claiming the High-Performance Mustang had 'the feel of a 2+2 Ferrari' – an unusually soft Ferrari presumably.

By 1966 Ford had dropped the huge and heavy 390 cu in (6.4-litre) V8 into the Mustang, leading *Car and Driver* to expect the nose-heavy 350 GT (the weight split was 60/40) to suffer terminal understeer, to 'plow like an Ohio farmer' as they put it. It didn't but its handling was best described as clumsy. Performance was another matter as the happy road testers went on to recount: 'Driving as laconically as we ever do in a car like this, we knocked off 15.2-second quartermiles with the air-conditioner and the sterio tape deck going full blast and letting the XPL 3-speed automatic shift when it felt like it'.

The Shelby programme continued until

1969 by which time Shelby's independent spirit was becoming tired of working with large corporations. He felt he had gone about as far as he could go, which if you take a look at his GT 500 KR (for King of the Road, what else?) seemed reasonable. The GT 500 KR was built in limited numbers in both fastback and convertible form and boasted a truly staggering performance. Its four-barrel Holley carburettor pumped air into the 428 cu in (7-litre) V8 at the rate of 735 cubic feet a minute, producing over 400 bhp – just about the right amount of power when you recall that the weight had crept up with the power to as much as 3700 lb (1680 kg).

When Shelby had finally had enough Ford brought the really high-performance Mustangs in-house. In 1969 the whole range had been restyled, becoming longer (by four inches/10 cm), lower and slightly wider. That distinctive scalloped side treatment of

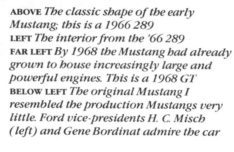

> *'The 351... far better and smoother than... the 289s and 302s...'*

the early cars disappeared to the detriment of the whole design, although the Mach I did have simulated rear three-quarter scoops to show it meant business. It also had the strange feature of an air scoop mounted directly to the air cleaner and poking out through the bonnet where high rpm vibrated it enough for Ford engineers to christen it The Shaker.... That would have been merely amusing if the car had only had pretensions to performance but speed was guaranteed even with the standard engine, the 250 bhp 351 cu in (5.7-litre) Windsor V8.

The 351 was regarded as a far better and smoother engine the the 289s and 302s but as *Motor Trend* observed in late '68, 'No matter what you say about the 351 it is not a Cobra Jet and if you're going to be in the Mach I dream you may as well have the genuine article.' The heavy 428 cu in (7-litre) V8 referred to meant that 'of course there is understeer but you can easily, very easily, bring the rear end into line with the throttle'. Of course you could, with more than 355 bhp on crossply tires. At that time American companies still measured horsepower in SAE gross terms (in other words power at the flywheel discounting any of the energy-absorbing ancillaries like the water pump or dynamo, let alone the transmission). The 355 bhp quoted would be more like 300 bhp in European terms. Nevertheless it was still a healthy power output although obviously nowhere even near the street limit for such an engine despite the high (10.6:1) compression ratio. No, the Cobra Jet's potential was indicated by the torque output of 440 lb ft at 3400 rpm.

That torque was fed through a three-speed Cruise-o-Matic transmission although a four-speed manual was available as an option. Either way the top speed was quoted at 127 mph (205 kph) and the standing quarter mile took only 14 seconds to cover with 60 mph coming up in 5.7 seconds.

Although the Mach I still had basically the same suspension as the very first models the rear was transformed by a simple trick lifted

from the Shelby cars. The rear dampers were staggered, one mounted ahead of the axle, the other behind with both inclined toward the centre of the axle. There was a new and much improved Traction Lok limited slip diff to go with that modification and the excessive liveliness of a live axle was overcome.

By this time, however, Americans were obviously becoming blasé about horsepower alone as *Motor Trend's* Eric Dahlquist went into raptures about the interior, '…your hand reaches out to see if the teak-

TOP *The Mustang II could be made attractive, like this 1977 Cobra*
ABOVE *A late version of the Mach I, from 1972. The '71–'73 Mustangs were the largest of all, 8 in (20.3 cm) longer, 6 in (15.2 cm) wider and almost 600 lb (272 kg) heavier than the first Mustangs*
RIGHT *Early Mach Is were not quite so gross. This is a 1969 example being put through its paces on the test track*
BOTTOM *400 bhp of real muscle in the form of the 1968 Shelby GT 500 King of the Road*

dinosaur age; they were well developed, extremely powerful, ponderous and doomed. They roamed around for a few years and then died in the ice age of the first energy crisis. Evolution only took a step sideways when the Mustang II appeared in 1974. It was a foot shorter than the '73 car and even five inches (12.7 cm) shorter than the original Mustang, but the fuel fright meant that the standard power plant had become the small 2.3-litre overhead-cam four-cylinder. When the Mustang II first appeared the new Mach I had to be content with a 2.8-litre V6 which reduced its 0-60 time to a yawning 14 seconds plus. Discerning critics disliked the Mustang II and consequently it led a quiet life until the next generation of Mustang appeared in 1979. That had far cleaner styl-

wood grain panels are real.... It is as if some native had gone off into the forest and felled a teak and carried it back through the undergrowth to the river where it was lashed to others of its kind and floated down to the saw mill.' As he implied, and presumably as most of America agreed, who needs natural materials when the world has plastic?

The Mustangs grew yet larger in 1971, but for the performance cars, the Mach I and Boss 351, the increase in track (3 inches/7.6 cm at the front and 2.5 inches/6.5 cm at the rear) far outweighed the increase in weight. Not surprisingly it made the handling of the new Boss 351 with the Cleveland engine far more secure than that of the Boss 302; the 351 went through most corners with virtually no roll and had so much power that it over- rather than understeered.

As America entered the '70s the Mach I and Boss Mustangs were entering their own

ing, almost as exciting as that of the last Cortina. A live rear axle was retained as was the rack and pinion steering that had come with the Mustang II, but the new styling and strut front suspension were sufficient excuse for Ford to dub the range 'A New Breed of Mustang'. There was nothing new about the engines as the lifeless 2.3 struggled on and although the 302 V8 was still available it was strangled by emissions controls.

Nevertheless the high-tech that was eventually to rescue the Mustang had begun to make an appearance in the form of a turbocharger for the four-cylinder engine, and low-profile Michelin TRX tyres. Unfortunately the turbo installation was a disaster of the first order and Ford's first excursion into turbocharging for the masses was quietly buried.

As worries about fuel supplies receded and the new breed of electronic engine

EVOLUTION

Mustang I prototype introduced in 1962 to test public desire for a small sporty Ford. It was an open two-seater powered by a mid-mounted 90 bhp 2-litre V4 and had front disc brakes, magnesium wheels and a top speed of 115 mph (185 kph)

1964 Mustang production car introduced as a '65 model with a 2.8-litre in-line six-cylinder engine as standard with three-speed manual gearbox. Optional engines included the 3.3-litre six and 4.3- and 4.7-litre V8s. The large V8 was available with a four-speed manual gearbox as standard. Three body styles were available – hardtop, convertible and coupé

1965 Shelby Mustang GT-350 introduced with 289 cu in (4.7-litre) V8

1966 Base engine became the 3.3-litre

1967 Optional 390 cu in (6.4-litre) V8 with 320 bhp introduced. Track and body widened by 2.5 in (635 mm) and fastback body redesigned to eliminate the awkward step in the earlier design. Front suspension modified. Shelby GT-500 introduced with 400 bhp 428 cu in (7-litre) V8 and either four-speed manual or three-speed automatic transmission

1968 302 cu in (5-litre) with 230 bhp and 390 bhp big-block 427 cu in (7-litre) V8 introduced as options. Later in the year the 428 cu in Cobra Jet V8 became available. Suspension slightly modified

1969 Mustang Grande introduced as luxury version. Mach I introduced as new high-performance variant. Styling revised once more, making the Mustang longer, lower and wider with the distinctive body side-scalloping removed. Mach I was available with either the 250 bhp 351 cu in or the 355 bhp 428 Cobra Jet V8 and included the GT Equipment option package which featured staggered rear dampers. Two ultra high-performance models were introduced – the Boss 302 and Boss 429

1970 GT suspension package discontinued except on Boss and Mach I models. The big-block 390 cu in (6.4-litre) V8 discontinued

1971 Mustang range restyled and the cars grew longer, wider and considerably heavier. Boss 302 and 429 were dropped and replaced by the limited-production Boss 351 with Traction-Lok limited slip differential and four-speed Hurst transmission

1974 Mustang II introduced. It was far smaller than the '73 model and even shorter than the original Mustang. Base engine was the overhead-cam 2.3-litre four while the Mach I was powered by a 2.8-litre V6. Rack and pinion steering introduced

1979 Third generation Mustang introduced with completely new styling and MacPherson strut front suspension. Base engine was still the 2.3-litre four with the 2.8-litre V6 and 5-litre V8 as options. A turbocharged 2.3 was optional equipment and standard on the Mustang Cobra, along with four-speed manual transmission

1982 Mustang GT reintroduced with 5-litre V8

1983 Mustang Convertible reintroduced with 3.8-litre V6 or in GT form with the 5-litre V8. Five-speed manual gearbox standard on GT

1984 SVO Mustang introduced with turbocharged 2.3-litre four with intercooler

management control systems meant that Ford and GM could meet the Federal fuel economy requirements known as CAFE, North America and the Mustang began to rediscover high performance.

By 1985 the Mustang GT was once more a reasonable car and Ford brochures were allowed to mention power outputs once again. The four-barrel 302 produced 210 bhp (SAE net) at 4400 rpm, a figure

---

> *'… the Mustang began to rediscover high performance… '*

---

that's grown steadily from the trough of around 150 bhp just three or four years before. Some judicious strengthening of the bodyshell meant that it was even possible to have a Convertible GT once again (introduced in '83 as an '84 model) and although the chassis still felt rather more flexible than a purpose-built open sports car it was acceptable and its performance even more so. Once again there was a Mustang that could turn in 7-second 0-60 times and reach a top speed near 120 mph (193 kph).

The five-speed manual gearbox was delightfully light and precise to use and the power steering direct and not overly boosted, although it was still rather insensitive.

The years since the Shelbys and Mach Is have seen some rear suspension development too. From staggered dampers and semi-elliptic springs Ford have progressed to a full belt-and-braces affair in locating the GT's axle. Two lower trailing arms are supplemented by two upper angled torque arms, a Panhard rod, an anti-roll bar and four dampers cunningly arranged to form what Ford call their Quadra Link system. The second set of dampers is inclined almost to the horizontal, like upper trailing arms, to cushion the shock of fierce gear changes and mask axle tramp.

Although the GT convertible looks the part and has a superb powertrain offering smooth and instant acceleration, the driver is seated far too high and the car is still too vague for European tastes. That problem was addressed (and almost solved) with the SVO Mustang introduced in 1983. As rear-drive Mustangs are scheduled to go out of production in '86 or '87 the SVO represents the pinnacle of Mustang design, its creators trying to achieve through 'high-tech' what was done with cubic inches years ago. Ford's electronic engine management control has permitted the use of up to 14 psi of turbo boost, enough to force 175 bhp out of the 2.3-litre four at 4400 rpm along with 210 lb ft of torque at 3000 rpm. Fuel injection and in-

tercooling also play their part, the intercooler bringing down the temperature of the air flowing into the engine down from around 300 degrees Fahrenheit to 175 degrees F to make that air more dense. That alone gave the turbo 2.3 a 20 per cent power boost. That makes it very slightly slower than the 5-litre GT with 0-60 times nearer 8 than 7 seconds, but it's faster over the standing quarter (15.8 seconds, 89 mph/143 kph) when the engine

'...faster over the standing quarter when the engine...gets going...'

really gets going. There are echoes of Shelby in the use of Koni (gas-filled) dampers all round (even in the Quadra Link system) while braking is by ventilated discs. Its cast alloy wheels are covered by 225/50VR16 Goodyear Eagles, the same unidirectional 'gatorback' design pioneered by 1984 Chevrolet Corvette. Such low profile tyres give

LEFT AND BELOW LEFT *The distinctive lines of the SVO Mustang. The SVO is the most sophisticated Mustang built so far, with a 2.3-litre intercooled turbocharged engine producing 175 bhp*

the Corvette and the SVO incredible grip.

Although the power peak is only 4400 rpm the 8.0:1 compression ratio means that the engine has to be kept boosted and certainly over 2500 rpm to produce the sort of performance the chassis craves. On the ordinary streets with a new car where the Hurst gear change is still stiff and notchy the result is extreme frustration as the revs drop. Around a test track such as Ford's Dearborn handling course where stop-start motoring is hardly called for the result is far more pleasing, the only mild criticism being that the SVO's small engine cannot match the wide spread of torque from the GT's 5-litre V8. While it lacks the GT's sheer punch, it fortunately lacks the larger-engined car's propensity for terminal understeer, making it almost the equal of the '84 Corvette through the slalom course. *Road & Track,* however, were prompted to wild enthusiasm, concluding that the Ford SVO team '...could hardly have done a better job of improving the car to world-class GT standards. This may be the best all-around car for the enthusiast driver ever produced by the US industry...'. They may be right – after all not many American cars can boast such sophistication or its ability to reach over 130 mph (209 kph) and still return near to 25 mpg. At least the Mustang will go out with its head held high after 20 years. KB

Since its launch in the troubled '70s, the Jaguar has proved itself to be the flagship of the British grand tourers, a true 150 mph cruiser, comfortable and superbly engineered and styled

LATE IN THE 1960S, a major worry crept into the Jaguar camp at Coventry. The E-type was getting old, yet what was to replace it? To put the age question into perspective, you have to remember that the XK150 which preceded the E-type was produced for only four years from 1957 to 1961, while the whole history of the XK series from the original 120 spanned only 13 years from 1948. Yet here was the E-type which, even if it had been streets ahead of its time when launched, was clearly going to see out its tenth birthday prior to replacement. And, in any event, how was it to be replaced?

The XJS was the result of that debate. It emerged at a difficult time for Jaguar. It was the result of those difficulties which meant that, in the end, the XJS did not replace the E-type production in 1973 and the launch of the XJS in 1975. Thus the E-type survived for 12 years, no less, although in practice the final two years' worth differed notably from those that went before, the Series 3 cars being powered (with a few exceptions) by the new V12 engine.

What, then, of those difficulties? The first and most obvious was the energy crisis which hit the world in the wake of the 1973 October War in the Middle East. Petrol prices rocketed and cars with big engines and high performance suddenly became very hard to sell. It spelled a premature end to the V12 E-type even though its successor was far from ready. It cast a doubt over the very future of that successor, and certainly played some part in determining its final form.

Then there was the British Leyland situation, into which Jaguar had been dragged via the original British Motor Holdings agreement with Austin-Morris. By the early 1970s BL was in a totally parlous state, losing money hand over fist, its management increasingly appalled at the magnitude of the task it had taken on, overseen by politicians who still saw it principally as a job-factory rather than a car manufacturer, and very thoroughly demoralised. What money remained in the kitty for new model development, it seemed, was more likely to be released in the direction of a Mini replace-

RIGHT *The balanced and purposeful lines of a 5.3-litre V12-engined XJS*
BELOW *The first production XJS ever built, pictured with some of its illustrious forebears: (left to right) a Jaguar E-type, XK 120 and XK 150*

ment than spent on a high-performance V12-engined sports car which could never hope to be built in large numbers. Yet, in the end, the Jaguar influence – and especially that of Sir William Lyons – won through and the XJS was produced anyway.

Among the arguments certainly marshalled in its favour were the amount of work already done on the project, the existence of the V12 engine and the proposed use of parts in common with the XJ saloons. Serious work on the XJS actually dated back to 1969 under the XJ27 project number, and the original intention, before BL's problems and management shuffles got in the way, was to launch it in 1972 with the V12 engine. As for the engine itself. its main intended purpose in life had been to power an E-type replacement, and if the project was not proceeded with, much of the investment already made in the Radford V12 factory

J A G U A R
XJS

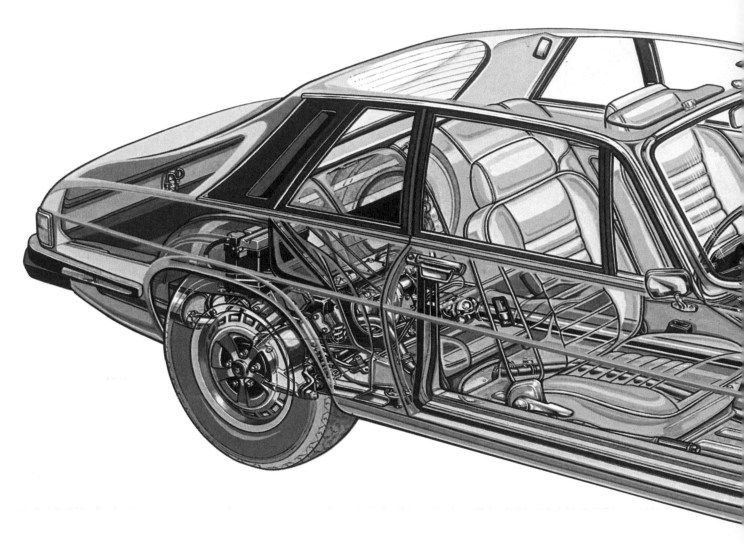

MODEL
Jaguar XJS (1975)
UK price when introduced:
£8900.19p

ENGINE
Location: Front, longitudinal
Type: Water-cooled V12 with cast alloy block and heads and seven-bearing crankshaft
Cubic capacity: 5343 cc
Compression ratio: 9:1
Valve gear: Two overhead, in-line valves per cylinder operated by single overhead camshafts
Fuel supply: Lucas Opus Mk II electronic fuel injection
Ignition: Lucas Opus contactless electronic ignition
Maximum power: 285 bhp at 5500 rpm
Maximum torque: 294 lb ft at 3500 rpm

TRANSMISSION
Layout: Gearbox in unit with engine
Clutch: Hydraulic torque converter
Gearbox: Three-speed Borg-Warner Model 12 automatic transmission
    1st 1.44:1   3rd 1.0:1
    2nd 2.39:1
Final drive: Hypoid bevel limited-slip differential
Ratio: 3.07:1

SUSPENSION
Front: Independent, with wishbones, coil springs, hydraulic dampers and anti-rollbar
Rear: Independent, with lower wishbones, driveshafts acting as upper links, trailing lower radius arms, twin coil springs, twin hydraulic dampers and anti-roll bar

STEERING
Type: Power-assisted rack and pinion

BRAKES
Type: Discs front and rear, servo-assisted

WHEELS AND TYRES
Type: Cast alloy 15 in (38 cm) wheels fitted with 205/70VR 15 steel-belted radial tyres

BODY/CHASSIS
Type: Cast alloy 15 in (38 cm) wheels fitted with 205/70VR 15 steel-belted radial tyres

DIMENSIONS AND WEIGHT
Length: 187.6 in (4749 mm)
Width: 70.6 in (1793 mm)
Wheelbase: 102 in (2591 mm)
Track front: 58.6 in (1488 mm)
    – **rear:** 59.2 in (1504 mm)
Weight: 8370 lb (1755 kg)

PERFORMANCE
Maximum speed: 152 mph (245 kph)
Acceleration 0-60 mph: 6.75 seconds
Fuel consumption approx: 16 mpg

BELOW The sophisticated engineering of the XJS revealed, much of it shared with the XJ6 saloon range. The effortless power of the 5.3-litre V12, which completely fills the large under-bonnet area, required extremely efficient suspension and braking, and the wishbone front suspension incorporates anti-dive geometry to maintain stability the car's stability under heavy braking. The body has a very strong passenger compartment, and although its styling was somewhat controversial when first introduced, its aerodynamic efficiency was notably better than the E-type's. Smooth, fast and comfortable, the XJS is now rightly regarded as a true successor in Jaguar's long tradition of 'Grace...Space...Pace'.

would have been made in vain. Finally, although the XJS was not an obvious XJ saloon derivative, it was much closer to the saloon than the E-type in concept and there was a measure of commonality between them though more in the mechanical than the body engineering area. No doubt it was also stressed that while everyone was finding it difficult to make money with small economy cars (and mostly still does) a specialised model for sale at a very high price stood more chance of paying back its development cost.

Thus when the XJS finally emerged in time for the 1975 Motor Show, it was very far removed from the ultra-advanced mid-engined sports car some were anticipating. It was no E-type for the 1980s but rather used a conventional unitary-construction body instead of the E-type's central monocoque and forward space frame. The running gear might easily have been taken from the saloon though it differed in important details (notably the provision of anti-roll bars at both ends of the car); there were the same noise-insulating sub-frames, wishbone front suspension and uniquely Jaguar rear suspension with the drive shafts acting as upper links, and twin coil spring/damper units per side. There too was the V12 engine without even the pretence – as there had been in the Series 3 E-type – that the 4.2-litre XK engine was offered as an alternative; and there was the Borg-Warner automatic transmission *without* any manual option!

It was this last feature as much as anything which gave the game away. The Jaguar tradition of genuine sports cars had died

with the E-type; the XJS was an alternative form of transport for the well-heeled who wished to cut more of a dash than the XJ saloon implied. In 1975 we had to think back only a few years to 1968 and Ford's Car You Had Always Promised Yourself; here now was the XJS playing Capri to the XJ6's Cortina, the same exercise moved significantly higher up the social (or at least income) scale. What nobody had ever really explained is why Jaguar should have thought it necessary (or got away with?) the almost *parallel* development of the XJS and the handsome two-door XJ Coupés which en-

---

> *'...virtually designed by the American safety regulations...'*

---

joyed a brief burst of production from 1974 to 1977, bracketing the years of the XJS introduction.

It was equally obvious that the XJS was aimed squarely at an American market just beginning to climb out of its post-energy-crisis despond. The car had in some respects been virtually designed by the American safety regulations: massive strut-mounted bumpers to meet the 5 mph requirement, single fuel tank well protected from rear impact, but above all, no convertible version. The mid-1970s were the era when it seemed to most car designers, on both sides of the Atlantic, that the Federal safety regulations had written *finis* to the soft-top

(Triumph's TR7 was laid out on the same basis).

To say that the XJS was received less ecstatically than the E-type would be an understatement. There was simply no comparison. The E-type had been startling not only in its looks but in being well ahead of its time. The XJS was a state-of-the-art device and deliberately so for all manner of reasons; and its looks were at once called into question. Plenty of withering comments rolled off the presses about it seeming that the front and back ends had been designed by two men who weren't on speaking terms. The back end was especially awkward, and if the 'rear buttress' approach was intended to echo certain Italian inspirations, it didn't succeed. Malcolm Sayer, whose genius had largely shaped the E-type, had long since died an untimely death. Even so, wind tunnel test results quoted at the time showed the XJS to have a drag coefficient of 0.39 compared with the 0.455 quoted for the E-type; a remarkable difference when you consider, for instance, how much better a nose shape the E-type seems to have. Maybe those buttresses either side of the rear window were more effective in cutting base drag than they seemed, though as we shall see, direct comparisons on the basis of actual performance (especially achieved maximum speeds) was made difficult for other reasons.

In any case the XJS drawbacks were more apparent than real. What some of the doubters failed to see was that the XJS designers had managed to combine all the needs of the 'regulation market' with the traditional

virtues of the marque. True, the XJS was heavy because the XJ saloon was overweight. It scaled 3,700 pounds at the kerb – as nearly as makes no difference two tons with full tank, two hefty occupants and some luggage – but it had both the engine and brakes to deal with it. The V12 with its new fuel injection, effectively the Bosch L-Jetronic adapted to those extra cylinders, produced 285 bhp and 280 lb-ft of torque. As for road behaviour, the XJ had always been a quality chassis and the XJS was in many respects better still with its lower centre of gravity and higher roll stiffness. It was quite adequately shod with high-geared power steering as standard. It was also more nimble, since its wheelbase had been cut back to 102 in (259 cm); but it still felt like a big car.

Only a few months after its launch, the XJS lost its automatic-only tag, at least officially. There must be some suspicion that the manual-gearbox car was offered partly to enable the more authoritative press road testers to record suitably elevated maximum speeds. Thus *Autocar's* first XJS test was carried out early in 1976 on a manual-transmission car which yielded a top speed of 153 mph (246 kph) and a 0–60 mph time of 6.9 sec. The test also pointed out that it was possible to start the car from rest in top

BELOW & RIGHT *Views of an XJSC 3.6, the luxurious and very well-styled cabriolet model introduced in 1983. The engine,* **TOP,** *is tilted at 15 degrees in order to fit under the low bonnet, and the interior,* **RIGHT,** *maintains Jaguar's long tradition of high-quality leather and wood trim*

EVOLUTION

Introduced at the 1975 Motor Show, the Jaguar XJS two-door coupé was designed to be the long-awaited replacement for the E-type Jaguar. It was fitted with the 5.3-litre V12 and fitted with automatic transmission as standard

1976 Four-speed manual transmission was offered as an option and the Borg-Warner automatic transmission was replaced by GM's THM400 unit. In manual form the car was capable of 153 mph (246 kph), with a 0-60 mph time of 6.9 seconds

1981 The XJS HE was introduced, with the engine heads modified to give improved fuel consumption, more low-speed torque and a power output of 300 bhp. Maximum speed was 153 mph (246 kph) and 0-60 mph took 6.5 seconds

1983 The XJS 3.6 was announced, fitted with the 3.6-litre straight six and available in coupe and convertible form. It was fitted with a five-speed manual transmission and capable of 145 mph (233 kph)

1985 The XJSC-HE was introduced, the cabriolet version fitted with the 5.3-litre V12. Maximum speed was 148 mph (238 kph) and acceleration to 60 mph took 7.8 seconds

gear, clutch fully engaged, by operating the starter motor and still reach 120 mph in less than 50 sec. This, presumably, was enough to excuse the relevance of the road test as a whole for a car of which nearly 10,000 automatics were sold in the first three full years of production compared with just over 200 manuals!

One of the problems of the manual car, apart from the fact that most buyers preferred automatic anyway, was the need to fit the old Jaguar four-speed gearbox whose ratios were horribly stretched to cover the spread of speed. The *Autocar* testers commented that in the form presented, with Salisbury's 3.07:1 limited-slip final drive, the XJS was still well under-geared for best performance since maximum speed took the car 700 rpm beyond peak power. In theory an even higher ratio would have helped but not without painful effect on the acceleration. A five-speed gearbox was the real answer; what was not public knowledge at the time was the existence of a so-called '88 mm' five-speed gearbox (88 mm being the distance between the main and layshafts, the box being one of a 66/77/88 mm BL corporate 'family' of which the only one to reach production was the 77 mm one for the Rover SD1). With this box, the XJS would probably have been a genuine 160 mph (258 kph) car even without the assistance of the 6.4-litre version of the V12 on which Harry Mundy was working...

Another of the reasons why the first XJS road tests were carried out on manual cars was that the Borg-Warner Model 12 automatic with which the car had been launched was a stop-gap. In little more than a year it had been replaced by the General Motors THM400, a far superior device in terms of

change quality (and standard fitting also on all contemporary Rolls-Royces). Even so, there was an inevitable effect on performance with only three speeds. A 1977 *Autocar* road test of the CM-transmission XJS showed that maximum speed had fallen to 142 mph (229 kph) while the 0–60 mph time was up to 7.5 seconds. Overall fuel consumption was also 10 per cent worse.

None of this might have mattered so much but for the second great energy crisis of 1978/79, in the wake of the Iranian revolution, when petrol prices again doubled almost overnight. It became essential, if the XJS was to survive at all, to project it not as a

---

'... a high-swirl design which promised very high efficiency...'

---

thirsty symbol of over-affluence but rather as high technology with an eye to an energy-efficient future. That in turn called for a significant revision of the engine.

Harry Mundy and the Jaguar engine team had for some time been interested in the 'Fireball' combustion chamber devised by Swiss engineer Michael May. It was a high-swirl design which promised very high efficiency in exchange for a certain amount of extra investment and the need to maintain very tight production tolerances. That was less of a problem for the V12 factory at Radford with its small production volumes than it would have been for a truly large-scale manufacturer. The energy crisis provided the impetus needed to adopt the system and the result was that in 1981, the

V12 Jaguar range (XJS *and* saloons) were announced in HE – High Efficiency – form with Fireball chambers formed under recessed exhaust valves. The effectiveness of the May heads can be judged from the raising of the compression ratio from 10:1 (whither it had crept in the intervening years from the original 9:1, taking the power up to 296 bhp) to 12..5:1, bringing the peak power up to 300 bhp, with 302 lb ft of torque, while at the same time specific fuel consumption was also improved. The result was that when *Autocar* tested the XJS-HE in 1982, it found a maximum speed of 153 mph (24.6 kph), a 0–60 mph time of 6.5 seconds and an overall fuel consumption of 16 mpg compared with the previous 14 mpg.

While this effort was being applied to the V12 powerhouse, two other important strands of development were being followed with respect to the XJS. First, there was a perceived need for a new smaller engine – as long as it had sufficient power and the right kind of image. Second, it had long been obvious that the American regulations *did* leave room for convertibles, and the XJS was Jaguar's candidate.

The two strands of development eventually came together in October 1983 when the XJS 3.6 was announced in both Coupé and Convertible forms. As far as the engine was concerned, the new AJ6 unit differed in many ways from the V12. It was certainly not the case, as many had expected, that the AJ6 would be 'half a V12'. On the contrary, the 3.6-litre engine had a twin-cam, four-valves-per-cylinder head with pent-roof combustion chambers. There could hardly have been a greater contrast with the V12's single overhead camshaft per bank and in-line valves: still less with the original V12 layout

LEFT *An XJS, a big seller in the USA*
ABOVE *The Tom Walkinshaw/Chuck Nicholson XJS at Donington in 1983*
RIGHT *The Walkinshaw XJS leading the pack at Donington in 1982*
BELOW *A 1983 Jaguar XJS HE coupè*

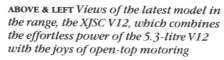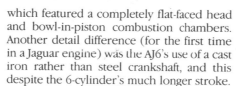

ABOVE & LEFT *Views of the latest model in the range, the XJSC V12, which combines the effortless power of the 5.3-litre V12 with the joys of open-top motoring*

which featured a completely flat-faced head and bowl-in-piston combustion chambers. Another detail difference (for the first time in a Jaguar engine) was the AJ6's use of a cast iron rather than steel crankshaft, and this despite the 6-cylinder's much longer stroke.

With its 3.6-litre capacity the AJ6 was bound to produce much more than half the power of the V12 which had, in the meantime, been slightly retuned to gain more torque (321 lb ft) for a small sacrifice in power (295 bhp). The equivalent AJ6 figures were 240 lb ft and 225 bhp, giving the new engine much higher specific power – 62.5 bhp/litre against the V12's 55. Such are the benefits of four valves per cylinder.

As one might expect, the changes needed to turn the original coupé body shell into a convertible were considerable. Even then, the result was not a 'fully topless' cabriolet but one which essentially retained the frame of the roof in order to transmit bending and twisting stresses without having to take them all through the floor and sill panels. Provision was made for rigid targa-type panels to fill in the roof opening as an alternative to erecting the hood. While the coupé was always fitted as a 2+2 – however small and lacking in headroom the rear seat might have been – the XJS 3.6SC was strictly a two-seater with an extended rear luggage platform, its standard equipment even including a discreet placard warning against a rear passenger!

In many ways, therefore, the AJ6-engined XJS was more nearly a sports car than the V12 had ever been, especially in cabriolet form. Here you had a two-seater with a deliberately high-output engine. The point was strongly underlined by Jaguar in offering the 3.6 only with *manual* transmission

(the manual 'option' on the V12 had been allowed to die in 1978). The switch of policy was made possible through the use of Getrag's excellent five-speed box which made the smaller-engined XJS a far more saleable proposition in performance-conscious Germany, then becoming another key market for Jaguar. Despite the ever-present weight penalty, the performance was certainly there in fair measure. The *Autocar* test of 1983 showed a 136 mph (219 kph) maximum, and 7.4 seconds to 60 mph, for the 3.6-litre coupé, with a fuel consumption of 17.6 mpg.

What had happened with the appearance of the AJ6 engine and the convertible was in fact that the XJS range had very nearly split into two lines. One was the plush, automatic-only, V12 grand tourer while the other was more nearly a sports car, which at least helped to excuse some of the un-Jaguar-like roughness from which most testers felt the engine suffered at low and very high speeds. All that remained was to complete the range of options by fitting the V12 engine to the cabriolet body, and this was duly done in 1985. By this time Jaguar (once again a fully independent company) had taken hood fitting onto its own production line to meet the demand which had materialised. What did *not* happen was the re-emergence of any manual gearbox option for the new V12 car.

In truth, the XJS has come a long way from the dark days of 1980 when production dwindled to little more than a thousand for the year. By 1984, with the emergence of the 3.6-litre versions to help, that figure was already back to more than 6,000 units, while the current Jaguar plan calls for at least 8,000. In other words the XJS is doing better than at any time in its history which already extends back, at the time of writing, more than ten years. Its rate of production does not compare with the E-type's, of which over 72,000 were made, but it looks as though the XJS will continue for a long time yet and claim classic status in terms of longevity. JRD

It was, in many ways, an unlikely cast, but together its members built the most stunning supercar of the '60s. There was Ferruccio Lamborghini himself, the short, thick-set Italian industrialist who started amassing money by rebuilding war surplus armoured vehicles into tractors, and there was his physical antithesis, Bob Wallace, a blond-haired, lanky New Zealander who went to Modena to be a racing mechanic and ended up chief test driver and engineering troubleshooter with Italy's newest, and probably most exciting, exoticar manufacturer.

Wallace was only 25 when he joined Lamborghini, in the summer of 1963. Even younger was the brilliant Parma-born engineer Gianpaolo Dallara, the holder of a degree in aeronautical engineering who had worked for both Ferrari and Maserati. He was in charge of chassis design and development. Dallara's assistant, Paolo Stanzani, was only one year older. Wallace, Dallara and Stanzani nurtured the idea of building a mid-engined supercar for the road which, in 1964, would make it the world's first. Lamborghini, a born showman who himself had long dreamt of building the ultimate road car, agreed with alacrity and enthusiasm. And, finally, there was another young man: 25 year-old Marcello Gandini. Following the departure of Giorgetto Giugiaro to Ghia in 1965, Gandini was reckoned to be Bertone's best stylist. He clothed the dream and made it the most sensational looking sports car of its day.

Rumour has it that Lamborghini went into the supercar business because he was dissatisfied with the service he received as a Ferrari customer and especially because Enzo Ferrari once made him wait a long

Twelve cylinders, four cams and 350bhp all clothed by one of Bertone's beautiful bodies – it was no wonder that the Lamborghini Miura outshone even Ferrari in 1968

BELOW AND RIGHT *Two views of the P400 Miura, which burst onto the motoring scene in 1967 after a stunning debut at the 1966 Geneva Show*

time for a meeting. The story is almost certainly untrue; Ferruccio built supercars because they were to him the most exciting machines. When asked why he became a sports car manufacturer, Lamborghini once answered: 'In the past I have bought some of the world's most famous *gran turismo* cars. In each of these machines I have found faults – too hot – too uncomfortable – not fast enough; now I want to make a GT car without faults. Not a technical bomb; very normal, very conventional, *but perfect.*' A factory was set up in Sant'Agata Bolognese, a village between Bologna and Modena. And because Lamborghini was a young car manufacturer, Ferruccio – who liked to think of himself as 'Cavaliere Lamborghini' (as opposed to 'Commendatore Ferrari') – recruited keen young men.

The first Lamborghini, the 350GT, was previewed at the Turin Show in the same year as the new company was formed. A strange looking, some said downright ugly, front-engined *gran turismo* machine, the GT offered 155 mph (249 kph) top speed with 0–60 mph (approximately 0–100 kph) acceleration of some 6.5 seconds. Its most notable feature was its 3.5-litre engine. From the start Lamborghini insisted on manufacturing his own power unit rather than buying it in (which he rightly thought would spoil the new car's pedigree). More than this he wanted nothing less than a V12 and gave former Alfa Romeo and Ferrari designer Giotto Bizzarrini a commission to build one. It so happened that Bizzarrini had already done preliminary work on a four-cam 60-degree engine which ideally suited Lamborghini's requirements, the four-cam arrangement appealing to Ferruccio as a piece of

LAMBORGHINI
MIURA

one-upmanship over the contemporary twin-cam Ferrari layout.

Thus was born the first of the breed, but the classic work was yet to come. The three youngsters – Dallara, Stanzani and Wallace – wanted to build the ultimate GT car, one that could also be used for racing. Lamborghini himself persistently said no to sporting involvement, but the three got their wish and the Miura was on its way.

Dallara, the most important member of the team, was greatly impressed by the styling and construction of the Ford GT40 which appeared in 1964 and decided that a mid-engined car with a central monocoque was the way to go. Even more innovative was his idea of mounting the V12 and its transmission transversely with the latter behind the engine and direct cog drive from one to the other. The arrangement would take less fore-and-aft room (the same argument used by Alec Issigonis for the Mini) and thus leave more space for passengers and luggage. It was also argued that it would provide better access to some key mechanical items, not that access was ever a prime consideration in supercar design.

It obviously made sense to use as many parts as possible from the front-engined GT car and the suspension geometry and most of the parts were the same as on the 350GT.

> *' ... 350bhp at 7000rpm, but like all power units quoted by Italian supercar makers of the day that was optimistic! '*

There were front and rear wishbones, with integral coil springs and dampers. 12-inch solid Girling discs were used at front and back, as were anti-roll bars. The chassis, of course, was quite different from that of the front-engined machine. The Dallara design had a deep central monocoque of light-gauge steel to which were bolted box sections to support the drive-train and front suspension.

The power-train was a mechanical work of art. One of its most extraordinary features was the single aluminium alloy casting which combined the block, crankcase, transmission and final drive, with cast-iron wet liners for the cylinders. The engine itself was based closely on that of the 350GT, soon to have a name change to 400GT, thanks to a capacity increase. It was the new 4-litre version of the V12 that actually went in to the Miura. The four camshafts were chain driven and actuated the valves through inverted steel bucket tappets. The valves themselves were inclined at 35 degrees to the cylinder centre-line, and operated in hemispherical combustion chambers. The crankshaft was nickel chromed, machined from a solid billet, and ran in seven main bearings.

The 350GT had six twin-choke Webers, but Dallara, who was most responsible for the development of the V12, decided to fit a quartet of three-choke units to the Miura.

The carbs were downdraught Weber 40 IDL3Cs as used by Porsche on their 911 of the day. Wet-sump lubrication was chosen in preference to the dry-sumping as seen on the 350GT. The end result of this Dallara deliberation and Bolognese brilliance was a claimed 350 bhp at 7000 rpm and 271 lb ft of torque at 5100 rpm, but like all power output figures quoted by Italian supercar makers of the day that was rather optimistic! This Sant'Agata power was transferred to Lamborghini's own five-speed gearbox (with synchromesh on all gears, *including* reverse) by a three-plate clutch, placed before the input shaft of the gearbox. When production started, however, this arrangement was superseded by an arrangement more like that of the Mini. The clutch was changed to a simpler single-plate affair, placed at the end of the crankshaft, which drove the gearbox input shaft through a pair of helical gears. A very small pinion and large ring gear took the drive from the gearbox to the in-sump

ABOVE *An S model of 1969. This had a 370bhp engine and later cars featured improved braking and stiffened suspension. The distinctive 'eyelash' headlight surrounds were later deleted*

final drive, and then to the wheels via conventional splined halfshafts. Originally a hydraulic gear linkage was envisaged, but this was soon scrapped and a conventional metal linkage used.

The first Miura chassis, complete with engine and gearbox, was ready by November 1965, in time for the Turin Show. Even with no bodywork it attracted a vast amount of attention thanks to its transverse layout. Lamborghini admitted during the show that production would be strictly limited, and the boss himself told a gathering that he was making 'a dream car for a few crazy people'. Although many sceptics dismissed the display as a publicity stunt, others started to get out their chequebooks. Lamborghini took ten Miura orders in Turin. For a car still some twelve months away from production, and with no body, that was quite a feat.

Not only were the motoring press and the general public intrigued by the Lamborghini display, but Italian coachbuilders also took more than their fair share of interest in it. The identity of the stylist had still not been

made public and there was no doubt that the exciting new low-slung chassis offered real aesthetic possibilities. Touring of Milan, who built the 350GT bodies, would have been a strong candidate and had even begun work on a design but serious financial problems, resulting in bankruptcy, prevented their carrying on. After their demise, Bertone were considered the most likely candidates. The Grugliasco firm not only had a distinguished reputation, and the facilities, but they also had the important qualification of not being linked with either Ferrari or Maserati. Nuccio Bertone knew that a really stunning set of clothes on Ferruccio Lamborghini's new baby would act as a great boost for his company. And although his star designer, Giorgetto Giugiaro, had recently left to join Ghia, Bertone had another great young designer he could trust to come up with the goods: Marcello Gandini The Italian youngster and his small team worked crazy hours during the latter part of 1965 and early '66 as the design moved from paper to the wooden model stage. Early in 1966, the chassis and body were coming together at Bertone's factory with the Geneva Show of that year as the target. Lamborghini made it – just; but not only did the car have to be finished, a name had still to be decided upon. Until the '66 Geneva Show, the car was known as the P400: P for *posteriore*, and 400 for 4.0 litres. Miura, the name of one of the greatest strains of Spanish fighting bull was finally decided upon.

Quite simply, the Miura absolutely dominated the Geneva Show. Not only was it the first mid-engined supercar designed specifically for the road, with a claimed top speed of 187 mph (300 kph), but it already had the look of a future classic. Both the front and rear body sections were made from aluminium, with the centre monocoque and the doors of steel. There was no glass fibre anywhere in a Miura's bodywork. There was even practicality to match the beauty. The bonnet was hinged at the front, the rear engine cover at the rear. Both gave excellent access, and both could be removed totally to improve matters further. Although mid-engined cars have never been renowned for their luggage space, the Miura did have a useful, if hardly capacious, boot behind the engine. In overall length this Gandini masterpiece measured 171.6in (436cm) – about 2.0 in (50 cm) shorter than a Ferrari Boxer, or about the same as a Ford Cortina. It was certainly not as wide as modern exotics, being only 4.0 in (102 cm) broader than an everyday Cortina. If there was any one extraordinary specification of the Miura, however, it was its height – or rather lack of it. From just behind the windscreen to the bottom of the specially made Pirelli tyres it was barely higher than a dining room table – some 2 in (2.5 cm) lower than the ground-

They *looked* imposing but were poorly sited, just a little too low for the driver's natural line of sight. In the central cowled console were six additional instruments, all angled towards the driver. There were gauges for water temperature, oil temperature, oil pressure, fuel level, the ammeter and a clock. Mounted in the roof, behind the rearview mirror, were six toggle switches for lights, wipers and the like.

Getting the Miura ready for the 1966 Geneva Show had been a monumental task – but the really hard work was still ahead. Real testing began in May '66 with Bob Wallace doing most of the hard driving. The most common route for Wallace and the Miura was the highways between Sant'Agata and Florence, which combined *autostrade* with winding mountain roads. Wallace soon discovered that his work should be concentrated on two main areas: adjusting the suspension and solving engine and cockpit cooling problems.

the occupants' ears and one bank of exhausts perilously close to the driver's rear. Wallace later admitted that the engine's location did cause serious heat and noise problems – and, to be sure, the Miura was always a noisy and fairly hot car. These early problems were partly remedied by a special perspex sheet (instead of the original glass) between the cockpit and the engine, by the slatted rear cover (which extracted heat from the engine), and by four inches of polystyrene insulation behind the sheet metal bulkhead.

By the end of May the Miura had progressed well enough for Ferruccio Lamborghini to gamble on giving his new charge its second public airing. The Monaco Grand Prix was approaching. The Boss knew full well that among the Pierre Cardin set, who flock to the Grand Prix like aristrocrats to Royal Ascot, were prospective Miura owners. So Bob Wallace and a mechanic were dispatched to the Principality as Lamborghini had the Miura accepted as the course marshal's car. An equally overt publicity coup was arranged for the night before the Grand Prix. Ferruccio Lamborghini knew that the Place Du Casino was the place to be seen on that Saturday night and managed to park the prototype Miura right in the centre of the square, amid all the other exotic machines

ABOVE *The interior of the S was rather more luxurious than that of the P400, with superior carpeting and upholstery, revised switchgear and electrically operated windows*

hugging Turbo Esprit of today.

Visually striking features of the Miura included the uncovered headlights with their curious 'eyelash' surrounds, which were raised and lowered electrically, the vast raked windscreen (which made the cockpit of the Miura like a sauna on a hot day) the big rear three-quarter air intake louvres, novel ducted alloy wheels for brake cooling and (later in 1966) the Venetian blind-like heavily slatted rear window cover which helped extract hot air from the engine, helped cool the interior and did not restrict rear vision too badly.

The interior was equally striking. It was – like most Italian exotics – not lacking in instrumentation. Directly in front of the driver, but placed in separate circular housings, were the tachometer (to 10,000 rpm) and the speedo (to 200 mph or 320 kph).

Wallace soon found that the car was prone to rather sudden oversteer when pushed hard and also had rear toe in/toe out problems. Under acceleration there was excessive rear toe-in; under braking too much toe-out. Many of these problems were never in fact fully rectified until production was well and truly underway. They were eventually partially overcome by larger Pirelli tyres and reinforced rear trailing links. Front end lightness was also a problem when running at the sort of high speeds of which the Miura was capable. This was never fully cured either although it was partly solved by the introduction of a chin spoiler, by the larger tyres and by more efficient expulsion of the radiator air (which cured a pressure build up under the nose). A ZF limited-slip differential was tried but abandoned because of oil viscosity problems with the common engine/transmission lubricant.

When the car was shown at Geneva, critics were also dubious as to how noisy and hot the new Lambo would be – with all those Webers gulping for air only inches behind

> '*The snarling buzz of the twelve trumpets drew even more inquisitive glances and doubled the size of the crowd*'

which assemble there. Naturally the striking rarity with the charging bull motif stole the show that evening. In case anyone had failed to notice the car, Ferruccio Lamborghini fought his way through the crowd surrounding the Miura to start up the V12 for a curious friend. The snarling buzz of the twelve trumpets drew even more inquisitive glances and doubled the size of the crowd. Ferruccio didn't bother to take sales orders that evening, but it is a fair bet that when the new Lamborghini finally hit the streets in early 1967 a number of those Monaco Grand Prix goers were the first to part with the 75,000 Swiss Francs required.

One of the corollaries of this protracted development period and continuing pre-production publicity was that the order book suddenly became much bigger than the intended production run, envisaged at something like twenty a year. As it turned out, during 1967, the first year of proper production, 108 Miuras were delivered to increasingly impatient customers. Most stayed in Italy, but cars were also delivered to rich enthusiasts in the USA, Britain (where the price in 1967 was a whopping £8050 at a time when an E-type Jaguar cost nearly £6000 less), Sweden and even Venezuela.

In late 1968 the first major improvement to the Miura was effected when the P400S Miura went on sale. First shown at the Turin

MODEL

Lamborghini Miura, 1967.
UK price when announced: £7455
(£9165 inc. tax).

ENGINE

Location: Mid, transverse
Type: Water-cooled 60 degree V12
with aluminium alloy cylinder heads
and block
Cubic capacity: 3929cc
Bore x stroke: 82mm x 62mm
Compression ratio: 9.8:1
Valve gear: 2 inclined valves per
cylinder operated in hemispherical
chambers by twin chain-driven
overhead camshafts per bank of
cylinders
Fuel supply: 4 Weber 40 IDL3Cs
downdraught triple choke

carburettors
Ignition: Twin coil and distributor,
mechanical
Maximum power: 350bhp (net
DIN) at 7000rpm
Maximum torque: 271lb ft (net
DIN) at 5100rpm

TRANSMISSION

Layout: Clutch and gearbox
transversely mounted behind and in
unit with the engine with direct
gear drive
Clutch: Single plate, diaphragm
spring, hydraulically operated
Gearbox: Five-speed manual
synchromesh on all forward and
reverse gear

1st 2.520:1	4th 1.00:1
2nd 1.735:1	5th 0.815:1
3rd 1.225:1	

Final drive: Helical spur with
limited slip differential
Ratio: 4.08:1

SUSPENSION

Front: Independent by double
wishbones, coil springs and
concentric telescopic dampers and
anti-roll bar
Rear: Independent by double
unequal wishbones, coil springs
and concentric telescopic dampers
and top-mounted anti-roll bar

STEERING

Type: Rack and pinion, manual

BRAKES

Type: Girling discs front and rear

WHEELS AND TYRES

Type: 7 x 15in Atesia alloy with

radial-ply Pirelli Cinturato 210HS 15

BODY/CHASSIS

Type: Steel spaceframe chassis
with alloy body. Coupé body,
2 doors, 2 seats

DIMENSIONS AND WEIGHT

Length: 171.6in (4360mm)
Width: 69.3in (1760mm)
Wheelbase: 98.4in (2500mm)
Track – front: 55.6in (1412mm)
  – rear: 55.6in (1412mm)
Weight: (kerb) 2850lb (1292kg)

PERFORMANCE

Maximum speed: 172mph
(277kph)
Acceleration 0-60mph:
6.7 seconds
Fuel consumption: 14mpg

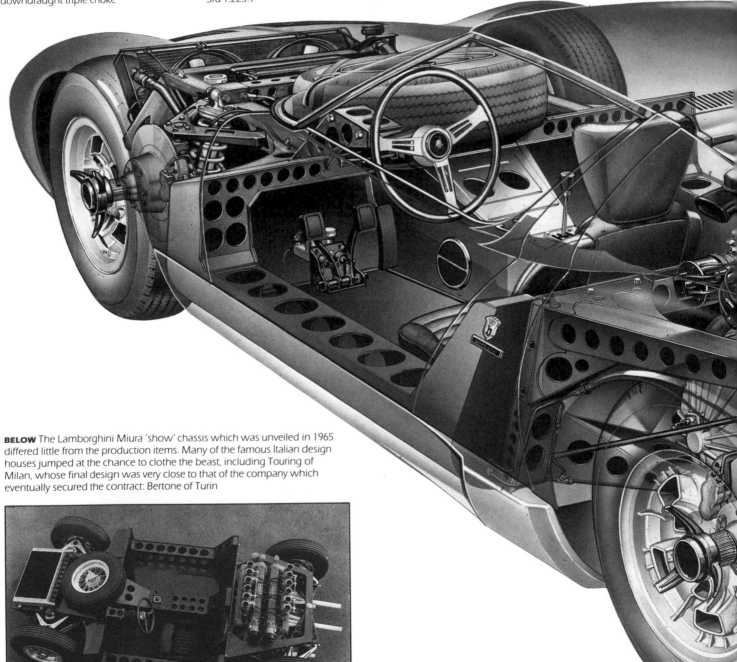

BELOW The Lamborghini Miura 'show' chassis which was unveiled in 1965
differed little from the production items. Many of the famous Italian design
houses jumped at the chance to clothe the beast, including Touring of
Milan, whose final design was very close to that of the company which
eventually secured the contract: Bertone of Turin

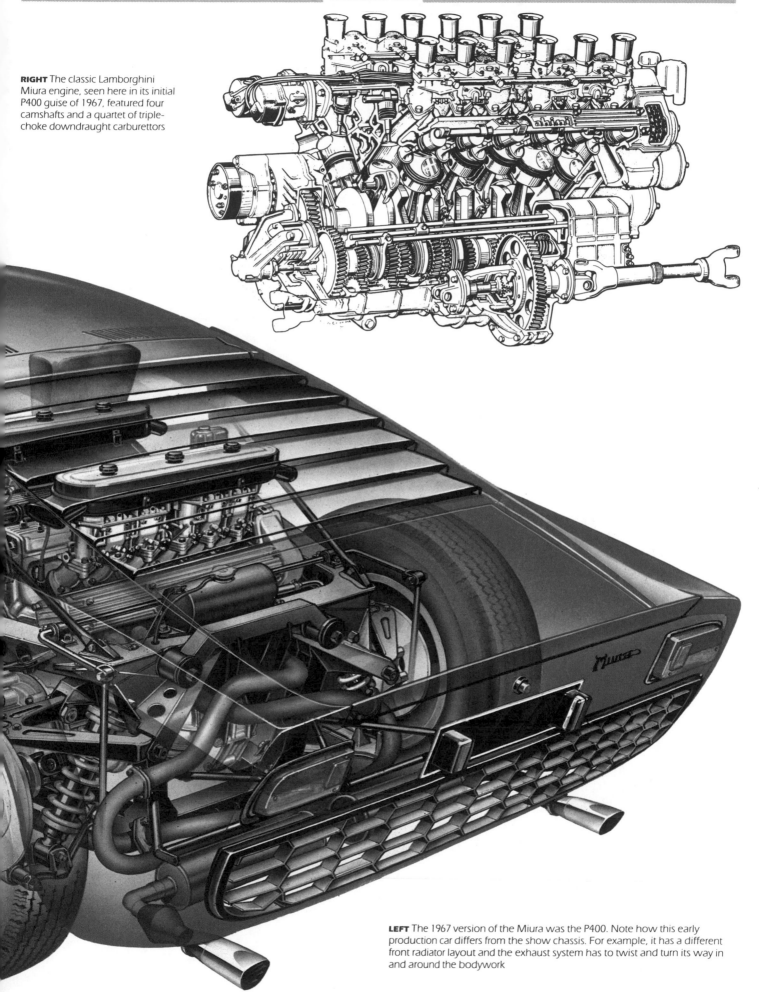

RIGHT The classic Lamborghini Miura engine, seen here in its initial P400 guise of 1967, featured four camshafts and a quartet of triple-choke downdraught carburettors

LEFT The 1967 version of the Miura was the P400. Note how this early production car differs from the show chassis. For example, it has a different front radiator layout and the exhaust system has to twist and turn its way in and around the bodywork

ABOVE *An SV variant of 1972 vintage. The SV is readily identifiable by its rather bulbous flanks, which were incorporated to cover wider wheels and tyres. With 385bhp, a stiffer reinforced chassis and improved suspension, with broader-based lower rear wishbones to reduce toe in changes, it was the most desirable of all the Miuras*

Show of that year, the S, besides getting 70 series Pirelli tyres which greatly increased the predictability of the handling, had more power, thanks to larger-diameter inlet porting and modified combustion chambers. The claimed output went up by 20 bhp, to 370 at 7700 rpm.

The carpeting and the upholstery were improved, with electric windows replacing the terribly low-geared window winders. The overhead toggle switches were replaced by rocker switches, as demanded by American safety standards. Externally the S was nearly identical to the original Miura – the main differences being chromed window and windscreen frames and headlight surrounds.

During the S's 2½ year life, ventilated discs were adopted to replace the solid variety, reinforcing links were employed on the lower rear wishbones to help overcome toe-in changes (although this was only done to a few cars) and the equipment level was increased.

In March 1971, when demand still easily outstripped supply, the most desirable of all the Miuras hit the showrooms. The Miura SV (V for *veloce*, or speed) was intended to be released in the late '60s but was held up by the labour problems which racked Italian industry at the time. Although it was somewhat overshadowed at its Geneva Show launch by the Countach show car on the Bertone stand (which was rumoured to be the Miura's successor), the SV still caused an enormous amount of interest. More different from the S than the S had been from the original P400, the Miura SV had modified styling (with wider hips to cover the wider Pirelli 60-section tyres; new tail lights; a different grille with new side lamps and different headlamp surrounds – without the eyelashes), some interior modifications and a number of mechanical ones. The most important mechanical change was the increase in horsepower (to 385 bhp at 7850 rpm) and torque thanks to an increase in the inlet valve diameter, modified cam timing and revised Webers (with bigger main jets). Miuras suffered from a lack of chassis stiffness when going very hard, so the SV had reinforcements put on both the front and rear extensions. Broader quadrilateral lower suspension arms replaced the

A-shaped lower rear wishbones, further to reduce toe in/toe out changes. A ZF limited-slip differential was also specified, necessitating a separate oil supply for the gearbox, but many SVs were built without the limited-slip diff. Some of these Miuras also had dry sumping.

Great car though it was, the Miura P400SV could not rightly claim to be the ultimate Miura. That honour must go to the Miura Jota. Initially conceived as a one-off, as the definitive high-performance Miura, the Jota project happened after Dallara had left the company.

His second in command, Stanzani, had assumed the role of chief engineer, and asked Bob Wallace to build a special car which could, if necessary, be raced successfully. Built to the Appendix J rules of the FIA (one of the reasons it was called Jota), the machine became a mobile test bed to evaluate a number of new components, some of which found their way on to the Miura SV. The project started in late 1970 and was much more than just a modified Miura. The suspension was pure racing car (with fabricated wishbones at the front), the chassis had a narrower and less massive backbone,

and both the front and rear subframes were different. Inside, the beauty of the Miura was discarded and replaced with a starkly functional alloy-sheet dash, gutted doors and fewer instruments. The wheels and tyres were also genuine sports car racing ware.

The beauty of the Bertone shape was sacrificed in the pursuit of better downforce (particularly for the sometimes suspect front) and a more slippery shape. The headlights were placed upright, behind perspex cowlings and canards (or small wings) were placed around the front corners of the nose

to increase downforce. An increased compression ratio (11.5:1, up from the 10.5:1 of the road car) and racing cams helped boost power to 440 bhp at 8500 rpm.

The original, and greatly prized, Jota was eventually sold in late 1971, never managing to turn a wheel in racing.

Naturally, some people wanted copies made. The factory, although initially unco-operative, eventually acquiesced and built what became known as SVJs, or Jota replicas. In most cases these cars were rebuilt versions of existing SV Miuras, although three

real SVJs were built from scratch (on SV chassis). These machines developed just over 400 bhp (thanks to larger inlet ports and free flow exhausts), and had a chin spoiler (as opposed to nose canards). They looked somewhat tamer than the original Jota but were far more practical road cars than the 'Wallace Wonder', albeit slower.

Miura production finished on 15 January 1973 when the last P400SV – painted white – left the modern Sant'Agata factory. 750 cars were manufactured during the six year production run, with 1968 being the most successful year (184 deliveries).

> **6 ... particularly impressive was the way the Miura would keep thrusting forward well after 125mph (200kph) had been registered. 9**

On the road, it should come as no surprise to learn that the Miura was one of the most exhilarating road cars ever built, as well as being one of the most trend-setting. *Autocar,* during a test on the P400S variant in August 1970, quoted its top speed as 172 mph (277 kph) which was then the highest speed they had ever attained on road test. It's doubtful whether an SV variant would have achieved a better terminal velocity (the extra power was counterbalanced by the bigger wheels and tyres), although the SV would probably have done better than *Autocar's* 0–60 mph time of 6.7 sec for the P400S. The maximum speeds in the first four gears were 59, 86, 121 and 153 mph, or 95, 138, 195 and 246 kph.

There were faults, of course. The driving position left a lot to be desired, particularly for those over about 5 ft 10 in (183 cm). Head room was very limited for tall men (the highest part of the car was actually just behind the windscreen rather than above the seat) and the steering wheel was angled a little too much, in typical Italian fashion. Quality control on the Bertone made coachwork was rather suspect – certainly inferior to the quality of contemporary hand-made

Aston Martins and Rolls-Royces. Glue stains, for instance, were quite common in the interior. Apparently a number of British buyers took their cars to local coachmakers for an interior refit. That's rather a sad commentary on the motto on the Lamborghini factory wall, *'Il prossimo collaudatore e il cliente. Fate in modo che resti soddisfatto'* (The next test driver is the buyer. Build it so he'll be satisfied).

The handling, in most situations, was as good as the mid-engined layout, with its perfect weight distribution, promised. Road test after road test lauded the high-speed behaviour of the mid-motored marvel and the ride, although firm, did show surprising suppleness over all except badly broken roads (when the low-slung Lambo would bottom). The Miura's cornering behaviour, when a driver was *really* motoring, however, could be a bit uncertain at the limit. This was largely rectified by the bigger tyres and rear suspension modifications which came with the P400S series, and was further improved with the SV – the sweetest handling Miura.

That V12 engine, apart from offering superb ultimate performance, was a gem in other ways too, particularly for its low speed tractability. You could pull away in top gear at 1000 rpm without any complaint, and keep accelerating until the 170 mph (273 kph) mark. Few cars have ever offered such flexibility. What was particularly impressive was the way the Miura would keep thrusting forward well after 125 mph

TOP LEFT *The roadster version of the Miura made its appearance at the 1968 Brussels Show*
TOP RIGHT *Extra compression and racing cams helped to boost the Jota's power output to 440bhp, which would have pushed the top speed towards the 200mph (320kph) mark*
ABOVE *The Jota racer was the ultimate in Miuras, with even sleeker bodywork and revised chassis, but it never turned a wheel in anger*

(200 kph) had been registered.

As *Autocar* put it 'At 3200 rpm on the accurate Jaeger rev counter the exhaust becomes a spitting spiteful, rasping bark and the car races forward. It stays like that unrelentingly all the way to 8000 rpm, the only change is that the noise is almost a scream at the top end'.

The engine was noisy, of course, but not unreasonably so for a motor that sits so close to the driver. Even at high revs, with the blended cacophony of cam chains, valve chatter, carburettor hiss, drive gear whine and the inevitable rumble of the wide Pirellis underneath, conversation was still possible and a radio was still considered a useful option.

The view out of the front of the Miura was nothing less than panoramic, with the large windscreen giving an extensive view of the sky as well as the road. Rear vision was a different story. Straight behind in the rearview mirror, a driver got a better view of the air cleaner on top of the Webers than he did of the road. Rear three-quarter vision was even worse and enthusiasts soon found out how inherently impractical mid-engined cars were.

It was a heavy car to drive, too. The steering was the only control which was reasonably light to operate. The brake pedal and the clutch both required tree trunk-sized thigh muscles to operate effectively. Even the throttle pedal was heavy, not helped by the tortuous throttle linkages, which made the job of opening the twelve throttle butterflies a real test of strength. The American magazine *Road & Track* criticised that aspect of the Miura in their first road test of the car, complaining that the gearchange from second to third was 'particularly slow. The 5-4 downshift was also slow and so clumsy as to require considerable diversion of attention'.

The worst aspect of Lamborghini Miura ownership, however, was undoubtedly the maintenance needed to keep one of these charging bulls on the road. Bob Wallace later admitted that the car went on sale well before all the development work had been carried out. 'They had a very, very bad maintenance life,' recalled Bob. The later cars – built in the early '70s rather than the late '60s – were much better, as development improved the quality of materials used.

Even though it did not always continue to run reliably on the road, there is no doubt it will be remembered as a classic. It was the first mid-engined supercar and as such sired a breed of exotics which began with the Ferrari Dino of 1967 (Ferrari's first mid-engined road car) and continues today with the likes of the latest Lamborghini Countach,

Ferrari Boxer and Lotus Turbo Esprit. It was also the fastest road car of its day, able to beat anything else on the road by a good 10 mph (16 kph) in ultimate speed, even if its claimed 187 mph (300 kph) top end was a bit optimistic. There is also little doubt that it was the fastest mid-engined car ever built specifically for the road.

Ferruccio Lamborghini himself, who sold the firm after financial problems some ten years ago, puts the Miura above all the cars he produced – including the Countach. Thanks to the Miura his infant company, with far more temerity than tradition, started to be recognised as one of the great Italian exoticar manufacturers able to compare with older firms whose histories were steeped in racing successes rather than tractor manufacture. GG

EVOLUTION

Introduced in chassis form at the 1965 Turin Show and available in 1967 as a two-seater, 4-litre, V12 mid-engined coupé .
Early production changes included the fitting of a chin spoiler at the front to help cure front end lightness at high speed. The glass section between the cockpit and engine was replaced with Perspex and insulation added to rear bulkhead to help reduce noise levels.

1968 P400S Miura, introduced at Turin Show with larger (70 section) Pirelli tyres and more power thanks to enlarged inlet ports and modified combustion chambers. Power now up to 370 bhp at 7700 rpm. Other changes included the introduction of electrically operated windows, improved trim and upholstery and rocker switches to replace the 'unsafe' toggle variety. Later the Miura S received ventilated disc brakes and a reinforced rear suspension to overcome toe-angle problems at the rear.

1971 Miura SV introduced at the Geneva Show with revised and wider bodywork to accept even wider (60 section) Pirellis. Other external differences included new tail and side lights. different headlight surrounds and a new grille. The inlet valve size was increased, bigger carburettor jets installed and the ccamshaft timing changed to produce a claimed 385 bhp at 7850 rpm. To cope with the extra power the chassis was reinforced further and the rear suspension changed as a new quadrilateral link replaced the lower wishbones. Some SVs were built with limited slip differentials and some with dry-sump lubrication.

1971 Miura Jota appears as a one-off prospective sports racer with narrower chassis, fabricated wishbone suspension and different subframes, and a more aerodynamicly efficient body. Compression ratio was raised to 11.5:1 and different cams installed to produce 440 bhp at 8500 rpm. The Jota spawned a number of Jota replicas with slightly less power (400 bhp) and chin spoilers rather than the canard wing of the true Jota.

1973 Miura production ends in January after 750 cars are produced.

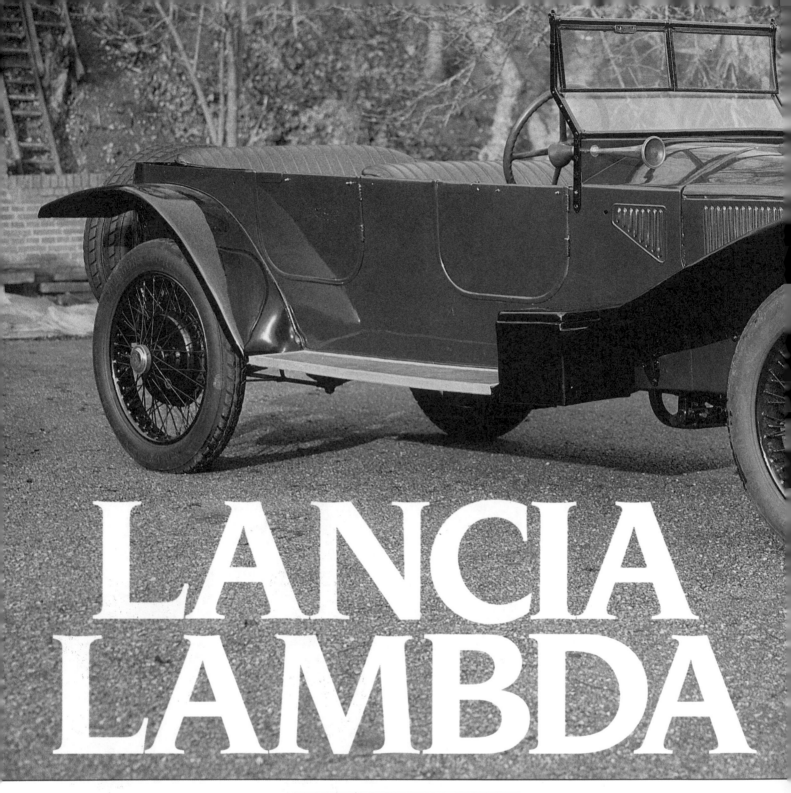

LANCIA LAMBDA

THE LANCIA LAMBDA was one of the great cars of all time, and one of the most prophetic. In an age when Renault, Sunbeam and Rolls-Royce were still offering side-valve Edwardian models to a car-hungry post-war world the Lambda had an all-steel body-cum-chassis, overhead-camshaft V4 engine and independent front suspension. It was that rarity, a car designed from first principles, and because those principles were right, Vincenzo Lancia's touring car would see off many a powerful sports car on long cross-country runs. Launched in 1923 the Lambda remained in production throughout the vintage decade, and the sliding-pillar independent front suspension which it made famous was not superseded in the Lancia range until

The prophetic design of Vincenzo Lancia's monocoque-hulled Lambda of the '20s has influenced cars ever since

1958 (on the Flaminia) when fashion at long last decreed greater deflections and softer springs and suspension.

The idea for a *scocca portante* or load-bearing all-metal hull came to Vincenzo Lancia towards the end of World War I, and he was granted a patent (no.171922) in March 1919. This patent covered 'a type of

car in which the chassis is eliminated, the connection between the back axle and the front axle comprising a rigid shell' and 'also the special form of this shell, which allows of its being lowered below the plane of the axles, and also confers strength'. In other words, Lancia had invented the propeller-shaft tunnel and was using this as a backbone for an all-steel shell. Passengers sat alongside the prop-shaft instead of on top of it, so that the whole car could be lower, with tremendous savings in weight and wind-resistance.

Independent suspension was added to the development programme during 1921 after a front semi-elliptic on a Lancia Kappa had broken while Lancia was taking his

run into by Walter Christie's unorthodox front-wheel-drive racer. He was thus brought into forcible contact with two original features of that car. One of them was independent front suspension by coil springs and sliding pillars, the other was a V4 engine. Did Christie memories linger in Lancia's mind for fifteen years, to be incorporated in his own masterpiece; was this why he chose this independent front suspension rather than one of the others in Falchetto's notebook?

By mid-1923 a definitive Lambda was ready for production. A first series of 500 cars was laid down and the model made its debut at the motor shows of that year, a low-built rakish four-seater touring car equipped with more interesting features than most journalists could comprehend. They passed over the independent front end for example, the virtues of which were not obvious at the time, but were intrigued by its novel engine and monocoque hull.

The all-steel hull which made the Lambda unique in its day was built like a ship. The sides of the body, from radiator to tail, comprised a skeleton framework of flanged 2 mm pressed steel members riveted together and covered on the outside with steel panels. Like a ship, too, it was crossbraced at frequent intervals. A channel-steel framework surrounded the radiator; next came the scuttle bulkhead. The backrest of the front seats was integral and used as crossbracing, giving immense strength amidships, and the rear seats acted in the same way, while aft of those seats the panelling converged to form a blunt pointed tail. The body in fact was a great steel box. Uniting the rear end with the scuttle bulkhead was the deep propeller-shaft tunnel mentioned in the patent – a most rigid backbone further strengthened by the seat pans and back-axle tunnel. All this was further stiffened by the engine-bearers, a stout pair of tubes running from bulkhead to radiator frame and front suspension assembly. A stout tube attached below the channel-section radiator frame was the bottom member of what Lancia literature calls the 'trapezoidal' framework which carried the jaws of the steering-head in which the tele-

This early series Lambda of 1923 is typical of the type, being a standard Torpedo. It featured a 2-litre V4 engine with overhead camshaft and a narrow angle of just 13 degrees, making it extremely compact both in width and length

mother for a drive. He discussed alternatives with Zeppegno, his chassis engineer from the beginning; also present was a young draughtsman named Falchetto, and the latter is on record as saying that he was so excited that he sat up all night, producing no fewer than fourteen suggestions for an 'independent' front end, including the one finally adopted.

Here an interesting historical point arises, which may explain why that particular system was chosen. Before starting his own company Vincenzo Lancia had been with Fiat, a member of their Grand Prix team and the fastest racing driver of his generation. In 1905 his Fiat had been all set to win the Vanderbilt Cup on Long Island when it was

MODEL
Lancia Lambda (8th series) 1928

ENGINE
Location: Front, longitudinal
Type: (Tipo 79) Water-cooled narrow-angle V4 with light-alloy block, cast-iron heads and cast-iron cylinder liners
Cubic capacity: 2570 cc
Bore × stroke: 82.57 mm × 120 mm
Compression ratio: 5.15:1
Maximum power: 69 bhp at 3500 rpm

TRANSMISSION
Layout: Clutch and gearbox mounted behind, and separate from engine
Clutch: Multiple dry plate
Gearbox: Four-speed manual
1st 3.19:1	3rd 1.44:1
2nd 1.89:1	4th 1.00:1
Final drive: Spiral bevel
Ratio: 4.45:1

SUSPENSION
Front: Independent with Lancia sliding pillar, combining coil springs and telescopic dampers
Rear: Live axle with semi-elliptic leaf springs and Hartford friction dampers

STEERING
Type: Worm and wheel

BRAKES
Type: Steel-disc brake drums with shrunk-on cooling fins

WHEELS AND TYRES
Type: Wire wheels with Michelin Bibendum 14 × 50 tyres

BODY/CHASSIS
Type: Steel platform chassis with various body styles available

DIMENSIONS AND WEIGHT
Length: 189.0 in (4572 mm)
Width: 65.4 in (1661 mm)
Wheelbase: 134.6 in (3419 mm)
Track – front: 55.0 in (1417 mm)
– rear: 55.0 in (1417 mm)
Weight: 2464 lb (1117 kg)

PERFORMANCE
Maximum speed: 75 mph (121 kph)
Fuel consumption: 19–20 mpg

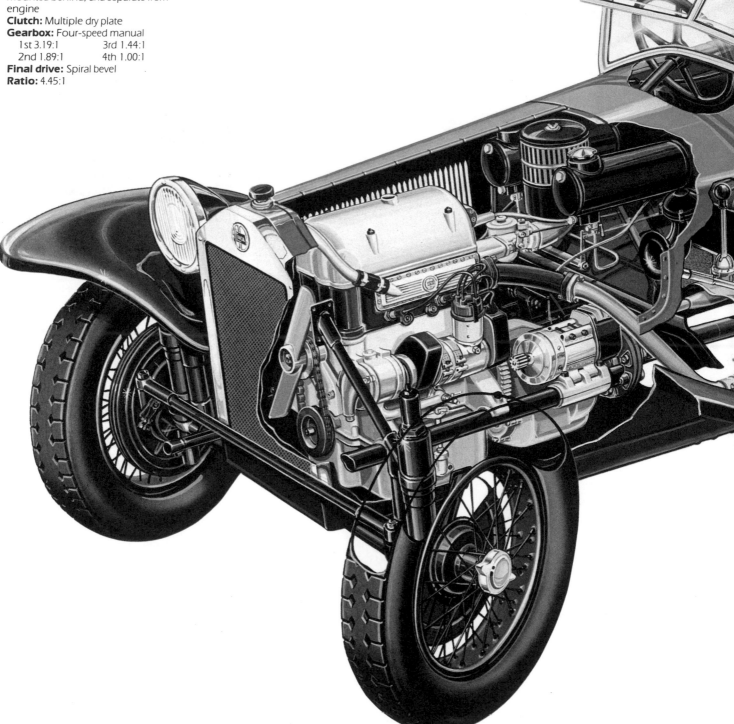

This cutaway drawing shows an Eighth Series Lambda, while **BELOW** is shown its body pressing, which contributes to a very stiff monocoque chassis

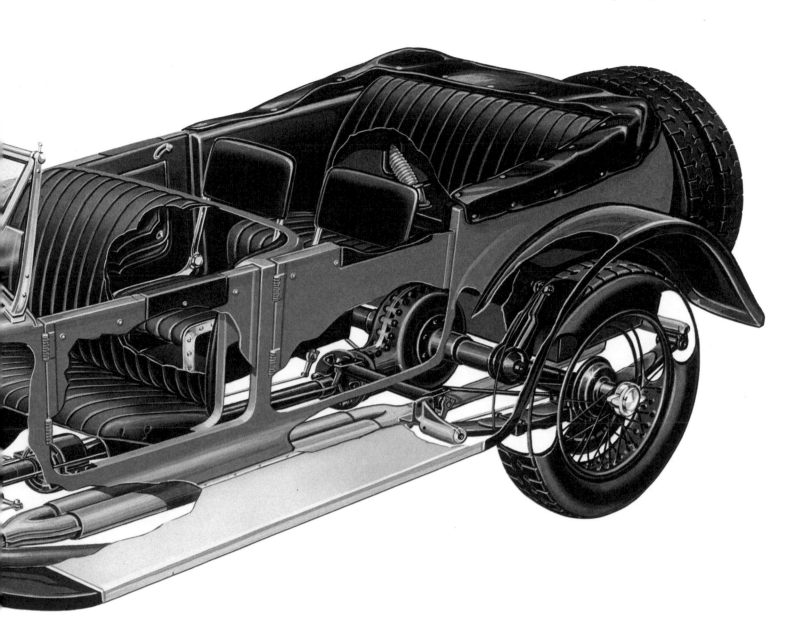

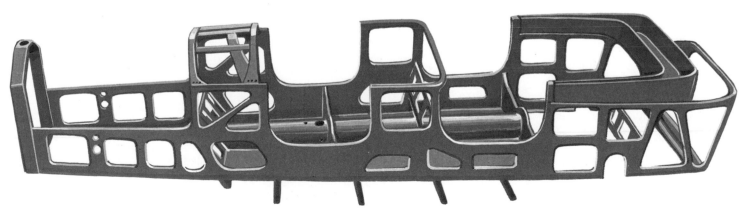

scopic oleo legs of the front suspension were held. Coil springs to control vertical movement of the wheels had been used several times in the past – by Christie, by Morgan and, in fact, by Decauville as long ago as 1899 – but it was Lancia who married the idea to the oleo legs of an aeroplane undercarriage. When he found that the front end of his original experimental car required damping, he added a dashpot, thus inventing the 'Lancia front end'.

For a description of this one cannot do better than quote Mr Geoffrey Robson, of the Lancia Motor Club. The suspension members consisted of 'a long hollow king-pin pivoting and sliding in guide tubes top and bottom, and integral with the stub axle. Two coil springs in compression bore upon a thrust-race above the stub-axle, and a short snubber spring in the bottom guide socket prevented the king-pin from bottoming'. By filling the king-pin with oil and installing suitable valves, Lancia arrived at the system which remained standard practice for as long as he remained in command. The steering-arms emerged forward from the stub-axles and were united by a one-piece track-rod in front of the radiator, and although theoretically this should have

> *'This was a clear reminder of the Grand Prix Fiats that had so often earned... fastest lap'*

caused tremors and kick-back, nothing of this sort occurred provided the tyres were good and the wheels in balance. Steering was beautifully sharp and precise, making a Lambda delightful to drive. Thanks to its independent front suspension it held the road far better than its contemporaries, especially when the going was rough.

In true vintage style the driver was seated amidships, his eyes a little aft of the midpoint of the wheelbase. Before him, scarcely higher than the lamps and wings, stretched a long and imposing bonnet; and beneath this great expanse, serene and isolated like a castle within its moat, was Lancia's strange but effective engine. The unit was certainly compact: the block was only 16.5 inches (41.9 cm) long and the whole thing, from flywheel to fan measured 22 inches (55.8 cm) overall, so that there was room under the bonnet for the gearbox as well. Perhaps this was to allow for growing; at least one surviving experimental car (known

as S1) is fitted with a 3-litre V8 engine.

Lambda production began in 1923 with a batch of 500 First Series cars, quickly followed by two further 500-car series. All these had the *Tipo* 67 engine, devised by designers Rocco and Cantarini, assisted by Scacchi, head of the experimental department, and no doubt by the *Padrone* himself. For whatever reason they chose a narrow V configuration, the bores converging at an angle of 13 degrees. Bore and stroke were 75 by 130 mm, giving a capacity of just over 2 litres (2120 cc) and the popular R.A.C. (British taxation) rating of 13.9 hp. Initial handouts claimed only 45 bhp (on a 5 to 1 compression ratio) but this power was soon exceeded. Production methods showed a mastery of foundry technique. Four flanged cast-iron cylinder liners were arranged in a mould in staggered V formation, and molten aluminium was poured round them to produce a single cylinder-block and crankcase casting complete with oil-filler, breather and

TOP *A First Series Lambda seen at the factory where wooden 'tyres' were fitted so the car could be rolled around*
ABOVE LEFT *Vincenzo Lancia, seen second from the right, with his prototype Lambda on the Sestriere Pass near Turin during trials*
ABOVE *An Eighth Series car on which the innovative sliding-pillar front suspension is picked out in chrome*
RIGHT *A Seventh Series with English saloon bodywork fitted*

oilways. The sump, too, was a single light-alloy casting. Having no external oil-pipes the engine was clean and architectural like most Italian engines. On the port side a magneto, dynamo and water-pump driven in tandem gave it a pleasantly powerhouse air, while to starboard there was nothing to mar the symmetry except the oil-filler.

The crankshaft had four throws (to avoid a need for forked connecting-rods) and was

machined all over, a truly delightful artifact. It ran in three white-metal main bearings and the big-end bearings were plain too, with tubular con-rods. For his overhead valve gear Lancia and his team used a vertical shaft at the front of the engine with bevel gears top and bottom to drive a single overhead camshaft operating two vertical valves per cylinder via needle-roller cam-followers and rockers. This was a clear reminder of the Grand Prix Fiats that so often had earned him fastest lap.

The *Tipo 67* cylinder head, like the block, was a piece of virtuoso foundry work. No manifolding was to be seen, all inlet and exhaust tracts being internal and hence water-jacketed. A Zenith triple-diffuser car-

---

> '*... a heavy flywheel to give the slow top-gear running that was so prized* '

---

burettor was bolted direct to the rear of the head feeding the inlet valves in the centre of the V, while two pipes emerged alongside it carrying away the exhaust. The lower face of this head finished flush with the valves so that it was flat-bottomed like that of the contemporary RL series Alfa Romeo. The combustion chambers were formed in the liners, and sparking plugs screwed into the aluminium block.

First, Second and Third Series cars had three speeds. The gearbox was not in unit with the engine but mounted close behind and braced to it by a strange 'overarm' casting. Ratios were 11.9, 7.3 and 4.16 to 1, or about 25 mph, 40 mph and 65–70 mph (40, 64 and 104–113 kph). It was fitted with a heavy flywheel to give the slow top-gear running that was so prized at the time. The clutch was a multiple dry-plate, and the gear positions were odd, with first and second in the front half of the gate. All Lambdas had right-hand drive and a central remote-

ABOVE *Another example of the classic First Series Lambda in Torpedo guise*

LEFT *The Lancia stand at the 1926 Paris Show with a Farina-bodied Roadster next to a Weymann six-light saloon; both are Eighth Series cars*

BELOW *Another Weymann saloon, this time a Ninth Series example*

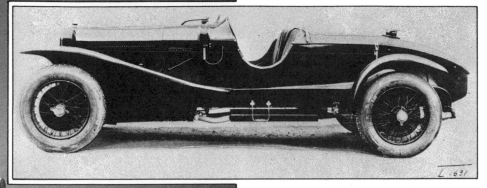

it Lancia brought out a long-chassis on a wheelbase of 123.6 inches (314 cm) which gave room for occasional seats amidships. The long-chassis is perhaps the best remembered Lambda recognisable by its length, its tail-high stance on the road and a phenomenal lock, which allowed U-turns in quite a narrow road and gave the impression that the car was describing a circle about its own back axle. The tourer cost £675, the saloon (a final version of the 'greenhouse' top) £750. The former weighed 2688 lb (1219 kg) and could do 70 mph (113 kph).

> **'... the Tipo 78 had almost one-third more power at maximum torque revs '**

At car no.15501, ie, after 5000 cars had been made, the Lambda underwent another transformation. This was the start of the Seventh Series. To accommodate true coach-built closed bodywork the structure was re-thought once more. By boxing the sides of the chassis Lancia was able to do away with the cross-bracing which had come from the structural front-seat squab. He could now use bucket seats and fit normal closed bodywork. Weymann fabric saloons were especially popular because their lightness

ing 22, 37, and 49 mph (35, 59, 79 kph) at the revs corresponding to 70 mph (113 kph) in top, and a delightful change. The fan drive was now taken from the crankshaft instead of from the nose of the camshaft, and the fan itself was now aluminium instead of being carved from wood like a vintage aeroplane propeller. Shorter valves and rockers brought a change from a flat rocker-box to a domed one. During the Fifth Series, too, Lancia went from narrow beaded-edge 675 × 105 Michelins to the new-fangled low-pressure 775 × 145 Michelin *Confort* 'balloons', which was achieved without causing the 'shimmy' or wheel-wobble which beset so many competitors.

The Fifth Series of 1925–6, last of the lightweight slimline Lambdas, was the nicest of all, being the final incarnation of the

TOP *One of the rare Sport Spyder cars built for the 1927 Mille Miglia and subsequently used for several later races. The privately entered Lambdas finished fourth and fifth in the 1927 event*
RIGHT *This heavily revised Ninth Series Car seen at Lake Como, has bodywork by Farina and is altogether quite imposing*

control gear lever.

In the early 20s motoring was still mainly an open-air pastime. The Lancia hull was so uniquely rigid however that the factory supplied various bolt-on greenhouses to convert one's Lambda into a saloon or indeed into a sedanca de ville. *The Autocar* tested a Third Series saloon conversion costing £695 complete in May 1925. They gave it a top speed of over 70 mph (113 kph) and a minimum speed of 5 mph (8 kph) in top thanks to that heavy flywheel. The weight, remarkable for a closed 2-litre car, was only 2464 lb (1117 kg). They found the four-wheel brakes wonderfully effective, giving a stopping power of almost 1 g.

With the Fourth Series (in the spring of 1925) the Lambda acquired a four-speed gearbox, with nicely spaced gear-ratios giv-

original stressed hull. Lancia now had other plans for the Lambda, and without changing the name or the silhouette, subtly upgraded it. The market was changing. People wanted more room to spread themselves and were less interested in sport. The Sixth Series therefore was virtually a new car, although the engine and 122-inch (309.8 cm) wheelbase remained the same. Introduced in 1926, the Sixth was three inches (7.6 cm) wider in track and no less than 13 inches (33 cm) wider overall. It was quite different in other respects too; the famous stressed hull, with its panelled steel pressings gave place to a stressed skin construction in 16-gauge steel, the metal being doubled below the doors, which were wider, deeper and closer together. The structure was even stronger than before, and as though to prove

matched that of the chassis; they often had wicker front seats. Even on these bodies the tail was still boxed, for reasons of stiffness.

Weight had been creeping up and so, more importantly, had frontal area. Seventh Series cars therefore had a new engine, *Tipo 78*. Piston stroke remained the same but the bore went up to 79.37 mm, giving 2370 cc and increasing the RAC rating from 13.9 to 15.6 hp, so that the annual tax went up by £2. This may not sound much, but in 1926 would have bought some 30 gallons of petrol. On *Tipo 78* engines the vee angle was 14 degrees and there were other changes: counter-balanced crankshaft, an added camshaft-damper, and the tubular con-rods replaced by I-section rods of nickel-chrome steel. At the same time the 'flat-bottomed' cylinder-head gave way to a

competitive. The recipe – later adopted by 'Special' builders in every land – was to take a lightweight early-series car, shorten it, install a highly tuned late-series engine, fit the latest brakes and add a large fuel-tank.

Very different from these delightful specials was the Eighth Series, which came out the following year, 1929. There was now a platform chassis with stout lateral box longerons, plus the famous tunnel of course, and the boxed boot. An Eighth Series on the long chassis was a car of formidable size, almost as long as a Phantom II Rolls-Royce at 189 inches (480 cm) overall, and carrying luxurious coachwork. The Eighth looked

Cazaro were a Torinese coachwork company who worked exclusively with Lancia. This is one of their Spyders based on a 1924 chassis and one which was first owned by Count Zborowski of 'Chitty-Bang-Bang' fame
RIGHT *Note the primitive 'dipping' mechanism on its Carl Zeiss lamps*

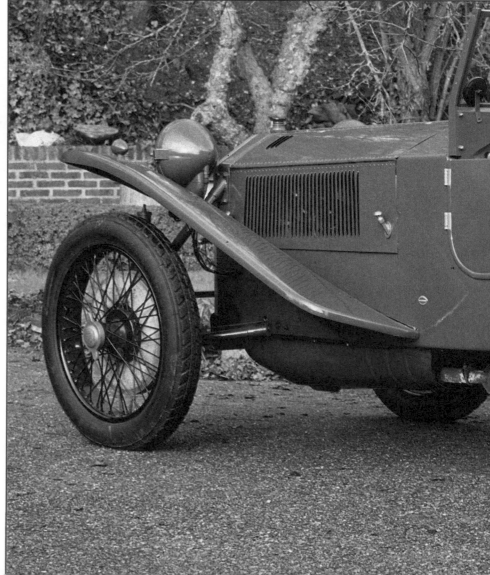

normal one, complete with combustion chambers and sparking-plugs. The carburettor was mounted further away from the head to keep it cooler, and maximum-power revs rose from 3000 to 3250. Maximum output went up from 50 at 3000 to 59 bhp at 3250. More important, in view of the weight and frontal area, the *Tipo 78* had almost one-third more power at maximum torque revs – 48 bhp at 2250 instead of 38 at 2125. What is more, the new crank and rods allowed a rev limit of 3600. All these changes brought their due reward: more than 3000 Seventh Series cars were sold, half as many as all the previous series put together.

The year of the Seventh Series, 1927, was the year of the first Mille Miglia. Although officially against racing, Vincenzo Lancia was delighted when privately entered Lambdas finished fourth (Strazza/Varalla) and fifth (Pugno/Bergia) behind three works OMs. In January 1928 he drove round the course himself at racing speeds with Gildo Strazza, seeking ways to make the Lambda more

more massive than the Seventh because the radiator and scuttle were three inches (7.6 cm) higher.

With the Eighth Series came the *Tipo 79* engine, largest of them all, although still only 2.6 litres. The bore had gone up to 82.55 mm, bringing the fiscal rating to 17 hp and the capacity of 2570 cc. The V angle was now 13 degrees 40 minutes, and other changes had been made: thicker valve-stems, modified con-rods, improved lubrication to the main bearings, a 38 mm Zenith instead of a 36 mm and a better exhaust manifold. All this raised the power to 69 bhp at 3500 rpm, gave a respectably flat

torque curve, peaking at 2300 revs, when there was 53 bhp available for acceleration, and pushed the rev limit towards 4000. Maximum speed (maker's figure) was 75 mph (121 kph), maximum gradient climbable 1 in 3½, and fuel consumption 19–20 miles per Imperial gallon.

Once again Lancia had his sums right. Although its launching coincided with the Wall Street crash of 1929, the Eighth sold better even than the Seventh had done and by 1931 despite the Depression sales totalled 3929, not counting Ninth series cars which differed only in having coil ignition.

And so the Lambda advanced into the post-vintage period – larger, roomier, more imposing but still very similar to that remarkable signpost the First Series tourer. Production continued into 1931, by which time 12,530 had been made, not counting the Ninth Series.

When finally the Lambda was withdrawn it took three models to do the same job: the Artena, the Astura and the Dilambda, respectively a 2-litre four, a 3-litre eight, and a majestic 4-litre eight. They all had the narrow-V engine layout and the independent front suspension which Lancia pioneered. The world was slow to catch up. In 1931 virtually no other manufacturer offered independent front suspension; today there is virtually none that does not.   DBT

EVOLUTION

Introduced in 1922 at the London and Paris motor shows, as a four-seater torpedo-bodied touring car with monocoque body and chassis. It also had independent front suspension and an overhead-cam V4 engine which produced 50 bhp. The engine was so short that the three-speed gearbox was mounted under the bonnet. First, Second and Third Series were mechanically identical

1925 Fourth Series Lambdas were fitted with a four-speed gearbox. Fifth Series cars were fitted with low-pressure balloon tyres and Marelli electrics instead of Bosch

1926 The Sixth Series Lambdas were wider and roomier, with a new and stronger stressed skin construction.

1927 The Seventh Series was introduced, with a separate chassis offered as an option. This model was fitted with the new 2370 cc Tipo 78 engine, which produced 59 bhp

1929 The Eighth Series was introduced, with platform chassis as standard, and long-wheelbase version available as an option. The new 2570 cc Tipo 79 engine was fitted, producing 69 bhp

1930 Ninth Series Lambdas introduced, identical to Eighth Series cars except for coil instead of magneto ignition

1931 Production ended. Total sales: 13,000

LOTUS esprit

In the '70s, crisis-hit Lotus could only move one way – up-market, to
Ferrari territory; the result was the Giugiaro-styled Esprit

ABOVE *The now defunct Lotus badge*
BELOW *The distinctive Esprit Turbo*

THE ENIGMATIC ESPRIT has come a long way. It started as an impractical Giugiaro show car before becoming the Hethel firm's more upmarket replacement for the Europa Twin-Cam (and with just as many reliability and quality control problems). Nevertheless from these inauspicious beginnings greatness was to emerge. The wedge-shaped wonder gained a turbocharger, quality was improved and the Esprit became Lotus's first road-car to rival those of their long-time race-track protagonists, Ferrari. The buzzy sports car became a supercar, and since the Esprit Turbo first made its mark in 1980, Lotus's claim to be quality car makers has also come on in leaps and bounds.

Lotus is a firm well used to crises, and the Esprit was launched in the midst of their most difficult-ever period. In the early '70s, chairman Colin Chapman decided the only way the small company would survive – let along prosper – was to move upmarket, for he knew that expensive cars were less susceptible to economic vicissitudes than cheap ones. A firm with Lotus's engineering excellence were capable, figured Chapman, of building a genuine British alternative to a Porsche or Ferrari – something no other UK company was doing. It was part pragmatism, part pride, and the consequence was that the

> *'The car was a spiritual successor to the Europa Twin-Cam...'*

type of car on which Lotus's reputation had rested for 15 years was ditched. Out went the Elan; out went the Europa. Instead of chasing people who aspired to a Porsche but couldn't afford one, Lotus went after people who could. The young, fast driving set which had formed the majority of Elan/Europa owners was ignored, and older, less impecunious buyers were sought.

The first stage was the four-seater Elite, launched in 1974. Thanks to its hefty price (£5749) and its introduction during the worst of the '70s oil crises, the Elite was never a great showroom success. The company's difficulties were exacerbated by the fact that at that point Lotus was only a one-product company, awaiting the launch of the Esprit, and the poor sales forced a decision to slash both production and workforce (the latter down from 830 in early '74 to less than 400 in '75). The change-over from being makers of cheap sports cars to makers of prestige cars was never going to be easy but in reality it was more difficult than Chapman ever imagined.

The Esprit helped, as he knew it would. The car was a spiritual successor to the Europa Twin-Cam, even though both its price-tag and equipment levels were always to be higher, but this was because the Esprit was really intended to be the car to lift Lotus into the Ferrari league. Code-named the M70, the mid-engined machine had first featured in Lotus's long range plans drawn up in 1970. The idea was to use as many parts from the yet-to-be-released Elite as possible, including the 16-valve four-cylinder engine then being developed, and a futuristic wedge-shaped body.

Chapman must have been wondering who was the best person to design that futuristic body for the M70 when, at the 1971 Geneva Motor Show, he was approached by Giorgetto Giugiaro. The master Italian stylist told Chapman that he wanted to do a show-car design based on a Lotus. With a background that included work for Bertone and Ghia – frequently on two-seater supercars – Giugiaro's qualifications were beyond dispute. Chapman agreed, and the Esprit's modern but simple lines took form.

A cut and reworked Europa chassis of intended M70 dimensions was delivered to Giugiaro's Torinese studio to be clothed, and in November 1972 a prototype was shown to the world at the Turin Show, a very angular wedge-shaped design with an extraordinarily steeply raked windscreen. Lotus were enthusiastic about the shape but also bemused by what would be its inherent production problems. The Esprit theme had been set, but the practical 'productionising' of the car had yet to begin. Chapman was also suspicious of the car's aerodynamics, and soon asked for a second prototype to be made complete with interior and decent aerodynamics. He wanted a car capable of being produced in glassfibre (in line with Lotus tradition) rather than one merely to be ogled at. The second car would thus be built in glassfibre, the first time Giugiaro had worked with this substance. Long hours and late nights followed.

Some of the important Lotus executives moved to Turin to work close to Giugiaro, including stylist Oliver Winterbottom, who

> **‘**Tests… confirmed what Chapman had suspected… bad lift problems… **’**

supervised the construction of the Esprit and who also designed the 1974 Elite. Others, including Chapman and Mike Kimberley (later to become chief engineer and managing director) made frequent private aircraft flights from Norfolk to Italy. A quarter-scale model of the original Giugiaro prototype was made and then taken to the MIRA wind tunnel in England. Tests there confirmed what Chapman had suspected – there were bad lift problems, which were as undesirable to a high speed sports car as an ugly body. The changes effected during this period of development included decreasing the rake of the windscreen by three degrees to comply with US roll-over strength legislation and reducing the size of the rear opening door, which had been a full-length hatchback type on early designs. There were also numerous subtle styling differences, both to help Lotus build the body and to enable the car to penetrate the air with less

ABOVE & ABOVE RIGHT *Giugiaro's prototype was known, for obvious reasons, as 'the silver car'*
BELOW RIGHT *The Esprit entered production looking rather different. This is an S1*

drag and lift. This second prototype almost identical with the production Esprit, was finished in 1973. Thus, two years before the Esprit made its world debut, the shape had nearly been finalised.

Lotus had always intended to use their new four-cylinder 16-valve engine in the Esprit, a unit which had been designed by former BRM engineer Tony Rudd, who had joined Lotus in 1969. This engine produced 140 bhp from 1973 cc, and was the first all-Lotus-designed production motor. It had been used first in the Jensen-Healey sports car, and as well as being high-revving and powerful, the all-alloy unit had a terrible thirst for oil – a characteristic which went down well neither with Jensen nor their customers – and it took Lotus some time to sort out this problem. Furthermore, the engine was inordinately harsh at high revs, the result of an inadequately stiff crankcase, and Lotus also had to do a lot of work on the motor's emission levels to make it acceptable in America, Japan and Australia.

The engineers had always anticipated that one of the most difficult problems with their new mid-engined car would be where to locate the rear-mounted transaxle. Lotus found an unlikely saviour: Citroën were about to discontinue production of their idiosyncratic Maserati-engined SM, a front-engined front-drive supercar. Nonetheless the French firm were able to guarantee Chapman a long-term supply of their five-speed gearboxes, and even production of tailor-made ratios. Fitting the transaxle, however, was not an easy task. It was mated to the engine via a Lotus-made bellhousing, which joined the centre line of the differential. The gearchange involved a rod to select the gears and a cable to work the across-the-gate movement, and was a complex fitting which 'broke every known engineering law,' according to one Lotus engineer. Nonethe-

MODEL
Lotus Turbo Esprit (1985)

ENGINE
Location: Rear, longitudinal
Type: Water-cooled all-aluminium in-line four-cylinder, five main bearings
Cubic capacity: 2174 cc
Bore × stroke: 92.29 mm × 76.20 mm
Compression ratio: 7.5:1
Valve gear: Four valves per cylinder operated by belt-driven twin overhead camshafts. Exhaust valves sodium-cooled.
Fuel supply: Two twin-choke Dellorto 40 DHLA H carburettors and Garrett AiResearch T3 turbocharger, set at boost-pressure limit of 8 lb per square inch
Ignition: Electronic
Maximum power: 210 bhp (DIN) at 6000 rpm
Maximum torque: 200 lb ft (DIN) at 4000 rpm

TRANSMISSION
Layout: Clutch and gearbox in-unit with engine
Clutch: Single dry plate, 9.5 in (24 cm) diameter, hydraulically operated
Gearbox: Five-speed all-synchromesh manual

1st	2.92:1	3rd	1.32:1
2nd	1.94:1	4th	0.97:1
		5th	0.76:1

Final drive: Hypoid bevel
Ratio: 4.375:1

SUSPENSION
Front: Independent with unequal-length upper and lower wishbones, separate anti-roll bar, coil springs and telescopic dampers (pre-1985 models had upper wishbone and single lower link assembly)
Rear: Independent with double unequal non-parallel transverse links with radius arms. Plunging drive shafts with aluminium hub carriers

STEERING
Type: Rack and pinion

BRAKES
Type: Discs all round, inboard at rear

WHEELS AND TYRES
Type: 15 in alloy wheels with 195/60 tyres at the front and 235/60 tyres at the rear

BODY/CHASSIS
Type: Galvanised steel backbone chassis with aerodynamic two-seat glassfibre sports body

DIMENSIONS AND WEIGHT
Length: 165 in (4191 mm)
Width: 73 in (1854 mm)
Wheelbase: 96 in (2438 mm)
Track – front: 60.5 in (1537 mm)
– rear: 61.2 in (1554 mm)
Weight: 2690 lb (1220 kg)

PERFORMANCE
Maximum speed: 152 mph (245 kph)
Acceleration 0–60 mph: 5.5 seconds
Fuel consumption: 21 mpg

This cutaway is of an American spec Turbo Esprit, hence the left-hand drive.
Early Turbos like this one shown had single-link lower front suspension

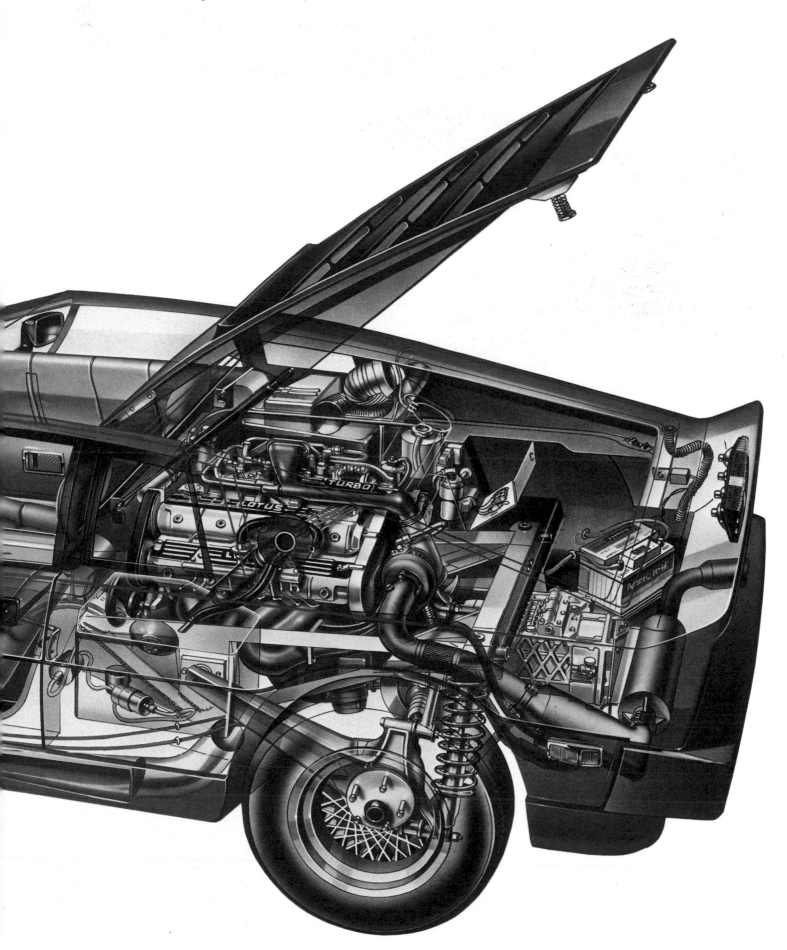

less, it worked. One of the priorities had been to give the Esprit a good gearchange, particularly after the atrocious cog-selection problems which had so blighted the Europa fitted with its Renault gearbox.

In between trying to get the new Elite ready for production and curing the problems inherent with the 16-valve engine, Lotus worked like Trojans in 1974 to get the Esprit developed for Chapman's Christmas deadline. Tony Rudd took overall responsi-

> *... one day ahead of the deadline, the team had a car to show the boss...*

bility, including specific engine and suspension work, Colin Spooner was responsible for the chassis and body and his brother Brian concentrated on adapting the Citroën gearbox. On Christmas Eve, one day ahead of the deadline, the team had a car to show the boss, although it was not a runner. The Esprit prototype's first real test in front of the boss was early in 1975, when Tony Rudd surprised Chapman by arriving to collect him in it at Heathrow Airport, after the first Grand Prix of the year. Chapman drove it part of the way back to Hethel before a hub

carrier broke.

By early 1975 it really had to: the Elan and Europa were gone and Lotus's only model – the new Elite – was selling at the meagre rate of 20-25 cars a month, worldwide. It was just enough to carry Lotus through to the launch of the Esprit at the Paris Show in October 1975. That was when, according to *Motor Sport*, 'the most exciting, attractive, series-production British sports car since the E-type' was unveiled.

The Lotus twin-cam 2.0-litre engine, mounted longitudinally at 45 degrees to the horizontal, now developed 155 bhp at 6580 rpm in the Series 1 Esprit, and 140 lb ft of torque at 4800 rpm, breathing through twin Dellorto carburettors. The car's glassfibre reinforced plastic body was made in two halves and then bonded together at the prominent waist-line, riding on a steel back-boned, tubular frame, partly sheet-braced. The front suspension used Opel Ascona double wishbones with integrated coil spring/damper units, and an Ascona anti-roll bar. Ascona front discs were also borrowed, and the steering rack was from the Elite.

At the back, the suspension was simple, unusual and flawed. The Esprit used its fixed-length driveshafts to form what was, in effect, its upper suspension links (Elite driveshafts and hubs were used). There were also box-framed trailing arms, a lower

were solved with the new S2; many were not. Lotus already knew that their rear suspension layout was inadequate for a car of this performance (even though it had worked adequately on the Elite), and they knew that the chassis had to be made stiffer. They reworked neither, however, for the S2. What they did do was improve the 16-valve engine and give it more mid-range pull (an improvement effected on some late S1 models, too) and better economy. New alloy wheels, made specially for Lotus by the Italian makers Speedline, replaced the off-the-shelf Wolfrace wheels which had looked so prosaic on the S1. A front wraparound spoiler was used, as were wider Rover 3500-borrowed tail lamps (subsequently used on all Lotuses).

The vague Veglia instruments were replaced by sensible Smiths ones, and the

> ' *... the standard of interior trim was massively improved...* '

standard of interior trim was massively improved. Mind you, the trim should have been revised, for with the launch of the S2, the price of the Esprit had rocketed to £11,124. The one-time kit car makers were now selling, truly, a Porsche-priced car, but they still weren't building cars as well as Porsche. The S1 had had many teething problems, and Tony Rudd later said, 'I reckon we solved 90 per cent of the problems before manufacture, but there were others who reckoned I solved 10 per cent and they did the rest trying to put it into production'.

Lotus also didn't do the Giugiaro shape any favours by some of the 'limited edition' styling kits they offered. The company are renowned for their tasteless decals, but the nadir probably came with their awful 1978 'World Champion' edition, to commemorate the Team Lotus World Championship title.

LEFT *Lotus were always quick to capitalise on their great Grand Prix success, adorning their road cars, such as this S2, with 'World Champion' decals*
ABOVE *The exterior styling was far more agreeable that that of the early interiors, which have dated badly*
BELOW *The turbo installation on the Esprit is one of the finest around; it is shown here under test in 1980*
BELOW RIGHT *The Esprit production line*

lateral link and integral coil spring/damper units. The rear disc brakes were inboard.

Inside, the Esprit was a mixture of good news and bad. The dash consisted of a futuristic wrap-around facia which contained the main gauges (which were hard to read) and the switchgear, and in between this and the driver was a cheap plastic two-spoke steering wheel. The interior ventilation was terrible, as it still is on the Esprit, and rear three-quarter vision was almost non-existent, but all these problems not withstanding, the Esprit got a deservedly good reception at its world debut, and when it went on sale in June 1976 it looked like Lotus had built a winner. Its success came not a moment too soon.

The Series 1 was in production for two years before being superseded by the Series 2 in May 1978. Some of the S1 problems

Painted black with thick gold striping and big 'World Champion' lettering down the side, the styling pack was a salient reminder of the intrinsic differences in quality and taste between Ferrari and Porsche (could either ever produce such a kit?) and Lotus. Unfortunately, when the excellent Esprit Turbo was first launched, in 1980, its body was similarly spoilt by its garish Essex livery.

Despite its initial paint-job, the Esprit Turbo marked the long-awaited turning point for Lotus. At last here was a car that was good enough to take on – and beat – a Ferrari 308GTB. The high-speed Esprit variant had been originally scheduled to have a V8 engine, rather than a turbo four-cylinder. If one looks at the chassis' engine cradle in the Esprit, one can see plainly that there is room for an engine with two banks of four cylinders. Nonetheless, powertrain engineering manager Graham Atkin favoured the idea of a turbo four, largely on the grounds of cost, and his voice eventually won through. Such engines were starting to gain favour then thanks to the work of

> *'...the engine was strengthened to take the greater...pressures...'*

companies like Porsche and Saab.

In typical Lotus fashion (they've always been better at engineering than they have at aesthetics), the turbo transformation was extremely clever. The design of the car involved a massive revision of the S2 specification. To make it look more aggressive and increase the downforce, Giugiaro was asked to add some addenda to the Esprit body, and replied by designing wraparound bumpers, large front and rear spoilers and deep skirts under the door sills. The changes to the engine were far more extensive. A longer-stroke crankshaft increased its capacity from 1973 cc to 2174 cc and a Garrett AiResearch T3 blower rammed pressurised air into the two twin-barrel Dellorto carburettors. The compression ratio was lowered (a necessary adjunct to turbocharging) and the engine was strengthened to take the greater internal pressures. The power went up by 35 per cent, to 210 bhp at 6000–6500 rpm, and torque rose by 43 per cent, to 200 lb ft at 4000–4500 rpm. The clutch diameter was increased by an inch (2.4 cm), although the gearbox and final drive remained unchanged.

The chassis and suspension were also extensively altered. The chassis, in fact, was new with Lotus-designed and built upper wishbone/lower transverse link front suspension (replacing the Opel system) attached to a new front box section. At the rear, where there had always been a handling problem on the S1 and S2, short top suspension links were added to take the loads imposed on the driveshafts. The trouble with the old system had been that to a large extent the engine mounts' compliance

had determined the handling. If good road-holding was to be maintained the result was excessive engine noise and vibration. The new chassis also had 50 per cent better torsional rigidity than that of the S1/S2, which also helped to explain the better handling composure of the Turbo when compared with earlier models. Bigger 60-aspect ratio tyres were fitted front and rear, the interior was leather-trimmed, (although this later became optional), air conditioning was standard and a better steering wheel was fitted. Top speed was 152 mph (245 kph) compared with the S2's 135 mph (218 kph), with 0-60 mph in 5.5 seconds (7.5 seconds for the S2). In April 1981 the mechanically identical but less luxuriously equipped 'normal' Esprit Turbo came out to replace the colourfully adorned Essex machine. At less than £17,000 – compared with £21,000 for the Essex – it was a far more sensibly priced.

Numerous road tests soon verified that the Turbo was one of Europe's most competent supercars. Its beautifully engineered turbocharged engine gave silken yet strong

EVOLUTION

Introduced in 1975 at the Paris and Earls Court Motor Shows, the Esprit was a mid-engined two-seater with an aerodynamic glassfibre bodyshell on a steel backbone chassis. It was fitted with the 2-litre 16-valve Lotus 907 engine which developed 140 bhp and 140 lb ft of torque. Braking was by discs all round and suspension was all-independent

1978 Limited edition Esprit S2 was launched to celebrate the Team Lotus World Championship title. 100 were built for each of the company's three markets, and the cars were available only in black with gold coachlining and insignia. The engine of the S2 Esprits was improved and there were minor body and trim changes

1980 Essex Lotus Turbo Esprit launched at the Royal Albert Hall, London. The first 100 were built in Team Essex racing livery. Engine size was increased to 2.2 litres, which in normally aspirated form produced 160 bhp and 160 lb ft of torque and in turbo form delivered 210 bhp and 200 lb ft. Top speed of the Turbo Esprit was 152 mph (245 kph), with 0-60 mph in 5.5 seconds. The bodyshell was competition-modified to improve the aerodynamics, with scoops under the nose and on the sills (the latter to feed air to the engine) and aerofoils on the roof and tail. The chassis was galvanised and suspension modified, and bigger tyres were fitted. The Esprit S2.2 was launched with the normally-aspirated 2.2-litre engine but without the chassis and suspension modifications

1981 Launch of 'normal' Turbo Esprit and Esprit Series 3, the latter incorporating the chassis and suspension modifications of the Turbo model

1983 Esprit Turbo was given larger boot and offered with option of removable glass roof

1985 Suspension modifications to Esprit range, including ventilated discs fitted at the front, larger rear disc calipers, and front anti-roll bar separated from front suspension

performance, it had razor-sharp handling, prodigious roadholding and the brakes were superb. It still didn't have the ultimate status or sheer beauty of the Ferrari 308GTB, but as a sheer driver's car it probably beat the Italian stallion.

The Esprit Turbo technology also helped to procreate a better normally-aspirated Esprit. Although the Series 2.2 – launched not long after the Turbo, in April 1980, to replace the Series Two – was nothing to write fan letters to Hethel about (it used the non-turbo 2.2-litre engine in the existing – and flawed – S2 chassis), its replacement, the Series 3, launched in early 1981, was an altogether superior machine. At last Lotus had given the car the strong chassis and suspension of the Turbo. The exterior was also neater than the S2.2, with no obtrusive matt black paint, and the quality control was noticeably better. Lotus's standards have improved in leaps and bounds since 1980, and to compare an S3 or Turbo with an S1 is like comparing a plastic model built by a child with one built by an expert, differences which are also very apparent when the cars are taken on the road.

Lotus thus achieved their goal and became makers of expensive luxury sports cars. That reputation is due, more than anything else, to the Esprit Turbo. With that model, Lotus grew up. TO'B

RIGHT *The Turbo Esprit never looks spectacular when put through its paces on the track, staying very stable at all speeds* **BELOW** *Esprit interiors have grown steadily more luxurious, particularly on the Turbo* **BELOW RIGHT** *An '84 Turbo Esprit*

MAZDA RX7

Smooth and sleek styling helped make the RX-7 the world's first really successful rotary-engined sports car

IN THE 1970s Japanese car styling had about the same reputation as their whisky; it was a poor substitute for Europe's best. Mazda built their fair share of, to us, bizarre looking cars before they saw the light and realised that a change had to be made to make their cars acceptable outside Japan. When Project 605 (the code for the RX-7) got underway in 1970 the first requirement was for 'functional styling'; in other words looks were ranked above such essential sports car features as 'quick acceleration' (ranked second) and 'sports car handling' (third).

The new car was obviously directed at the US market where the 240Z had made Datsun's reputation (which made it rather surprising that ride was only ranked fourth in Mazda's scheme of things) and indeed the RX-7 was an immediate hit all over North America.

Yet apart from its beautifully smooth Wankel rotary engine and its very good looks (an in-house design incidentally rather than a product of Bertone, Pininfarina or Ital Design) there was really nothing all that special about the car – Mazda surely knew of what they spoke in saying that looks came first.

The RX-7 was by no means Mazda's first rotary-engined model but it was the first to be taken as more than a curiosity. Preceeding models looked odd, were not particularly reliable and suffered from the appalling thirst which was a feature of rotary engines. The Cosmos 110S of the late 1960s was, to the few who cared to look, a sign of what was to come. It was attractive, albeit in an overly fussy Oriental fashion, it was fast and it was a challenge to drive; to add to its Porsche-like oversteer, it was also a noisy car. All those things would be fundamental

drawbacks in a saloon but could almost be considered advantages in a sports car.

Despite its performance the Cosmos was never produced in great numbers and was never part of Mazda's export armoury. Consequently when the RX-7 appeared in 1978 it was a revelation.

By that stage Mazda had 17 years experience with the rotary engine, longer than any other company, and the company's director of Research and Development (and now company president) Kenichi Yamamoto had become the world's leading authority on the engine with Audi/NSU and GM having lost faith in the concept. He had gradually overcome most of the fundamental problems which had doomed the NSU Ro80, the very short life expectancy and the seemingly insurmountable sealing problems. The 12A twin-rotor engine used in the unattractive RX-2 was already a major improvement over the NSU's engine and for the RX-7 it was further modified in those vital areas.

The various sealing problems in conventional engines had long since been overcome – valves had springs to assist their seating while piston rings which went up and down in cylinder bores were a relatively simple technical challenge, made easier by the engineer having the option of using several per piston. In the rotary engine the problems were a little trickier; the engine made up for its lack of moving parts with numerous problems for what movement there was. The three tips of each trochoid rotor had to double as compression and oil

ABOVE *The interior of the original RX-7*
RIGHT *The RX-7 was introduced on the UK market in 1979 with alloy wheels as standard equipment*

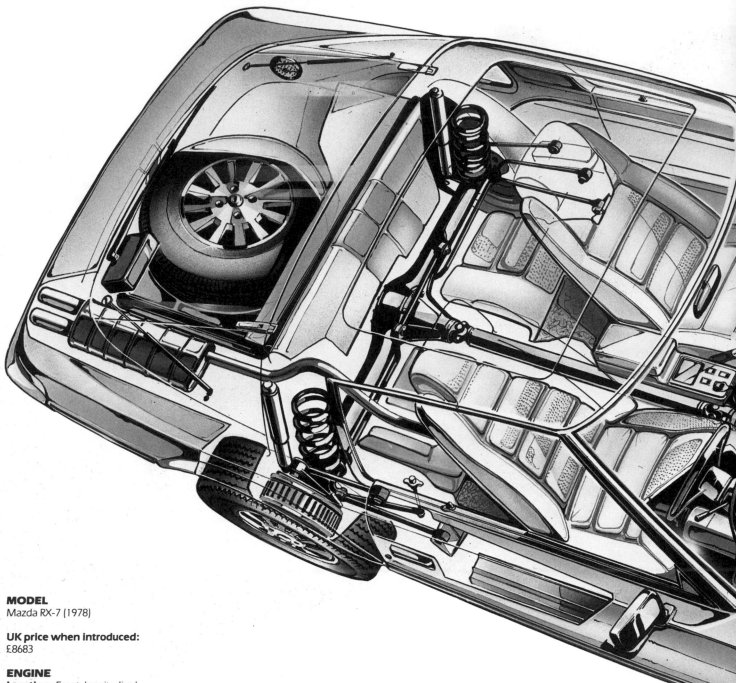

MODEL
Mazda RX-7 (1978)

UK price when introduced:
£8683

ENGINE
Location: Front, longitudinal
Type: Twin rotor Wankel
Cubic capacity: 2292 cc
Compression ratio: 9.4:1
Valve gear: Side inlet,
circumferential exhaust
Fuel supply: Downdraught two-
stage, four-choke Nippon
Ignition: Electronic breakerless
Maximum power: 105 bhp (DIN)
at 6000 rpm
Maximum torque: 106 lb ft (SAE)
at 4000 rpm

TRANSMISSION
Layout: Gearbox in unit with
engine
Clutch: Single dry plate
Gearbox: Five-speed manual
   1st 3.674:1   4th 1.000:1
   2nd 2.217:1   5th 0.825:1
   3rd 1.432:1
Final drive: Hypoid bevel
Ratio: 3.909:1

SUSPENSION
Front: Independent with
MacPherson struts and anti-roll bar
Rear: Live axle with Watts linkage,
upper and lower trailing links, coil
springs telescopic dampers and
anti-roll bar

STEERING
Type: Recirculating ball, variable
ratio with 4.3 turns lock to lock

BRAKES
Type: Discs front and drums rear,
8.94 in (22.7 cm) diameter front and
9.0 in (22.8 cm) diameter rear

WHEELS AND TYRES
Type: 5½J alloy wheels with 185/
70HR13 Pirelli Cinturato CN36 radial
tyres

BODY/CHASSIS
Type: Integral steel chassis with
two-door 2+2 coupé body

DIMENSIONS AND WEIGHT
Length: 168.7 in (428.5 mm)
Width: 65.9 in (167.5 mm)
Wheelbase: 95.3 in (242.0 mm)
Track – front: 55.9 in (142.0 cm)
         – rear: 55.1 in (140.0 cm)
Weight: 2258 lb (1024 kg)

PERFORMANCE
Maximum speed: 115 mph
(185 kph)
Acceleration 0–60 mph:
9.5 seconds
Fuel consumption: 18 mpg

Engine apart the RX-7 was a very simple design without even independent rear suspension. The live rear axle was, however, well located with trailing arms and featured a distorted form of Watts linkage with unequal length arms for lateral location. The original RX-7 featured drum brakes at the rear, slightly surprisingly in view of its performance; the switch to rear discs was made in 1981

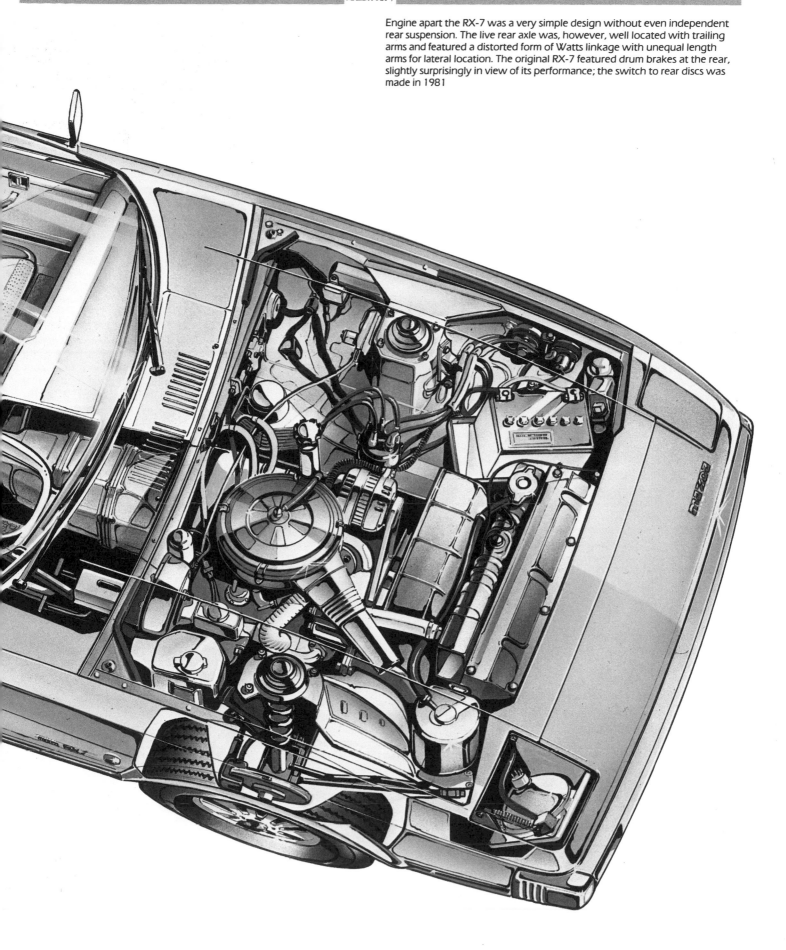

control piston rings and there could obviously be but one tip on each of the three apexes. On the 12A there had been a problem with leaks past the sides of the apex seals so they were made shorter to lessen their side area on the RX-7 and new, expanding, corner-apex seals were introduced. At the same time the seal material itself was improved; it was the same form of iron used for piston rings but the rubbing surface was given a new treatment to crystallise the iron, better to withstand the enormous heat of combustion.

Another of the rotary's problems is the considerable swept area of the side plates. It's an area that has to be sealed and yet not at the expense of excessive friction and wear and that's a bigger problem than it could be in that the rotary is a relatively high-speed engine. 12A engine revisions saw a new gas nitriding treatment given to the side plates to form a long wearing iron-copper-nickel layer. At the same time the combustion chamber surfaces were treated to a new chroming process that allowed them to retain oil and resist wear.

In an effort to improve power and economy, the combustion chamber shape was revised; in the rotary engine the combustion chamber is formed by an identation in the rotor itself – in other words it's similar to the Heron type combustion chamber formed in the top of a conventional piston and used in conjunction with a flat cylinder head. For the RX-7 the chamber was reshaped and biased towards the leading edge of the rotor.

Engine displacement was just 1146 cc, that is both of the coaxial rotors swept 573 cc. That, however, gives a quite misleading impression of the 'true' engine displacement. It's now accepted under FISA's equivalency formula that the Mazda's engine was equal to 2292 cc in a conventional piston engine. In those terms, and considering that it had a compression ratio of 9.4:1, the rotary seemed have little going for it. 105 bhp at 6000 rpm and 105 lb ft or torque at 4000 rpm is not particularly impressive.

> **❛ ... a warning buzzer, set at 6800 rpm was necessary to warn the driver... ❜**

It's a figure easily beaten by fairly old, and smaller, twin-cam designs from Fiat, Lotus or Alfa Romeo and just about equivalent to the output of the TR7's very ordinary 2-litre single-overhead-cam engine. But in the words of the song, 'it's not what you do but the way that you do it . . .' and while a driver might well struggle to get the theoretical maximum from a conventional engine, staying clear of the red line through mechanical sympathy, the Mazda engine would spin around with ease, to the extent that a warning buzzer (set at, in rotary terms, a fairly conservative 6800 rpm) was necessary to warn the driver because the engine noise certainly would not.

Although maximum torque wasn't available below 4000 rpm the engine was never regarded as annoyingly peaky in the way that some turbo units can be frustrating devices before the blower begins its work. Indeed as one writer observed rather speciously, as there was no camshaft the engine didn't suffer any 'camminess'. Like many turbo units, however, best results were achieved by keeping the engine spinning at over 3000 rpm.

Mazda may have succeeded in producing adequate power, torque and longevity but their record on fuel consumption (another nail in the Ro80's coffin) wasn't all that good. Relatively gentle crusing at steady motorway speeds might see 25–26 mpg but more varied conditions could easily drive fuel consumption below the 20 mpg mark. Had the RX-7 appeared a few years earlier, at the time of the first oil crisis, or been aimed solely at the European market, it would have been doomed. Luckily the Americans for whom it was intended didn't blink an eye at such figures and it was never handicapped by its lack of economy.

One very definite advantage of the engine was its sheer compactness, stripped of its ancillaries it was very small and light which gave great freedom to the chassis designers who chose to mount the engine well back in what they described as 'front, midships'. That, in turn allowed an excellent weight distribution, nearly neutral at 51% front and 49% rear and permitted the low bonnet line which helped to give the RX-7 its sleek low lines.

Because the rotary took up so little space it allowed almost every worthwhile front suspension option to be considered. In the end the choice fell on MacPherson struts with transverse arms and one trailing link

per side, along with an anti-roll bar. It echoed the TR7 in being a sports car with 'saloon car' front suspension rather than a traditional sports car set-up such as double wishbones. It was felt that the struts would give adequate location, and produce acceptable handling while at the same time having sufficient travel from low spring rates to give a ride tailored to the vital American market.

That was virtually the same rational that Triumph used in their US-bound TR7 and in fact the parallels with the TR7 are many and interesting. At the rear of the car for example Mazda also opted for the simplicity and strength of a live axle. At first glance that appeared to be a retrograde step in that the Cosmos had used a de Dion axle but the extra complexity and manufacturing expense did not seem to offer any worthwhile advantage over a well-located live axle, and the RX-7's *was* tied down pretty well. Lower trailing links and upper torque arms were complemented by a (slightly lop-sided) Watts linkage to take care of transverse

The RX-7 proved a very successful race and rally car in Europe and North America **TOP** *John Wolf's car at Pike's Peak in '81* **RIGHT** *Win Percy and Tom Walkinshaw enjoyed great success in the European Touring Car Championship, winning here at Spa, for example, in the 1981 24 Hours* **BOTTOM** *More ETCC Action, from 1982*

location; Watts linkage and gass pressurised dampers apart, it was the very same layout as the Triumph and the Mazda even made do with rear drum brakes too, just like the TR7. At the car's launch one respected journalist was sufficiently impressed by the RX-7's live rear axle that he compared it favourably with that of the Bertone-styled Alfa Romeo GTV coupés which had been honed over many years. That impression was gained on a test track where 'real world' results are notoriously hard to duplicate and in later road tests some complaints were made of axle tramp under hard acceleration and of less than perfect location.

A more fundamental weakness than the live axle, however, was the steering; the *sine qua non* of a sports car, at least to British eyes, was rack and pinion steering as nothing else offered its precision, certainly not the recirculating-ball system Mazda were committed to.

Close scrutiny shows that Mazda had settled, engine apart, for the adequate rather than the spectacular but they had done it in

---

❝… more important… was the way in which the RX-7 attained such speeds ❞

---

such a skilfull fashion that the whole was far greater than the simple sum of its parts. That showed in all manner of ways, in both its image and performance and to demonstrate the point the unfortunate TR7 should be dragged back into view. Similar specifications aimed at exactly the same American buyers produced two models which are now hardly ever mentioned in the same breath. The Mazda was soon regarded as far more up-market, as a viable alternative to the Porsche 924 because it was better looking, better built and, rather strangely, quicker than the Triumph. From its very similar power and torque output the RX-7 could produce a maximum speed of 121 mph (205 kph), accelerate from 0–60 mph in under 9 seconds, reach 80 mph (129 kph) in a fraction over 15 seconds and cover the standing quarter mile in 17 seconds. It should be noted, however, that not every magazine managed to return such good figures; *Motor*'s test car could not better 10.1 for the 0–60 sprint or a maximum speed of 113 mph (182 kph).

Perhaps more important than the actual figures was the way in which the RX-7 attained such speeds. There was a steady flow of acceleration up to around 110 mph (177 kph) and only the last 10 mph or so of maximum speed proved hard to extract, although it could be reached in both fourth and fifth gears. Even at 100 mph the absence of engine harshness was matched by the lack of wind noise which, along with that impressive top speed, indicated that the RX–7's drag coefficient of 0.36 was more effective than that figure suggested.

Not only was the RX-7 agreeably quick

but it was firmly in the Japanese tradition of being very easy to drive. All the controls were light and easy to use, particularly the clutch and gearlever, so much so that diehard sports car fans could criticise the car for being almost soulless. The rather soft nature of the suspension and the disappointingly vague feel of the steering tended to mask the car's very considerable abilities. After driving their long-term test RX-7 for 12,000 miles (19,000 km) *Car* found the same thing, concluding that there was '...no excuse for the dead feel or the lost motion around the straight ahead' but went on to admit that it was more a subjective problem than a real weakness of the car. When they drove an RX-7 around Donington Park immediately after two Maseratis (a Khamsin and Merak) they admitted that 'It did not matter that the Maseratis accelerated faster, braked harder, steered better and held on longer. What mattered most was that all three cars were exciting, rewarding – and safe.' Their admission that a Japanese car could be that good was quite a breakthrough, coming as it did from perhaps the most anti-Japanese publication in the country at the time.

Motor Sport was never as biased against things Japanese but did have the odd quibble along the lines that, '...its solid handling, taut though it is, could do with a bit more liveliness.' Nevertheless they found that its handling was actually better than that of the Porsche 924. Where the 924 would switch abruptly to roll oversteer the Mazda would carry on unperturbed; the RX-7 would oversteer but the driver was given sufficient warning to make it enjoyable rather than harrowing. Yet another writer found that its oversteer could be '...provoked at will; merely slightly backing off or as far as a real tailslide is concerned, by

tightening the lock and pouring on the power immediately.'

That predictability was partly due to the live axle; there were no sudden camber changes to throw the car off line in sudden manoeuvres while at the same time the chassis designer was able to get away with relatively soft suspension bushes to minimise noise and harshness. Such an approach did, of course, mean that the Watts linkage was a vital component to provide transverse location.

When the RX-7 first appeared Japanese tyre technology was not what it is today and it wasn't surprising that in Britain the Bridgestone RD106s were replaced by Pirelli CN36 in the mildest of low-profile formats,

LEFT *Elford Engineering's turbo conversion used a Garret T3 turbo down-stream of an SU HI44 carburettor and produced around 160 bhp using a boost pressure of between 5 and 6 psi*
BELOW *The RX-7's elegant lines were an in-house design and its styling one of the keys to its success*

185/70HR13 which proved far superior in the dry, less so in the wet when they broke away too quickly for some drivers' liking. Rather attractive 5½J alloy wheels were also made standard for Britain but in the North American market the base model appeared with conventional steel wheels and skinnier tyres which made the whole car look disproportionately cheaper – as of course it was. In the US the Mazda was very competitively priced; just like the Datsun 240Z before it, the RX-7 was a bargain; at just $7200 (a mere £3500 at the time!) it was in direct competition with the TR7. It says a lot for the car that it was still highly regarded in Britain despite costing some £8549 when it was introduced here in 1979 and that meant that it had to sell

against the likes of the 924 (£9103) or the BMW 323i (£7550). Some of that price differential was accounted for by the fact that Britain only got the top of the line specification (if you are limited by import quotas you really have to maximise your profit on each car sold), and that transport costs to Britain were greater. Even taking that into account the fact remained that Mazda knew perfectly well that the British buyer was used to paying *far* more for his car than were US drivers....

Price was one good reason why the RX-7 was never that common a sight on British roads. In 1981 Mazda decided to do something about that and for just another £150 introduced an improved version which was far closer to being value for money. A lot of

the changes were essentially cosmetic – the addition of a sun roof, rear wash/wipe, electrically operated windows, more instrumentation and a far better stereo. Cosmetic changes were made to the body too with the urethane covered bumper recessed further into the body. A reshaped air dam at the front was complemented by a rear spoiler, the combination of which was claimed to reduce the Cd to an excellent 0.32. The rear light clusters were also remodelled.

Rather more fundamental were such features as rear disc brakes, replacing the original drums, and more power and torque. Further fine tuning of emissions controls (even the British spec cars had the full US emissions controls, they were such an integral part of the engine's design) and of other sensitive areas like the rotor seals and inlet shape resulted in a power output of 115 bhp at 6000 rpm. That was an improvement of 10 bhp while torque was also increased, to 112 lb ft. Although these were not enormous improvements, along with the improved aerodynamics they helped increase top speed to 122 mph (196 kph) and meant that 60 mph *could* be achieved in 9 seconds (always somewhat problematical in the earlier car) and the standing quarter mile covered in 16.5 seconds. The extra torque helped top gear performance too but that was still the area where the RX-7 lagged behind such rivals as the 2-litre Alfa Romeo GTV, the Datsun 280ZX and even the TR7.

More power could be obtained from the rotary, and fairly easily too. Win Percy's 1980 RAC British Saloon Car Championship winner was tuned to produce 200 bhp although, naturally enough for a racer, it was all top-end power. Rather more practical were the turbo versions, private conversions by Elford Engineering and Mazda's own model which unfortunately never made it to these shores. By 1985 the combination of a turbocharger and electronic fuel injection was helping the engine to produce 165 bhp

---

> **' ... did wonders for the top speed which climbed to 143 mph (230 kph)... '**

(according to the slightly optimistic JIS standard) at 6500 rpm along with 166 lb ft of torque at the normal 4000 rpm. That did wonders for the top speed which climbed to 143 mph (230 kph) and to help cope with the extra performance the turbo versions were given adjustable dampers front and rear and ventilated disc brakes.

Although it continued to sell very well, by 1985 it was time for a change and the new RX-7 owed very little to the old car apart from its name (retained for marketing reasons). Its styling owed a lot to the Porsche 944 according to most observers (to the

A completely new RX-7 was introduced in 1985. The only similarity to the old model was that it was rotary powered and rear-wheel drive. Its engine was the larger 13B 2616 cc unit which produced 150 bhp at 6500 rpm and 136 lb ft of torque at 3000 rpm. The car's most notable feature was its rear suspension, which was independent where the previous car had used a live axle. It was designed to eliminate oversteer and gave the new RX-7 prodigious roadholding

annoyance of Mazda) and even the rotary engine was not the same as the original RX-7. Instead of the 12A the new car had the larger 13B 2616 cc engine originally used in the RX-4, suitably improved with a Teflon coated rotor housing, lighter rotors and further revised rotor seals. With Mazda's own fuel injection, UK-bound cars produced 150 bhp at 6500 rpm and 136 lb ft of torque at 3000 rpm. US buyers, however, could (and for approximately the same price) get the turbo version which produced a very impressive 182 bhp and 183 lb ft of torque.

Where the old car was simple, for example in its use of a live axle, the new one was deliberately more complex, particularly in its rear suspension. The 'dynamic tracking' rear suspension's main feature was the 'triaxial floating hub' which, somewhat like Porsche's Weissach axle, varied the toe in and out of the rear wheels depending on cornering load. At low speeds there would be some toe-out to give better 'bite' or turn-in to the corner but at higher speeds that would be replace by toe-in to prevent oversteer. Whereas Porsche used a mechanical linkage Mazda rather daringly opted for carefully chosen compliance in strategically located bushes to achieve the same ends.

As that, and such devices as the optional semi-automatic damping system (the front dampers switched to a harder setting at speeds over 75 mph/120 kph) indicated, the new RX-7 had moved into a different bracket. The original model had paved the way and its much more expensive replacement was set to reap the benefit. KB

MERCEDES-BENZ
S series

The S series cars of the '20s, with their Porsche-designed six-cylinder engines, were powerful, handsome and fast, and when supercharged well nigh unbeatable

WHEN STIRLING MOSS, navigated by Dennis Jenkinson in a Mercedes-Benz, won the 1955 Mille Miglia, it is fair to say that Italy was impressed and the rest of the world delighted. There had for too long been an assumption, bordering upon a superstition, that a foreign driver could never win this most Italian of races, that a foreign car could not do so either, and – although this was incidental and not at all xenophobic – that whoever led at Rome would not finally win at Brescia. By shattering all these illusions Moss did the race a considerable service, as everybody was keen to recognise; but their acclaim for him betrayed a sad dismissal of history. The race had been won before by a German, Rudolf Caracciola (the name was

> *Caracciola... his support crew consisted of his wife and three men* >

Italian, but removed by some hundreds of years from Italy), in a German car, a Mercedes-Benz SSKL, in 1931.

Maybe the celebrants of 1955 did not want their euphoria disturbed. After all, Moss did have a navigator to advise him of what lay ahead, and he had the support of a large army of Daimler-Benz mechanics, technicians and administrators who had made thorough preparations for the event through months of practice. Caracciola, by contrast, drove with a mechanic for company, and his support crew consisted of his wife and three men – one of whom had to drive over partially blocked roads from Siena to Bologna since the route demanded more refuelling points than the team had

men available. Times were hard....

They had been hard for all Germany since the end of the Great War in 1918. They were especially hard for motor manufacturers, who were numerous, over-ambitious and under-capitalised for reasons that had as much to do with the history of Germany as a loose aggregation of principalities in former centuries as with her history as industrial titan and failed warfarer in the twentieth. At the beginning of the 1920s there were 86 different firms in Germany producing at least 144 different cars. There was also a luxury tax of 15 per cent imposed on their products, yet import duties had been cut and so foreign cars could flood the market. What with poverty and inflation running riot as the

> *One car factory would have sufficed to supply the whole market...* >

victors stripped Germany of her wealth for reparations, one car factory would have sufficed to supply the whole market: accordingly, Benz & Cie and their erstwhile competitors the Daimler Motoren Gesellschaft entered into an association of common interest leading, after three years progressive collaboration, to their complete amalgamation as a new company, Daimler-Benz AG, at the end of June 1926.

Did they then attempt to market a car that would serve all the German people? Wisely, they did not. Both firms had traditionally cultivated high technology and high quality, and the new managing director Dr Hans Niebel (from Benz) insisted on the maintenance and furtherance of this tradition. Of

MODEL
Mercedes-Benz 38/250 SS TT (1929)

ENGINE
Location: Front, longitudinal
Type: Water-cooled straight six with cast light-alloy crankcase and block. Four main bearings
Cubic capacity: 7069 cc
Bore × stroke: 100 mm × 150 mm
Valve gear: 2 valves per cylinder operated by single gear-driven overhead camshaft
Fuel supply: Twin Mercedes-Benz carburettors with Roots-type supercharger
Ignition: Coil and magneto
Maximum power: 220 bhp at 3000 rpm

TRANSMISSION
Location: Clutch and gearbox behind engine with torque tube location to rear axle
Clutch: Multi-disc type with central spring

Gearbox: Three-speed manual
  1st 3.15:1   3rd 1.36:1
  2nd 1.81:1
Final drive: Spiral bevel
Ratio: 2.76:1
(2.50:1, 3.09:1 optional)

SUSPENSION
Front: Non-independent with solid axle, semi-elliptic leaf springs and friction dampers
Rear: Live axle with semi-elliptic leaf springs and friction dampers

STEERING
Type: Screw and nut

BRAKES
Type: Internal-expanding drums all round

WHEELS AND TYRES
Type: Knock-on wire wheels or wooden artillery-type, with 20 × 6.5-inch tyres

BODY/CHASSIS
Type: Pressed steel channel chassis with two side rails and five cross members. Open four-seater tourer body

DIMENSIONS AND WEIGHT
Length: 200 in (5080 mm)
Width: 68 in (1727 mm)
Wheelbase: 134 in (3403 mm)
Track – front: 56 in (1422 mm)
      rear: 56 in (1422 mm)
Weight: 4704 lb (2134 kg)

PERFORMANCE
Maximum speed: 115 mph (187 kph)
Acceleration 0–60 mph: 8 seconds
Fuel consumption: 7-11 mpg

The Mercedes S series cars were essentially simple; note, for example, the non-independent suspension by semi-elliptic leaf springs and friction dampers. The underslung rear springs, however, contributed to the car's handling and road holding. The S series was surprisingly good in both respects considering the weight and upright stance of the cars. Later SSKL models had the chassis side rails drilled for lightness

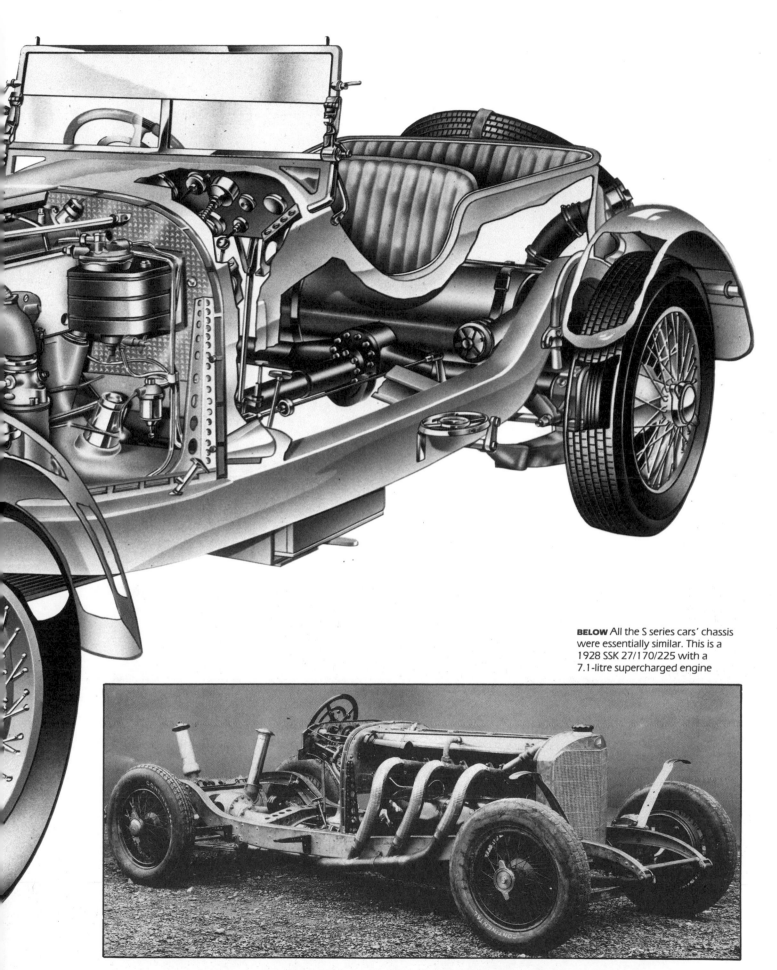

BELOW All the S series cars' chassis were essentially similar. This is a 1928 SSK 27/170/225 with a 7.1-litre supercharged engine

all Germany's surviving manufacturers, from Adler to Wittekind, theirs was the name least likely to perish. For steady business they had a more reliable stock-in-trade than any canny little cobbler of economy runabouts: they made lorries and public service vehicles that would remain economic necessities, however parlous the purchasing power of the private individual. Their cars, built for those individuals who still carried some weight, would be the heavy but flexible 16/50 Benz and the supercharged Mercédès.

Supercharging was something with

> *'the compressor... driven from the engine through a multi-disc clutch'*

which Daimler had been experimenting as early as 1915 for aero engines, at a time when the importance of high-altitude operation for military aircraft was becoming apparent. It would not appear in Grand Prix racing until Fiat introduced it in 1924, but as early as 1921 Daimler had added it to their catalogued 28/95, a 7¼-litre fast tourer that had been announced in 1914 and was put into production after the Armistice. In 1922 supercharging featured in their purpose-built competition cars too, still with the same arrangement which they were doggedly to persist with in some of their production cars until 1939. That is, the supercharger was for occasional use only, and was not continuously in engagement.

The compressor chosen was of the Roots type, driven from the the engine through a multi-disc clutch which was forced into engagement when the driver, having already reached the full-throttle position of the accelerator pedal, pressed further and harder. When that happened, a flap valve diverted air from the long intake pipe feeding the carburettors and fed it to the blower, which returned it to the original route further downstream, just ahead of the carburettors themselves, simultaneously pressurising the fuel feed to maintain its flow. When the driver eased his foot the supercharger was immediately bypassed again and the engine reverted to atmospheric induction, which was why the carburettors had to be downstream from the compressor, and why the acoustics of the system produced such an eerie and sometimes frightening high-pitched scream when the blower was working.

The system was evolved under the guidance of Paul Daimler, chief engineer of the firm and son of pioneer Gottlieb who had actually toyed with the idea of forced induction for his engine back in 1885. In 1922 Paul left, and his place was taken by a fellow from Austro-Daimler called Ferdinand Porsche. To make his mark, he promptly produced some new engine designs including a big six-cylinder 6-litre supercharged touring device which was known as the 24/100/140 hp model. This triple rating displayed the German fiscal rating, the power unblown and the power with the blower engaged, and was to be applied to a long series of supercharged machines – so was the style of the engine, constructed in very different fashion from the aviation-inspired engines of Paul Daimler.

Porsche gave it, for the first time in the firm's experience, a one-piece crankcase and cylinder block cast in light alloy. The cylinder liners were cast iron, which was reasonable enough; so was the cylinder head, which was unfortunate – as indeed was the very fact of its being separate when

ABOVE *Manfred von Brauchitsch winning at Avus at an average 120.7 mph in an SSKL with specially designed streamlined coachwork by Baron von Faschenfeld* LEFT *One of Rudolf Caracciola's greatest drives was in the 1929 Monaco GP when he took the massive SSK to third place* BELOW AND BOTTOM *A 1929 38 250 SS originally built for Lord Cholmondeley. The instrumentation was comprehensive*

the best rival engines still enjoyed integral heads with no gaskets interposing their potential treachery. It was the only flaw in an otherwise impressive design, which numbered an overhead camshaft (driven by silent helical gears), an integral cooling fan, generous coolant passages, a vast sump and a properly robust four-bearing crankshaft (better than seven) among its virtues. The engine was very good-looking for its time, and was carried with its gearbox in triple bearers between the channel-section longerons of the chassis.

It was a big engine, but it was a very big chassis: the wheelbase, nearly 12 ft 4 in (376 cm) long, was appropriate to the six- and seven-seat bodies intended to be carried. Yet the temptation was there to run the car in competitions, and in 1926 a short-chassis version known as the K model (*kurz* – short) appeared, with a wheelbase of 11 ft 2 in (340 cm). It was still known as the 24/100/140, but in fact the true power figures were more like 110 and 160 bhp, for the engine had been enlarged to 6240 cc, with bore and stroke of 94 mm and 150 mm and a modest rev limit of 2800 rpm. In Britain, where the taxation system was different and where exaggeration of power figures was common, it was known as the 33/180, following the 33/140 of the long-chassis car; in Europe it figured in a number of races, though without any really noteworthy successes. In 1926 this was the world's fastest production tourer, but although it could go hammering on for hours at high speeds on the ill-maintained roads of the day it was far from being the best-handling or braked.

These deficiencies were very quickly cured. The chassis was lowered drastically: it would have been a shame to lose the superbly designed Daimler front axle, a lovely curved forging that put everything from brake-shafts to kingpins and spring-pads in what looked like just the right places; but behind it the side-rails were sloped down, with a sharper rise again over the rear axle which was now carried on underslung springs. The wheelbase was the same as in the K model before, but the engine had been enlarged internally, bores larger by 4 mm bringing the displacement to the memorable figure of 6789 cc. With stronger supercharging than before, and now with two carburettors instead of one, this engine really did produce 180 bhp; the British agents called it the 36/220, but in Germany the car was known as the 26/120/180, or

simply as the S model.

It was also known as a car blessed with far better behaviour than might have been anticipated from its sheer mass. Its straight-line performance was beyond dispute: in top gear it could do anything from walking speed up to as much as 110 mph (177 kph), the figure it set as a German sports-car record soon after its introduction. What really amazed people was its evidently superb roadholding, and those who actually drove it were equally enraptured by its steering. Obviously the geometry of the latter was inherently very good and was not corrupted by the motions of the suspension; less obviously the lowering of the chassis and the rear springs had produced just the

right suspension geometry, probably by lowering the rear roll centre (by adopting underslung springs) to compensate for the rear springbase ·being much wider than at the front. Balance was surely the secret of it all: that huge cylinder block being largely hollow and almost entirely of silumin, Germany's favourite silicon-aluminium alloy. The car was not by any means as heavy as it looked, and was low in relation to its length – or, more precisely, its centre of gravity was low in relation to its wheelbase, reducing pitching moments as well as roll.

Nothing less would have been good enough; the car looked so beautiful that it had to behave beautifully. Promptly pitched into the sporting arena it gave an exemplary

LEFT AND TOP *A supercharged SSK from 1928. SSK stood for Super Sports Kurz, or in other words it was the short-wheelbase Super Sports. With the supercharger the power output was raised to 225 bhp*
ABOVE *This 1929 SSK engine is rated at 250 bhp merely because the British importers tended to exaggerate....*
BELOW *The Cholmondeley 1929 SSK*

account of itself in the numerous hillclimbs (long Alpine pass-storming affairs, quite different from the briefly explosive sprints popular in Britain) which made up a large slice of the German sporting calendar. Outstanding drivers in these were two: one was Adolf Rosenberger, a wealthy Jewish amateur who had been closely involved with the rear-engined Benz GP cars of 1922 and was at that time probably the fastest driver in Germany; the other was a newcomer, young Rudolf Caracciola.

The two met in the German Grand Prix, held on the very fast Avus track at Berlin in 1926. The official Mercedes-Benz team chose to enter a race at San Sebastian instead, but Rosenberger entered the Avus race privately and Caracciola persuaded the factory to let him run as a semi-official or works-supported privateer. It was the young man's first Grand Prix (he had been a reserve driver for the team in earlier and less straitened seasons) and he won it – but only after Rosenberger, in the lead on the seventh lap of the rain-slicked track, had lost control at the tricky 105 mph (169 kph) Nordkurve and crashed. Years later, the famous Rennleiter or team chief Alfred Neubauer let the cat out of the bag, saying that the accident had been caused because Rosenberger had been affected by fumes from a leaking ether tank under the bonnet.

So what was he doing with ether? The same as Pierre Levegh was doing with a tank full of a blend containing equal parts of petrol, benzol and alcohol when he crashed his Mercedes-Benz at Le Mans in 1955: he was trying to enlist chemistry as an ally with physics to achieve the best possible performance. Daimler-Benz never missed a trick in the rule-book (they were disqualified from a couple of races in 1928 and '29 for tricks that were not in it) and in those days when racing formulae were pretty free they experimented just as much as some other firms with the fruits of science.

Was this why the works-entered cars were always so convincingly fast, and why so many private owners were disgruntled by the slowness of their production cars? Not entirely: the customers' cars were always turned out well trimmed and with bodies built heavily enough to be reasonably enduring, whereas the works cars went out stripped nearly naked and no heavier than they needed to be to last the length of the race. Every competent factory in those days did the same, except perhaps Frazer Nash who did not believe in giving the customer more than they had to. The fact remains that there was many an S model, doubtless overbodied and festooned with all the fashionable trappings that induced so much extra drag, that could not do much more than 90 mph (145 kph) – and many more customers who could not drive.

In any case, there was more performance forthcoming in 1928, when the cylinder bores were enlarged to 100 mm to make the displacement 7069 cc. The triple rating told most of the story: the new car, known as the SS, was listed as 27/140/200. At the same time there was a new short sporter, the SSK (Super Sport Kurz), within the 9 ft 8 in

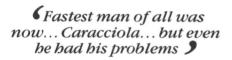

> *'Fastest man of all was now... Caracciola... but even he had his problems'*

(295 cm) wheelbase of which was a more highly tuned engine rated as 27/170/225. As far as the British agents were concerned the 36/220 had grown into the 38/250!

As far as the sporting drivers of Germany were concerned the big blown six had grown almost entirely convincing. Almost? The bonnet was taller, perhaps because the radiator needed to be bigger; the brakes were alleged to be less good than on the S, and, when driven as hard as only maybe five men drove it, it could be heavy on tyres. Fastest man of all was now unquestionably Caracciola, probably the only racing driver in history to rank with Jim Clark for smoothness and equilibrium; he could make a set of tyres outlast anyone else while still going faster, but even he had his problems. Most memorable of these occasions was also one of the most memorable feats ever accomplished by the big Mercs or by Caracciola, when he drove an SSK into third place in the first Monaco Grand Prix. Starting from the back of a grid full of such fancied little jewels as the 2.3-litre Bugatti, the huge SSK was ridiculed; the jeers faded as it fought its way around the houses and harbour of the 'race of a thousand corners' until it was in the lead. Only the need to stop for fresh tyres caused that lead to be lost to a couple of Bugattis. For so big and supposedly heavy a car it was a preposterous performance, suggesting that not only were the steering and roadholding as good as legend would have us believe but also that the brakes were a lot better than some would have us suppose.

The following year saw the car competi-

EVOLUTION

1922 Ferdinand Porsche moved to Mercedes and designed the 24/100/140 hp 6-litre Mercedes which featured a Roots-type supercharger.

1926 Mercedes K introduced – the K stood for kurz or short as it was built on a short (134 in/ 340 cm) chassis. It was fitted with a larger, 6240 cc, engine which produced 110 bhp, or 160 bhp with the supercharger engaged. It was the world's fastest production tourer

1927 Mercedes S introduced with engine enlarged to 6789 cc and twin carburettors fitted. Power output increased to 180 bhp, supercharged

1928 Engine displacement increased to 7069 cc to form the SS with a maximum power output of 200 bhp supercharged. SSK introduced on the 116-inch (295 cm) wheelbase with tuned version of the 7-litre engine producing a maximum power output of 225 bhp

1930 SSKL introduced. It was the same size as the SSK but had a much lighter chassis and a larger supercharger to boost power output to 300 bhp

tive there again, but not for long: clutch slip forced retirement. People said that clutch slip was one of the weaknesses of the model, but a lot of people (especially Englishmen and Frenchmen, and worst of all English Francophiles) used to be very sniffy indeed about the big Mercs, casting upon them every imaginable aspersion. Sometimes it was jealousy, more often it was political prejudice and occasionally it was simply an aesthetic distaste for the allegedly aggressive styling of the cars. When, in that same 1930, the lone long SS Mercedes-Benz retired at Le Mans after leading two full teams of Bentleys a very merry dance indeed, the cause was dynamo failure leading to a discharged battery. The way the headlamps faded while the car was in the pits at 2.30 am demonstrated the truth of the official statement, but the British tried to insinuate a gasket failure,

saying that if a Merc was forced to use the blower much its head gasket also blew.

It was a gross exaggeration of the truth. The blower was not to be used except in conjuction with 50/50 petrol/benzol fuel, a reasonable precaution in those days when knock-resistance was a fuel quality little understood. It was not to be used in bottom gear, which was rather low and therefore involved a considerable torque multiplication, which would have been too much for the 'box if the torque were further amplified by the blower. Finally it was not recommended that the blower be kept engaged for more than 20 seconds at a time – but this instruction was for private owners chasing the horizon down the ruler-straight *Routes Nationales* of France, not for racing adepts chasing filigrees up the flanks of an Alp or chasing Bugattis down the echoes of the

FAR LEFT *The 7.1-litre 1929 38 250 SS TT which was driven by Sir Malcolm Campbell in the Ulster Tourist Trophy and at Brooklands where the car held the 7-litre Mountain Circuit record*
LEFT *The rather strange fuel filler cap; the car's thirst was prodigious*
BELOW *The instrumentation included a water temperature gauge, clock, tachometer, speedo and ammeter*
BOTTOM *The view that most other drivers had of the SS. Note the large-bore exhaust*

Nürburgring. In practice, the drill on ordinary roads was imposed by the sheer impossibility of going that fast for long: the top three ratios of the four-speed gearbox were all high (peak rpm were 3200) and after reaching a chosen cruising speed quickly with the blower one relaxed the foot and cruised unsupercharged.

The lie was given to all the snide critics at the end of 1930 when the SSKL was readied for the following season. Dimensionally the same as the SSK, but extensively lightened (most obviously by many holes in the chassis rails), it had an even larger blower known as the Elephant delivering a boost pressure of 0.85 atmospheres to raise the brake horse-power to 300. Caracciola took it out the first time for the last 1930 event, the Schwabenberg hillclimb, winning it and the European Mountain Championship. In 1931 he won everywhere he drove the SSKL: seven hill events (with an outright or sports car record at each one), two closed-circuit road races (the Eifelrennen and the German GP) at the Nürburgring, a track race (the Avusrennen at Berlin) and, most splendid of all, the Mille Miglia road race.

The following year he was beaten at the Avus. He was driving for Alfa Romeo now, and the car that beat him was an SSKL clad in a special streamlined body, the work of Freiherr König von Fachsenfeld, an aerody-

namics formalist of academic authority. The car was timed at 156 mph (251 kph), but the days of the big blown six were fading fast. It could be tossed about in a manner that belied its size but its little rivals kept passing it when it stopped for fresh tyres. Worse, it was out of keeping with the new breed of independently-sprung touring cars put into production from 1931 onwards. Racing an outmoded car did nothing to help sales of the new ones.

In any case, Daimler-Benz had withdrawn from racing. They said they could not afford it because times were hard. Actually they were preparing revolutionary new cars, supercharged, independently-sprung metallurgical marvels with Fachsenfeld-style bodies, for the new GP formula to come into effect in 1934. Soon they would be making times hard for everybody else.   LJKS

Classless and unique, the Mini was one of the most revolutionary cars ever produced in Britain and is still in production 26 years after its introduction

IF IN THE PRESENT DAY, in the middle of the 1980s, you saw your first Austin Mini, your impression would almost certainly be of a very small, cramped, noisy, harsh-riding car with poorly designed controls and twitchy handling; and you would be right. On the other hand, nobody in Europe in the 1980s ever sees a Mini for the first time. The shape, and the whole character, of the car is essentially as it was when it was launched in August 1959, and well over four million have been built since then.

The Mini is inescapably associated with one man, Sir Alec Issigonis. He was born in Turkey but had British nationality, and this brought him to these shores in the 1920s when he decided to study engineering and join the motor industry. His first real triumph was the Morris Minor of 1948, and indeed it was in some senses out of the Minor that the Mini grew.

Issigonis rejoined BMC, the monolith that resulted from the 1952 merger of Austin and Morris, after a period at Alvis during which he had designed an advanced and ambitious sports saloon that was rejected by the management. His return to Longbridge occurred just before the 1956 Suez crisis, and it was the sudden shortage of petrol which this caused that led BMC chairman Sir Leonard Lord to postpone all other projects and set Issigonis the 'crash programme' task of de-

RIGHT *The 1275 GT was introduced in 1969 with the longer Clubman body but it did not prove as popular as the Cooper*
FAR RIGHT *A 997 cc version of the Mini Cooper, introduced in 1961*
BELOW *A Mini in the '64 Monte Carlo*

MINI

signing a completely new economy car, something which might hope to assume the mantle of the Austin Seven of the 1920s.

Issigonis proceeded by using what has since become known as 'packaging'. He decided firstly the size of the smallest cabin which would accommodate four people in comfort, his chosen dimensions being 8 ft 9 in (267 cm) long, 4 ft 2 in (127 cm) wide and 4 ft 4 in (132 cm) high. Then, on the basis that the smallest and lightest – and therefore most economical – car would be arrived at by squeezing the engine, transmission and the rest of the mechanicals into the smallest possible extra box, he applied his undoubted engineering genius to finding the most compact arrangement. His task was complicated by having to use the existing A-series, overhead-valve engine which powered the Minor, since there was no time to develop a new one even if the money had been available. The decision to develop the Mini was taken early in 1957, and it says much for the speed of Issigonis' small engineering team that the car was in production and on sale within two and a half years. That, by the usual standards of the British motor industry in those days, would have been a remarkable achievement for a conventional model, let alone one which overturned as many cherished traditions as did the Mini.

> *'The cornerstone of Issigonis's layout was the transverse engine...'*

The cornerstone of Issigonis' layout was the transverse engine and front-wheel drive. By setting the engine across the car he reduced the overall length; by driving the front wheels he retained interior space usually devoted to a propeller shaft and rear axle, which would in turn have meant enlarging his precious minimum-sized cabin. In essence the Mini consisted of a tightly-cowled driving pod trailing that cabin behind it, the rear supported as simply as possible on plain trailing arms with the simplest but most ingenious of springing: the rubber units developed by Alex Moulton. Another iconoclastic decision concerned the use of 10 in (25 cm) wheels,

ABOVE The Cooper S of 1970 was essentially the same as the very first Mini of 1959 and, with its 76 bhp, proved just how conservative the original management had been in giving the first car the small 850 cc 37 bhp version of the famous A-series engine. This particular model has the hydrolastic suspension rather than the 'dry' rubber cone system of the first cars. The Mini was a superb piece of packaging, with the gearbox housed actually in the engine sump and the rear suspension so designed that it did not encroach on the passenger compartment

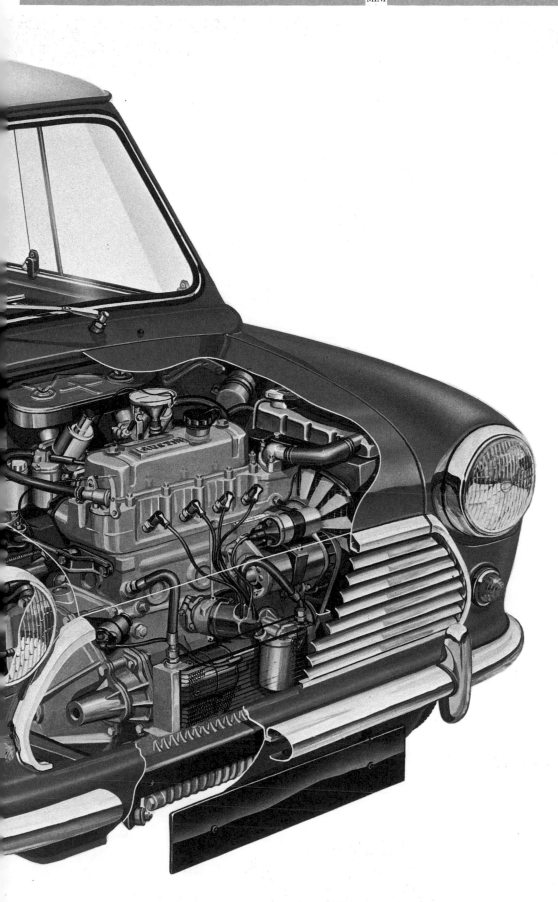

MODEL
Morris Mini Cooper S (1970)

UK price when introduced: £719

ENGINE
Location: Front, transverse
Type: In-line water-cooled four-cylinder with cast-iron block and head. Three main bearings
Cubic capacity: 1275 cc
Bore × stroke: 70.7 mm × 81.4 mm
Compression ratio: 9.7:1
Valve gear: Two valves per cylinder operated by single block-mounted camshaft, pushrods and rockers
Fuel supply: Two SU HS 2 carburettors
Ignition: Mechanical by coil and distributor
Maximum power: 76 bhp (DIN) at 6000 rpm
Maximum torque: 79 lb ft at 3000 rpm

TRANSMISSION
Layout: Gearbox mounted below engine in sump with clutch on end of engine
Clutch: Single dry plate
Gearbox: Four-speed manual

1st 3.200:1		3rd 1.357:1	
2nd 1.916:1		4th 1.000:1	

Final drive: Helical spur
Ratio: 3.440:1

SUSPENSION
Front: Independent with wishbones and hydrolastic rubber cone springs. Hydraulic connecting pipe to rear wheels
Rear: Independent with swinging longitudinal trailing arms, hydrolastic rubber-cone springs, connecting pipe to front wheels and pitch control tension springs

STEERING
Type: Rack and pinion. 2.33 turns lock to lock

BRAKES
Type: Discs front (7.48 in/190 mm dia) and drums rear, servo-assisted

WHEELS AND TYRES
Type: Steel wheels with 5.2 in × 10 in radial tyres

BODY/CHASSIS
Type: Integral steel with auxiliary subframes front and rear. Two-door four-seat saloon body

DIMENSIONS AND WEIGHT
Length: 120.24 in (3054 mm)
Width: 55.51 in (1410 mm)
Wheelbase: 80.16 in (2036 mm)
Track – front: 47.53 in (1207 mm)
    – rear: 46.31 in (1176 mm)
Weight: 1458 lb (661 kg)

PERFORMANCE
Maximum speed: 98 mph (157 kph)
Acceleration 0–60 mph: 10.9 seconds
Fuel consumption (approx): 30 mpg

EVOLUTION

Introduced in August 1959, the Mini, known as the Austin Seven and Morris Mini Minor, was available in basic and deluxe saloon versions, and was a highly compact four-seat saloon of integral construction powered by the 848 cc A – series four-cylinder engine

1960 The Mini Van, Countryman and Traveller estates were introduced, the latter two with ash-framed bodywork

1961 The Mini Super saloon was launched, fitted with an oil-pressure gauge, water temperature gauge, key-start ignition (instead of floor-mounted button) and Duotone paint scheme. The Mini Cooper was also launched, fitted with front disc brakes and, initially, a 997 cc version of the engine, later changed to 998 cc. The Riley Elf and Wolseley Hornet were introduced, with traditional radiator grilles, boots and wooden fascias

1962 The Austin model redesignated the Austin Mini. Deluxe and Super models replaced by Super Deluxe. A cheaper version of the estate car, without the wooden trim, also became avalable. The Riley Elf and Wolseley Hornet were fitted with the 998 cc engine

1963 The Mini Cooper S was launched, based on the Mini Cooper body but fitted with the 1071 cc engine, servo-assisted brakes and ventilated wheels

1964 The Mini Cooper S model's 1071 cc engine was replaced by the 1275 cc and 970 cc units. Improved gearboxes were introduced to the range, along with diaphragm spring clutch and Hydrolastic suspension on the saloons. Twin-leading-shoe front brakes were fitted to all but the Coopers. The Mini Moke was launched

1965 A four-speed automatic gearbox became optional (with uprated engine) on some models

1966 The Mk III Elf and Hornets were launched, with improved internal and external trim. All models were given a smoother clutch action

1967 The Mk II Mini Cooper, Standard and Super Deluxe saloons were launched, fitted with larger rear screens, larger grille and new exterior and internal trim. The new Cooper S model was fitted with an all-synchromesh gearbox. The Mini 1000 Super Deluxe was introduced, fitted with the 998 cc engine

1968 The Elf, Hornet and Mini Moke were discontinued. On other models the cable interior door-lock mechanism was replaced by handles. All-synchromesh gearboxes became standard. The Mk II models were replaced by a new series of saloons with wind-up windows, concealed hinges for the doors and dry-cone suspension

1969 The Mini Cooper Mk II was discontinued. Introduced were the Mini 1275 GT saloon with disc brakes and Hydrolastic suspension, the Mini Clubman saloon, with the 998 cc engine and Hydrolastic suspension, and the Clubman Estate, with dry cone suspension, replacing the 1000 Countryman and Traveller models

1970 Mini Cooper S Mk III introduced, fitted with wind-up windows, concealed hinges and new trim and seats

1971 Dry cone suspension fitted to the Mini Clubman. Cooper S discontinued

1973 Shorter-travel gearchange introduced

1974 Automatic gearbox only available on home market. Inertia-reel seat belts became a standard fitment

1975 The Mini 1000 Special (limited-edition) was announced, with distinctive interior and external trim. The Mini Clubman's 998 cc engine was replaced by the 1098 cc engine, except on the automatic versions

1979 Mini City 850 was launched, but then the 850 series was discontinued. Mini 1000 redesignated the Super. 1000 City introduced, with estate version, available in manual and automatic versions. The 848 cc pickup was discontinued

1980 The Mini Clubman was discontinued

1982 Mini 1000 estate discontinued, the City was renamed the Mini E, the HL the HLE, the HLE the Mini Mayfair. All van and pick-up versions were discontinued

1983 The limited-edition Mini Sprite was released, based on the City but with a special trim package

1984 The limited-edition Mini 25 was launched, commemorating a quarter of a century of Mini production; this model had a special silver and grey velour interior

1985 The Mini Ritz was announced, based on the City but with a special trim package

1986 New, colour-matched interior for the Mini Mayfair and City. The five-millionth Mini will be produced, celebrated with a special, limited-edition model

---

TOP LEFT *Minis racing with typical gay abandon at Crystal Palace in 1962*
FAR LEFT *The Hopkirk/Liddon car from the '63 RAC Rally*
LEFT *Action from the 1969 British Saloon Car Championship*
BELOW LEFT *Years later and the Mini is still competitive. The year is 1978 and the venue Brands Hatch*

smaller than anything previously seen on a 'proper' car, for the sake of smaller wheel arches which helped preserve under-bonnet space at the front and seat width at the back.

In theory it would have been possible to add the engine and transmission package at the back; indeed it would have been much more fashionable since the increasingly successful Continental mass-manufacturers of the day – Fiat, Renault and Volkswagen – were churning out rear-engined cars which were much admired. Alec Issigonis chose his layout not because of concern for stability and handling, but because his studies showed that he could make the Mini far more compact that way than by trying to squeeze the tall A-series engine under or aft of the back seat. Of course, as soon as it became available, the Mini's handling qualities quickly made people realise how lacking the rear-engine layout was: it died a lingering death as Europe's car designers raced to climb on the front-drive band-

wagon. No car has ever been so flattered by imitation as the Mini.

There have been arguments that the Mini layout was not original. Fiat's chief engineer recalled a pre-war paper in which he had sketched something similar in principle – yet when the Mini appeared, Fiat was building the 600 and preparing the directly competitive, rear-engined 850. Besides, Issigonis

> *'... the Mini's handling made people realise how lacking the rear-engine lay-out was...'*

made no claims for originality as such but rather for the efficiency and logic of his engineering package. Not all of its features were brilliant, since the gearbox was packed into the sump – a clever piece of width-saving and a layout which permitted the use of a central differential and equal-length drive shafts, but which condemned the gears to run in engine oil and meant using a complicated transfer-gear system that caused insoluble noise problems (it also meant there was no prospect of the Mini or any derivative being given a fifth forward speed, but that was only to become a headache 20 years later). While the transverse engine layout has become well-nigh universal, few

engineers ever adopted Issigonis' transmission layout. Most found the room to put a conventional two-shaft gearbox on one end of the engine, even if it meant having one drive-shaft longer than the other.

The Mini was not an overnight success, surprising though it may seem today. When *The Autocar* first tested one, its conclusions were that 'the manufacturers are to be congratulated on producing, at a truly competitive price, an outstanding car providing unusual body space for its size, and one in which four persons can enjoy comfortable, safe and economical motoring. It is far from being an underpowered miniature, and has a very lively performance; it is certain to interest the sporting motorist because of its fine handling qualities. It scores in heavy traffic on account of its size, and its minimum overhang, front and rear, makes parking an easy matter in congested cities.' If that sounds like praise, remember that the motoring magazines of the 1950s were sparing indeed of outright criticism. Note the absence of any positive suggestion that this might be one of the epoch-making cars of the generation.

If there was initial caution, compounded by the almost simultaneous appearance of Ford's 105E Anglia with its more advanced engine and refined rear-drive chassis, there might almost have been worse to come. By the time the winter of 1959/60 was over, there were many stories of water leaks through the Mini's floor, of breakdown caused by a drowned distributor every time it rained, and of high oil consumption. People grumbled about the crudity of the interior with its slide windows, pull-string door handles and carpet dropped in more or less at random, and the osteopaths were crying about the driving position and control layout all the way to the bank.

Yet it transpired that these criticisms amounted to nothing. The Mini *was* a success and there appear to have been two reasons for it. The first was a social attitude, a matter of taste. While the 105E Anglia was kept firmly in its place by the unwillingness of the 'right' people of the early 1960s to be seen dead in a Ford, it appeared that you could take a Mini anywhere. It was soon enjoyed by shopping housewives and short-distance commuters, and then celebrities began to use Minis to arrive at Claridges functions – the interiors, of course, suitably treated by Hooper or Wood and Pickett to remove those cheap pull-string door handles.

> *'... those close dimensions really did enable it to go where others could not...'*

Why should the Mini have appealed in this classless way? That is probably where the second and very logical factor comes in. The Mini was extremely easy to drive to high limits of cornering and adhesion – and that mattered to people who didn't in the least think of themselves as budding rally drivers. It quickly gained the classic reputation of a 'nippy little car' (always high praise in British motoring circles), enhanced by superb visibility from the driving seat and those close dimensions which really did enable it to go where others could not: city parking, for example, ceased to be a problem for

Mini owners. Also, not to forget its original purpose, it was extremely economical to the extent where *The Autocar*'s lead-footed testers achieved an overall 40.1 mpg (against which the 105E Anglia returned 36.1 mpg and the 100E Popular, just 29.6 mpg).

What manner of car was it in engineering terms? The A-series engine had had its stroke shortened to reduce the standard 948 cc to 848 cc, giving a leisurely power output claimed to be 37 bhp gross (say 34 bhp DIN). However, the car was extremely light at just over 1300 lb (590 kg), justifying the Issigonis approach, and the main reason for the outstanding economy allied with reasonable performance. It would hardly seem reasonable by today's standards, for the first Press test cars crept past 70 mph (113 kph) and needed nearly half a minute to reach 60 mph, but it was enough in its day – and improvements were already in hand which would transform the situation. The lower gears of the four-speed gearbox took the Mini to roughly 25, 40 and 60 mph (40, 64 and 97 kph). Suspension was by double wishbones at the front, the drive shafts articulated by Mr Rzeppa's constant-velocity joints, another of the technical keys to the design. Moulton's rubber-cone springs were used here as well as for the rear trailing arms. The 10 in wheels were shod with 5.20 section cross-ply tyres – radials were then still in their formative years. Braking was by 7 in (18 cm) diameter Lockheed drums all round; discs were still for high-performance sports cars. The fuel tank was a mere 5.5 gallons (25 litres), then and for many years after. The battery was housed under the boot floor, causing a notable maintenance problem, for the sake of making the car a little less nose-heavy and the rear brakes less inclined to lock prematurely.

That was the Mini when first launched, but it soon began to sprout versions. Initially, to suit the BMC sales and dealership policy of the day, it was offered either as a Morris Mini-Minor or an Austin Seven, but

ABOVE *A Mini hydrolastic unit*
BELOW *The utilitarian Mini Moke was introduced in 1964 and proved popular in quite a different market*
BELOW LEFT *With two engines this Moke had rather too much power*

ABOVE *The Wolsey Hornet, introduced in 1961, was more luxurious but rather pretentious, like its stablemate the Riley Elf* ABOVE RIGHT *which was mechanically identical*
BELOW *A Mini rear subframe*

the name Mini caught on and became universal more or less by public demand. An early extra model was the Mini-Traveller with a miniature version of the then-classic BMC estate-car body style with exterior ash framing. A van version, without benefit of framing, had appeared a matter of months after the original launch and had proved a great success, making the estate-car conversion a simple matter. A year after that the Mini-Cooper arrived with its 997 cc engine, all of 55 bhp (net), disc front brakes, and capable of 85 mph (137 kph) or so, with 60 mph coming up in under 20 seconds! In 1961 such performance made the Cooper the first choice of every club rallyist until the Cortina GT came on the scene, and BMC trumped that particular Ford card with its 1963 launch of the Mini Cooper S, originally of 1071 cc but soon with a choice of 970 cc (rare) for 1-litre class events, and 1275 cc (far more popular) for the 1.3-litre class and for brisk motoring generally.

The Cooper S models quickly established a reputation second to none in top-class European rallying in the hands of drivers like Makinen, Aaltonen and Hopkirk, and in racing under the gentle urging of characters like Sir John Whitmore. One outcome of all this sporting activity was that the Mini's general sales success boomed in the mid-1960s, when, by normal motor industry logic, after six or seven years in production it should have been waning sufficiently to turn engineering minds towards its successor. There had been developments other than the purely sporting ones, of course. The 1961 arrival of the Cooper had been accompanied by the Riley Elf and Wolseley Hornet, with new radiator grilles and vestigial boots which added far less in the way of luggage space than they did in presumed distinction. Oddly, the public didn't seem to want the distinction nearly as much as the familiar, well-balanced but cheeky Mini shape, and neither the Riley nor the Wolseley enjoyed real success despite the fact that for some time they were the only non-Cooper ver-

sions (from 1962) with 1-litre rather than 848 cc engines and useful extra torque. Official BL figures quote production of less than 60,000 Rileys and Wolseleys, compared with over 100,000 for the Cooper and nearly 45,000 for the Cooper S. The 998 cc engine finally appeared in the Mini 1000 in 1967.

> *'... its shortcomings were enough to cause speculation about its replacement '*

One of the more controversial moves in the Mini's history came in 1964 when the original 'dry' suspension was replaced by the Hydrolastic variety used with success in the bigger Austin/Morris 1100. The general consensus was that the Hydrolastic Minis traded a slightly more comfortable ride for slightly less crisp and predictable handling, but the overall value of the change was questionable. The following year the Mini formed the launching pad for the ingenious but largely ill-fated AP four-speed automatic transmission. Some customers may have bought this version because however much they loved the Mini, they had perpetual problems with the gearchange: throughout the 1960s there were detail changes to the synchromesh and the shift linkage, culminating in the adoption of an all-synchromesh box in 1968.

A major change in Mini policy became evident in 1969, following the Leyland merger with BMC that created the new British Leyland combine. By this time the Mini had been in production for 10 years and its shortcomings in some design areas were more than enough to cause speculation about its replacement. In the event, 1969 saw the appearance not of a replacement car but of a supposedly interim model, the Clubman, with a squared-off nose that added four inches to the famous 10 ft (305 cm) overall length, and a redesigned and updated in-

terior (the instruments were, wonder of wonders, in front of the driver!). The Clubman was offered in 998 and 1275 cc versions and supplanted the Riley Elf, the Wolseley Hornet and the Cooper. The 1275 Cooper S struggled on unchanged until 1971, but more significantly the original Mini shape also continued, in 850 and 1000 versions, with sufficient detail changes – like wind-up windows and flush door hinges – to warrant a change from the ADO15 designation to ADO20. Interestingly, the ADO20 also reverted to the original type of rubber-cone dry springing.

Partly because of BL's internal confusion about the future of individual marque names like Austin and Morris, there was a period during the 1970s when Mini became a marque in its own right, without any of the former badge distinction. This made some kind of sense as long as there were distinct basic and long-nosed Clubman models to form a range, but with the coming of the Metro (and the dropping of Morris) the Mini finally became an Austin again.

The question of a true Mini replacement was debated within BL throughout the 1970s, with various interesting prototypes like ADO74 and ADO88 failing on grounds of cost – or perhaps of lack of sufficient funds for development. The Mini and the Clubman soldiered on until at the end of the decade some 4.5 million Minis and derivatives had been made. By this time the Mini had become a legend, and there was no longer any question of replacing it directly.

Why so? In 1969, the Mini was 10 years old as a production model, rather elderly and fit for replacement by something better, but it was helped through the 1970s by two

LEFT *Where it all began, the original Mini introduced in 1959. This is a Morris Mini Minor version but the Austin Seven was identical*
BELOW LEFT *The 848 cc A series engine produced just 37 bhp (gross)*
BELOW LEFT *The interiors were spartan indeed to begin with, but quite functional*

great surges in demand for ultra-economy cars, after the 1973 Yom Kippur war and the 1978/79 Iranian crisis. By 1979 it was 20 years old, and cars which survive in production for that long, like the VW Beetle, the Citroën Traction Avant and 2CV, become motoring legends almost as of right, and so it was with the Mini.

> *'... the Mini survives 26 years into production, likely to make its 30th birthday'*

Then again, the question of outright replacement hardly arose by the end of the 1970s. Had Issigonis sat down at his drawing board in 1977 rather than 1957, his minimum cabin would have been bigger, because people have, on average, become bigger. People's expectations of higher standards of comfort and equipment make life difficult for any car like the Mini, unless of course it has legendary status to back it up. In any event, the Mini replacements of the 1970s gradually grew into a car of the so-called 'supermini' class – the Metro, substantially bigger and heavier, built less to replace the Mini than to slog it out in the market with the Ford Fiesta, Fiat 127 and Renault 5. When the Metro arrived in 1980, the Mini Clubman models were dropped.

It is an interesting commentary on the pace of motoring development, and its direction, that the last Mini 850 to be tested by *Autocar*, just before the small engine was discontinued, managed a maximum speed of just 70 mph, actually slightly lower than that of the original. The overall fuel consumption was worse too, at 38.1 mpg, but six seconds had been carved off the 0–60 mph time giving the later 850 acceleration similar to that of the first Cooper!

Today, the Mini survives 26 years into production and likely at least to make its 30th birthday. In its current form it retains a 1-litre A-series engine, though now tuned for extreme economy with the help of modern technical developments under the 'A-plus' designation. The basic Mini City E remains cheap, although the man who paid £529 for a Mini de luxe in 1959 might look askance at £3,298, at least until he studied the price of the cheapest listed Ford which has more than kept pace.

Yet in a sense, the Metro *has* replaced the Mini. In 1979, the last complete sales year before the Metro became available, the ever-green Mini stood third in the British sales charts and took nearly 5 per cent of the British market. In 1981 it lay 10th, and took less than 2 per cent of sales, and by 1984 it had slumped to 16th, and 1.3 per cent, while the Metro was up there with the front-runners. The writing may be on the wall for the Mini, yet there seems no point in Austin-Rover handing 25,000 British sales a year, and a useful number of European customers, to their deadly rivals by simply consigning their legend to history.   JRD

PORSC

The 1950's rear-engined 356 was fast, aerodynamic and very reliable, and pointed the way for Porsche. Yet it was a pre-war design...

WHEN PROFESSOR Ferdinand Porsche was released in August 1947 from the French prison where he had been interned after the war, he returned to the family home in Gmund, Austria. He found that his son Ferry and his old design associates Karl Rabe and Erwin Komenda were installed in a small design office and workshop in the outbuildings of the family house. They had begun by designing and building agricultural machinery, including a new design of tractor, as motor cars were out of the question in the immediate post-war days, and their workshop also carried out repairs on war-time Volkswagen cars, especially the cross-country vehicle which Austrian farmers were finding very useful.

By 1947 Ferry Porsche and his two experienced designers had begun work on a car to carry the Porsche name, based on VW components, owing much to a one-off streamlined coupé that Porsche had built in 1939 on a Volkswagen base. That coupé had been intended to take part in the Berlin-Rome race, but the war had put a stop to that. The prototype Porsche built at Gmund was an open two-seater sports car for the simple reason that Porsche's facilities were limited and they were unable to make a coupé. This was the prototype 356, and when Professor Porsche returned home he was well-pleased to see the family name on this sleek little sports car.

Before the war the Porsche design office and workshop had been in Stuttgart, and it was imperative that they returned there so that work could begin on producing Porsches again. Unfortunately the American military were in possession of the Stuttgart premises and it took a long time to reposses them (until 1950 in fact). While negotiations were in progress a batch of 50 cars was built in Gmund, each one hand-made and with a hand-beaten aluminium coupé body. When series-production of the little coupés was instituted, the Reutter body plant next door to the Porsche premises was given the contract to produce the chassis/body unit in steel, while Porsche looked after all the mechanical components, most of which were of Volkswagen origin. Thus did the Porsche 356 go into production, in Zuffenhausen in north-west Stuttgart.

The coupé 356 had first been shown to the public at the Geneva Motor Show in the spring of 1949, and it had proved to be an instant success among the sporting fraternity, even though its capacity was only 1100 cc. By reason of its air-cooled rear-mounted engine it had a very smooth front and consequently very low drag, so that its modest power output enabled it to reach a maximum of 84 mph (135 kph). By the time production was under way in 1950 the engine had been enlarged to 1300 cc and delivered 44 bhp, giving the car a speed of over 90 mph (145 kph), which was very impressive for such a small car. Thanks to the rear-mounted engine and smooth body the car was remarkably quiet cruising at 90 mph (145 kph) and set new post-war standards of the sort that are normally associated with much larger cars.

Almost at once customers used their Porsches for rallies and speed hill-climbs, and the factory soon began a very vigorous competition programme of their own. Racing and rallying cars similar to those on sale was good publicity, and offered the chance to feed development work into the production line and set a standard of known competence. The factory retained four of the aluminium coupés as a basis for their

gain momentum over the years until it reached a standard that everyone else tried to emulate.

The Le Mans success was followed by a similar performance in the rugged Liège-Rome-Liège rally, when Von Guilleaume and Count von der Muhle won the 1500 cc class and finished third overall. This was the first appearance of another major production step forward, in the form of a 1500 cc version of the ubiquitious flat-four air-cooled Volkswagen engine.

Through the 1950s the Porsche factory made more and more of the mechanical components, gradually phasing out the VW connection. Engine development had been continuous since the prototype was built in Gmund, but gradually Porsche began to produce the gearbox and final drive units, the shock-absorbers, suspension, brakes, steering, electrics and axles. It all went hand-in-hand with engine development aimed at more power and more performance, carried out in conjunction with the active racing and rallying programme. All these developments were passed into the production line, and whatever the engine it

> *'Porsche's idea of a competition engine was one that would last... Le Mans...'*

was always available in two forms, 'normal' or 'super'. The 'normal' engine was the basic unit and naturally the 'super' was a tuned version giving as much as 25 per cent more power, and although intended for competition could easily be used for everyday purposes, for Porsche's idea of a competition engine was one that would last the Le Mans 24 Hours, the Nürburgring 1000 Kms or the Mille Miglia. Although the 356 could give a good account of itself in sprints or hillclimbs, it really came into its own in the more rugged endurance events.

Naturally the feed-back to the production cars ensured that reliability and longevity were the keynotes on which the Porsche reputation was built. During the formative years of the mid-1950s the firm gave an attractive enamel car-badge to owners who had covered 60,000 miles (96,000 km) without having the crankshaft and connecting rods looked at, and a gold watch to those who reached 100,000 miles (161,000 km) without attention. Porsche engineers expected their production engines to cover 100,000 miles (161,000 km) without being stripped down, and today this mileage is the normal expected figure for a Porsche 928.

works team, and these cars made the name Porsche synonymous with winning at a very early stage.

In 1951 the Porsche 356 really established itself on the sporting scene when one of the cars was driven in the Le Mans 24 Hours by the Frenchmen Veuillet and Mouche, the first entry of a German car in the French classic since the war. With its 1100 cc engine tuned to give 44 bhp and with all four wheels enclosed by 'spats' the little coupé was capable of 100 mph (161 kph), using a special high axle ratio. The car ran like a clock and won the 1100 cc category with ease, starting a Porsche reputation for reliability that was to

By 1955 there had been so many development changes to the original design that the type number was changed from 356 to 356A. A change in bore and stroke increased the engine capacity to 1582 cc and the gearbox and transmission had little in common with the original VW, although outwardly the casing was similar. Swing-axle rear suspension was still used, just as the Porsche-designed trailing-arm front suspension was still like that of the VW, but it was built to Porsche standards of strength and geometry. The basic shape of the coupé was only changed in detail, and such things as bumpers, lights, windscreen and rear window were improved slowly as the years went

> *' Porsche sales in the USA were very strong almost from the beginning... '*

by. The little coupé, or Beetle as it became known, was the mainstay of Porsche production and was the 'real Porsche' in many owners' eyes. Concurrent with the coupé a drophead version was offered and by the end of 1954 a third model arrived in the form of an open two-seater, not unlike the Gmund prototype. As it was 135 lb (61 kg) lighter than the coupé, the Speedster, as it was known, was very popular among the racing customers, but for normal motoring the coupé was still favoured. The drophead model, known in Germany as the Cabriolet, was fairly popular in Europe and America, especially in the sunny climes of Florida and California, and Porsche sales in the USA

were very strong almost from the beginning. The Cabriolet was also favoured by the German police for use on the autobahns, as there was not much about in the mid-'50;s that could get away from a 1600 Super Porsche.

In the racing world it was clear that the basic Volkswagen pushrod-overhead-valve layout could not compete forever, and a new engine was evolved by the Porsche design team, headed by Dr. Ernst Fuhrmann. The flat-four layout and air-cooling were retained but the valves were operated by overhead camshafts driven by shafts and bevel gears from the crankshaft. While the pushrod engines reached their limit at a

little over 6000 rpm the new engine was designed to run at 7000 rpm, with the possibility of going to 8000 rpm if necessary. This project was given the Porsche design number 547, these numbers stemming from Professor Porsche's first design in his own drawing office in 1930, which he gave the number 7 in case his first customer should realize that nothing had gone before! The numbers were given to all projects, be they engines or gearboxes, complete cars or even tractors! The new overhead-cam engine was destined for production but was first of all used in competitions in the special two-seater sports-racer Type 550, known as the Spider. After proving itself in strenuous

events like the Mille Miglia and at Le Mans the Spider sports/racer was put into limited production. Its first racing appearance, apart from brief excursions in practice, was in the 1954 Mille Miglia, and the following year saw a production line of something like 100 built. There was more to follow, for the overall size of the 547 engine was not much more than that of the pushrod 1600 cc engine, so it was only a matter of time before a 356A body/chassis unit received the four-cam engine. There was a lot of racing activity in Europe for GT cars, and the 356A 1500 cc four-cam was ideal. Naturally the first ones went to customers who intended to race or rally, but soon the 356A/1500GS was in full production and was given the name Carrera (the Spanish word for 'race'), after the Carrera Panamericana, the road-race that ran the length of Mexico. Porsche had taken part in that race until it was abandoned after the 1954 event, and named the new GT after it in memory of their successes. Carreras really caught on with the public and the term Porsche Carrera began to be used as a term for outstanding performance.

The advent of the Porsche Carrera

> *'... the Porsche Carrera changed the whole sporting scene...'*

changed the whole sporting scene, but the normal pushrod engine was still the mainstay of production. By the time the four-cam engine was in full production it had been enlarged to 1600 cc (the international capacity class limit) and the roller-bearing crankshaft had been replaced by a plain bearing

PREVIOUS PAGE *A 356C Cabriolet*
ABOVE AND LEFT *One of the earliest 356s, from 1949, distinguishable by its split windscreen and very low bumper line*
RIGHT *A modified 356 chased by a Ferrari 166MM at the concours historic races at Laguna Seca in 1984*
BELOW *A 1498 cc works 356 from 1953*

MODEL
Porsche 356C (1965)

ENGINE
Location: Rear, longitudinal
Type: Air-cooled flat-four with plain bearings. Cast-iron block and alloy cylinder heads
Cubic capacity: 1582 cc
Bore × stroke: 82.5 mm × 74 mm
Compression ratio: 8.5:1
Valve gear: Two valves per cylinder operated by pushrods and single central camshaft
Fuel supply: Two Zenith 32 ND1X carburettors
Ignition: Mechanical by coil and distributor
Maximum power: 75 bhp at 5200 rpm
Maximum torque: 90.4 lb ft at 4200 rpm

TRANSMISSION
Layout: Gearbox ahead of engine
Clutch: Single dry plate
Gearbox: Four-speed manual
1st 1.765:1	3rd 1.130:1
2nd 1.309:1	4th 0.815:1

Final drive: Spiral bevel
Ratio: 4.428:1

SUSPENSION
Front: Independent with trailing arms, transverse torsion bars, anti-roll bar and telescopic dampers
Rear: Independent with swinging half axles, swinging longitudinal trailing arms, transverse torsion bars, telescopic dampers and optional transverse leaf spring fixed to differential

STEERING
Type: Worm and roller

BRAKES
Type: Ate discs front and rear

WHEELS AND TYRES
Type: 5.60 × 15 steel sport wheels with 165/15 crossply tyres

BODY/CHASSIS
Type: Integral with steel two-door coupé body welded to steel floor pan

DIMENSIONS AND WEIGHT
Length: 157.9 in (4011 mm)
Width: 65.8 in (1671 mm)
Wheelbase: 82.7 in (2101 mm)
Track – front: 51.4 in (1305 mm)
     – rear: 50.1 in (1273 mm)
Weight: 2040 lb (925 kg)

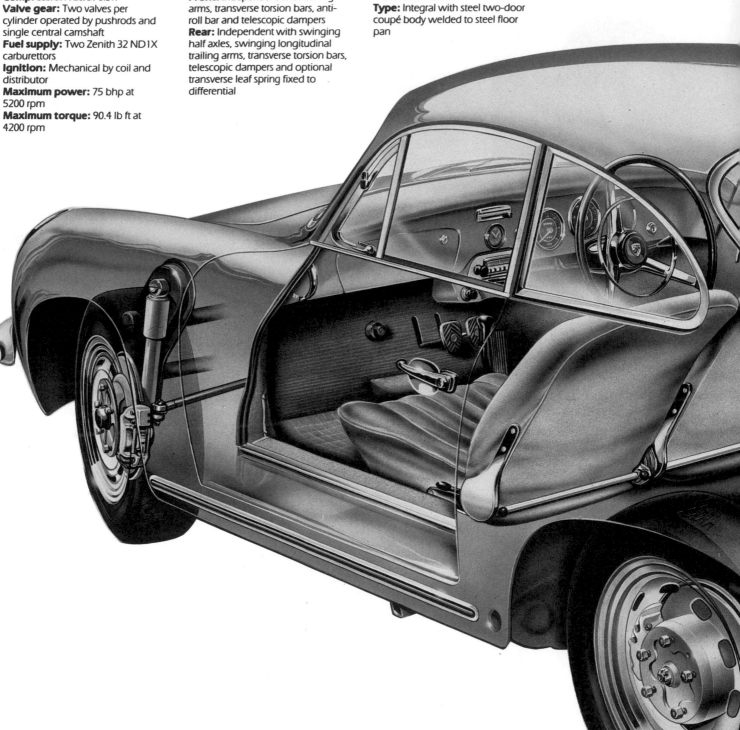

PERFORMANCE
Maximum speed: 106.6 mph
(172 kph)
Acceleration 0-60 mph: 13.5
seconds
Fuel consumption: 25.7 mpg

BELOW The layout of the last of the 356s, the 356C, still owed an obvious debt to the VW Beetle on which the original 356 was based. The 356 maintained the VW's torsion bar suspension front and rear along with a rear-mounted flat four engine

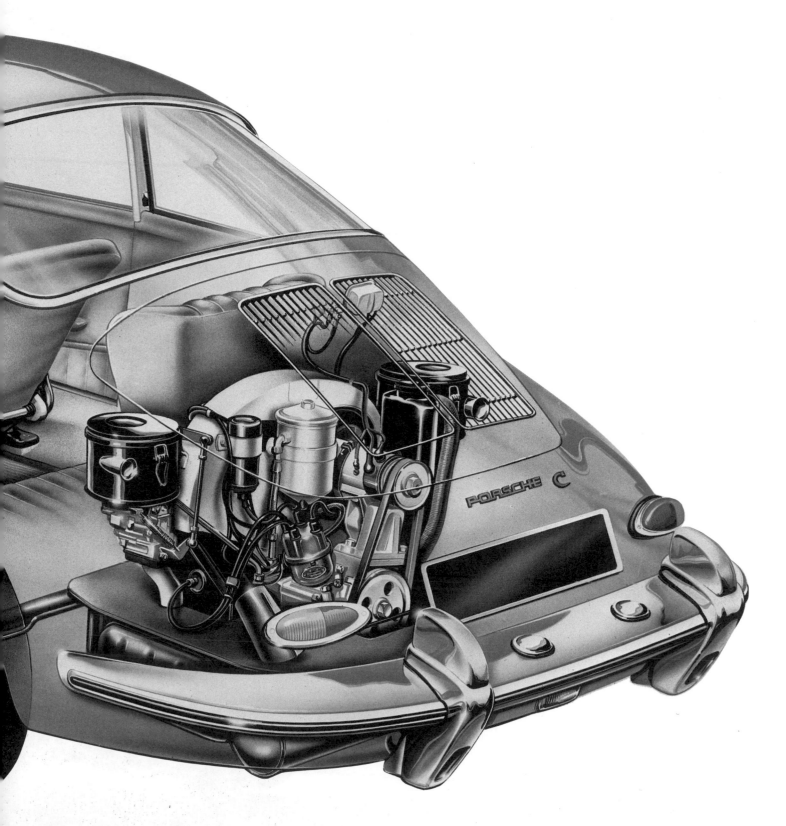

one. The compression ratio was lower on the production engine to make it more flexible and suitable for traffic, but even so it gave an easy 100 bhp at a time when the pushrod engines were giving 70 bhp. That meant that the Carrera buyers had a fully equipped fast-touring car that would do 125 mph (201 kph). From the early days the Porsche factory in Stuttgart-Zuffenhausen had been within sight of an autobahn, and naturally the cars were designed with high cruising speeds in mind. Even the simple *Damen* or standard 356 could be cruised flat-out, the gearing being such that it was

to 2 litres. The overall size of the car was still unchanged from the basic 356 coupé, and in the 2-litre form the Carrera was a landmark in the development of high-performance cars. In production form it was indistinguishable from a normal coupé, the only indication of its potential being the word 'Carrera' on the tail. The 2-litre version was known as the Carrera 2, but its production run was short as Porsche were planning bigger and better things in the shape of the new flat-six engine for the 911 series.

The development of the normal 356 series was continued right through until

ABOVE *The works Spyders of 1954-5*
ABOVE RIGHT *The functional cockpit of the 356 Speedster*
RIGHT *A 1959 356 Sprint. The flared rear wheel arches are a later addition, as are the slightly low profile tyres*
FAR RIGHT *A 356A Cabriolet. The 356As were built from 1955 to 1959*

impossible to over-rev the engine, even down an incline in top gear. The Carrera was geared in the same way in standard form, though naturally special gears were available for serious competition work. By 1959 the competition version of the Carrera could reach nearly 115 mph (185 kph), impressive performance for a 1600 cc coupé.

While all this high-performance activity was going on the normal customer was not forgotten, and the 1600 cc pushrod models were continually developed, improvements to body details eventually leading to the 356B model and later C and SC models. The horsepower of the production pushrod engine was increased steadily until 90 bhp was available, that model being known, reasonably enough, as the Super 90. Production figures had soared during the late 1950s and the personal touch at the factory inevitably suffered, but the idea of a Porsche family was still generated and extended by Porsche clubs forming all over the world.

With the success of the Carrera it was inevitable that Porsche would look for further fields to conquer in competition, and the first step was to enlarge the four-cam engine

1965 and the 356 could boast disc brakes by the time the factory stopped production and changed over to the 911.

The 356 was finally phased out in 1965, by which time 76,303 cars had been built,, not very many in Ford or Volkswagen terms but a very satisfactory number for a firm that had only started in 1948, making their first cars literally by hand. Production of the original 356 model, using Volkswagen components, had continued until 1955 with 7627 cars being built. Then came the 356A which was rapidly becoming much more of a Porsche; it was introduced in August 1955

and was in production for four years, during which time 21,045 cars were built. The 356B ran for the following four years and saw 30,963 cars built, and in 1963 the 356C saw the series through to the end with 16,668 cars built. Throughout its life the basic concept did not change. The cars were built on a steel platform chassis to which the coupé body was welded to become an integral monocoque, the various open versions being made from the same basic unit. The flat-four air-cooled engine was mounted behind the rear axle line while the gearbox was ahead of it. Front suspension was by

THIS PAGE & BELOW RIGHT *The last of the line in the form of a 356C Cabriolet. The 356Cs were built from 1963 to 1965* RIGHT *A true cutaway. This is a 356SC used as an exhibit at the motor shows of 1963, clearly revealing its VW Beetle origins*

origins of all of them can be traced back to the Berlin-Rome coupé of 1939.

It was the formative years of 1950 to 1960 that saw Ferry Porsche lead the firm towards the engineering giant it has become today. His father died in 1952 at the age of 77 years, his health having been weakened by the years of imprisonment, but he was able to appreciate that his son had inherited all his engineering talents and was well able to carry the family name towards greater things. Last year Ferry Porsche celebrated his 75th birthday, and though the Porsche empire is now run by new management and is partly publicly owned, Herr Porsche is still

> **' ...a tribute to the small band... who started making the cars in Gmund... '**

EVOLUTION

Prototype 356, an open two-seater sports, built in 1948

1949 The 356 was unveiled at the Geneva Motor Show, powered by an 1100 cc engine and capable of 84 mph (135 kph)

1950 Production commenced with the flat-four engine stretched to 1300 cc, producing 44 bhp and a top speed of 90 mph (145 kph)

1951 60 bhp 1488 cc engine introduced

1952 1500 Normal (N) introduced with plain rather than roller bearings. The 1500 Super (S) continued with roller bearings, producing 70 bhp. It was given larger brake drums and baulk-ring synchromesh to match the 105 mph (169 kph) performance

1954 356 Speedster introduced in 1300 and 1500 N and S form. Front anti-roll bar added

1955 Engine bored out to 1582 cc. 1600 N produced 60 bhp and 1600 S 75 bhp, giving a top speed of 100 mph (161 kph). 7627 cars were built before the 356A was introduced with revised body and chassis details including thicker torsion bars, more vertical dampers, thicker anti-roll bar and larger tyres. First 356 Carrera introduced with 1498 cc twin-cam engine and top speed of 125 mph (201 kph)

1957 Roller bearing crank discontinued

1958 Carreras given the 1600 engine. Speedster discontinued in favour of Convertible D. 21,045 356As were built in all

1959 365B introduced at the Frankfurt Show with raised bumpers and headlights, bigger rear seats and better brakes

1960 356 Super 90 introduced with the plain-bearing 1582 cc engine and transverse leaf spring attachment to improve rear suspension

1962 356 Carrera 2 introduced with 130 bhp engine, top speed of 125 mph (201 kph) and disc brakes all round. 30,963 356Bs were built.

1963 356C introduced in Coupé and Cabriolet form, both with the 1582 cc engine. 356SC introduced with 95 bhp.

1965 Porsche 356 range discontinued. 356C production totalled 16,668 and in total 76,303 356s were built

trailing arms with the transverse torsion bars which Professor Porsche had first designed for the Auto Union racing car, and rear suspension was by swing-axles also sprung on torsion bars. The 356 was essentially a two-seater sports car but two small 'jump seats' behind the driver and passenger gave the car a much wider appeal than a pure two-seater. The petrol tank, spare wheel and luggage space were located in the front, under the sloping nose, and because there was no radiator the penetration of the front of the car was excellent, as was forward visibility. Throughout its 14-year life the 356 was made in Coupé, Cabriolet, Speedster, Roadster and Convertible versions, but the

very much in the picture.

The 356 Porsche is now something of a collector's car and some really well-preserved examples are still in daily use in many parts of the world, while pampered and protected ones are preserved everywhere. The 356 is undoubtedly a classic but above all else it is a tribute to the small band of people who started making the cars in Gmund and had the courage and strength of purpose to return to Stuttgart and build the foundations of the present empire: solid foundations built on integrity and enthusiasm for the product, two aspects that are as strong today as they were in the beginning.   DSJ

It was a complete departure from traditional Porsche rear-engined practice and it took the 928 years to be accepted as one of the world's truly great supercars

TO STATE THAT the Porsche 928 has a Jekyll and Hyde character is to imply that one side of its nature is good and the other correspondingly bad…both are good; it's just that one side is docile, the other fierce in a manner unlike almost any other car.

Very few cars indeed can combine the gentle tractable nature of an expensive saloon and the sheer excitement of one of the world's ultimate GTs. Unfortunately for the 928's image far too few people have man-

aged to get past the first stage. Those with any sensibility drive a car slowly to begin with, especially an expensive car – do that with the 928 and it gives no hint of what's in store. Happy to trundle around as slow as you wish, it doesn't demand to be driven furiously like the Italian thoroughbreds.

That led one noted motoring writer to report, 'Nothing prepares you for the anticlimax of your first miles in a Porsche 928…' and the same man to conclude that it was a

'…strident, sometimes downright loud car for the person who will drive it firmly and with unfailing precision.' Granted, he was writing of the 928S but same was true of the first 928 of all which appeared at the 1977 Geneva Motor Show after five-years. of development.

Intended to replace the classic but elderly 911, it was as radically different as it was possible to imagine. Where the 911 sported a high revving, air-cooled flat-six in its tail

PORSCHE

the 928 was motivated by a relatively large and lazy water-cooled V8 at the front, with (shades of Detroit) hydraulic tappets. Where the 911 was light and nimble the 928 was wide and looked massively heavy.

Why so different? During the summer of 1970 Porsche had studied every possible combination of engine and transmission layout, the object being to have the handling of a mid-engined supercar without the drawback of awkward access and minimal cabin space. Coincidentally Alfa Romeo were doing the same thing and both came to the same conclusion – the engine should go in the conventional place, at the front, and the transmission in the rear to equalise weight distribution front to rear, albeit with the high-polar-moment-of-inertia approach which meant that theoretically neither the Alfa not the 928 would ever be as nimble as the best of mid-engined designs. They might both have quite neutral handling of course but nimbleness had been removed from the equation (see *Evolution of the Car*, Issue 51), at least in theory.

Perhaps both companies were overly concerned with appearances, after all other less prestigious companies managed to combine the boringly conventional approach of a front engine with the gearbox on the end of it with as near equal weight distribution as made no difference. It would be at the cost of having the transmission intrude somewhat into the cabin of course, but would otherwise seem to fit the bill as BMW, Aston Martin and others continue to demonstrate. For Porsche, however, there could be no compromise and the transmission had to go to the rear.

Water cooling was adopted for the engine as being intrinsically quieter than the exposed air-cooled engine could possibly be. The engine's displacement was larger than the flat-six too so that it could be made 'lazier', making it easier to meet increasingly stringent emission controls without being sapped of power. With the displacement envisaged the engine had to be bigger than a

928

BELOW *The latest in the line, the 1986 Porsche 928S Series 2*

MODEL
Porsche 928 S (1986)

UK price: £35,523

ENGINE
Location: Front, longitudinal
Type: Water-cooled, all alloy V8 with linerless cylinder bores and five main bearings
Cubic capacity: 4664 cc
Bore × stroke: 97 mm × 78.9 mm
Compression ratio: 10.4:1
Valve gear: Two valves per cylinder mounted in-line operated via hydraulic tappets by single belt-driven overhead cam per bank of cylinders
Fuel supply: Bosch LH Jetronic fuel injection
Ignition: Electronic
Maximum power: 310 bhp at 5900 rpm
Maximum torque: 295 lb ft at 4100 rpm

TRANSMISSION
Layout: Transmission in rear, with clutch in-unit with engine
Clutch: Single dry plate
Gearbox: Five speed manual or four-speed automatic

1st 3.765:1	4th 1.354:1
2nd 2.512:1	5th 1.00:1
3rd 1.790:1	

Final drive: Hypoid bevel
Ratio: 2.727:1

SUSPENSION
Front: Independent with wishbones, coil springs telescopic dampers and anti-roll bar
Rear: Independent with Weissach axle consisting of wishbones, semi-trailing arms, transverse torsion bars, coil springs and telescopic dampers

STEERING
Type: Rack and pinion. 3.13 turns lock to lock

BRAKES
Type: Discs front and rear. 11.1 in (28.2 cm) dia front, 11.38 in (28.9 cm) dia rear

WHEELS AND TYRES
Type: Alloy wheels with 7 in rims. 225/50VR16 tyres

BODY/CHASSIS
Type: Integral with two door 2+2 coupé body in steel and alloy

DIMENSIONS AND WEIGHT
Length: 175.2 in (445 cm)
Width: 72.44 in (184 cm)
Wheelbase: 98.43 in (250 cm)
Track – front: 60.98 in (155 cm)
– rear: 59.88 in (152 cm)
Weight: 3307 lb (1500 kg)

PERFORMANCE
Maximum speed: 158 mph (255 kph)
Acceleration 0–60 mph: 6.2 seconds
Fuel consumption (approx): 18 mpg

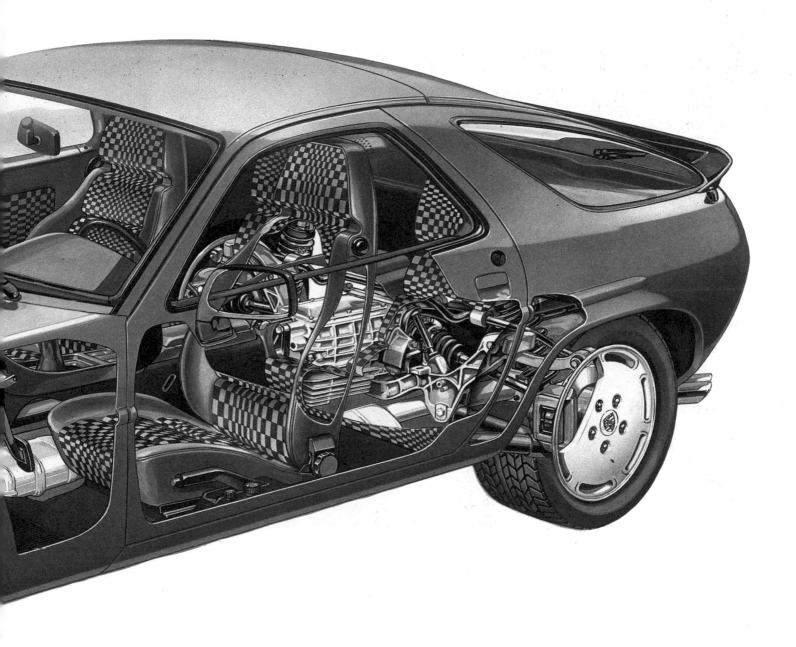

Locating the gearbox and final drive in-unit at the rear of the car allowed the V8 to be set well back in the engine compartment to give the ideal equal weight distribution. While the front suspension is thoroughly conventional with double wishbones (albeit massive ones) the rear suspension is the 928's most interesting technical feature with links so designed to decrease oversteer in high-speed corners by controlling the toe angle of the rear wheels

ABOVE *The smooth and totally uncluttered lines of the first 928*
LEFT *The V8 buried under the intake plenum displaced 4474 cc and produced 240 bhp at 5500 rpm with 250 lb ft of torque at 3600 rpm*
RIGHT *The interior was typical Porsche with an instrument panel which could be raised and lowered in-unit with the steering wheel*

six so a V8 it had to be. Hydraulic tappets or not, it was a world away from the typical American V8 with their cast-iron construction and single block-mounted camshaft. The Porsche engine had to be light and yet strong enough to withstand the extra power that future development would inevitably bring.

Porsche turned to American technology, to a process perfected by Reynolds Aluminium whereby the engine block was cast in extra-eutectic aluminium-silicon alloy. The idea was to eliminate the need for cast-iron cylinder liners (necessary in conjunction with alloy pistons) and that was achieved by acid etching the cylinder walls; the acid would eat away a layer of aluminium leaving the silicon standing proud which, in conjunction with the usual supply of engine oil, would provide the ideal surface for the pistons. The system had first been used in the totally unsuccessful engine of the Chevrolet Vega; the engine may have been a disaster but the linerless technique had proved itself.

Unfortunately as such an alloy is somewhat brittle Porsche could not permit themselves the luxury of a very deep one-piece casting which normally would give the block extra stiffness and instead had to split the crankcase along the line of the main bearing caps and have the bottom section cast in a more conventional alloy. The downfall of the Chevy Vega engine had been its very uneasy alliance of alloy block and iron head and Porsche's forced mixing of metals was a risk. In the event, however, it caused not the slightest problem.

The cylinder heads were more conventional alloy and in fact quite conventional in design. The two valves per cylinder were in line, operating in a pent-roof combustion chamber and operated by a single belt-driven overhead camshaft per cylinder bank, necessitating a quite extraordinarily long belt. Conservative or not, it certainly worked as a pre-production engine was fitted to a competition Porsche and happily revved to 8000 rpm, hydraulic tappets and all.

By 1975 Porsche had decided on the exact engine dimensions for the V8, opting for an oversquare configuration of a bore of 95 mm and a stroke of 78.9 mm to give a displacement of 4474 cc. The compression ratio was kept to a very conservative 8.5:1 (remember that some of the big American V8s used to run compression ratios over 10:1 when high octane petrol was readily available and emissions controls yet to be imposed) and Bosch K-Jetronic fuel injection was used. The combination produced 240 bhp at 5500 rpm along with 250 lb ft of torque at 3600 rpm. Obviously there was a lot of untapped potential; the original design envisaged four valves per cylinder and eventually turbocharging and even in 1986 the V8 has scope for more power.

Alfa Romeo opted to move even the clutch to the rear of the car in the Alfetta, saddling themselves with a heavy conventional propellor shaft always rotating at engine speed and increasing the inertia of the whole drivetrain to such an extent that Alfa's traditionally weak synchromesh had an almost impossible task. That was out of the question for Porsche – they were going to be feeding a far greater amount of torque through their drivetrain and decided that the only way was to retain the clutch (a two-plate affair) at the front with the engine and feed the drive to the transmission through a slim drive shaft running on bearings within a rigid torque tube connecting engine to transmission.

Despite the more elegant approach Porsche ran into similar vibration problems as Alfa Romeo with their propeller shaft and had to experiment with various numbers of bearings within the torque tube before settling on two, with a one-inch diameter shaft. Even that wasn't completely satisfactory and eventually Porsche resorted to a variation of an old American palliative, the 'tuned bumper'. That was simply a weight (the correct weight…) attached to the front bumper tuned to eliminate scuttle shake in open cars (a system used, incidentally, in the TR7 convertibles). Porsche used the battery as their weight or damper, mounting it at the rear of the gearbox, incidentally helping the weight distribution.

That went a long way to eliminating the remaining vibration and just left the problem of making the gear change to the rear mounted transmission as smooth as it should be in such an expensive car. That did come in for some criticism as *Autocar* for one noted, 'No amount of practice with the

ABOVE *The 928S could be distinguished by the discreet rear spoiler and the side rubbing strakes*

LEFT *The plan view of the 928 showing its width and bulbous rear*

ABOVE RIGHT *Snetterton circuit with Porsche's own 928S on its way to victory in the 1983 24 Hours*

Porsche gearbox enables one to make lightening changes across the gate, and particularly from first to second and from third to fourth is notably slow. But a less than completely perfect change was simply one of the prices to pay for the equal weight distribution, and one you didn't have to pay if you opted for the four-speed Mercedes automatic transmission rather than Porsche's own five-speed manual.

One of the drawbacks to the high-polar-moment approach is that when the (admittedly high) limits of cornering are reached and the rear starts to slide, to oversteer, it can be hard to stop. The last thing Porsche wanted was to perpetuate a reputation for evil oversteer with a brand new design and they applied an enormous amount of effort to devise an almost foolproof system. The end result was known as the Weissach axle (after the Porsche research centre) and was an intriguing assembly of wishbones, semi trailing arms and torsion bars.

It was so designed that in cornering the outer (loaded) rear wheel would toe-in safely, rather than toe-out to cause rear-wheel steering and oversteer as the car swung around. It is only the torque fed through the driven wheels which counteracts their natural tendency to be forced apart (to toe out) as the car moves forward. If the driver suddenly lifts his foot in a typical panic reaction on finding himself travelling too fast in a

> **'...no longer a car, it is a throne for the Gods...'**

bend, the rear wheel which is doing all the work suddenly loses that toeing-in torque, points outwards and oversteer sets in, usually quite sharply. It's an effect strengthened by the weight transfer to the front tyres when the driver comes off the power. Suddenly the front tyres have more grip, to turn-in more faithfully and the rear tyres loose a percentage of their grip just when they need it most. All of that Porsche hoped to eliminate and the trick to the Weissach axle was its slim transverse links connected to the forward mounting of each bottom arm and designed to pull the front of the wheel hub inwards under cornering force.

Of course such considerations were only necessary where the rear suspension was independent and there would of necessity be some compliance in the bushes holding the suspension arms to the body. In a live axle there would be no toe deflection – nor would there be with the de Dion system that Alfa adopted....

Thankfully the front suspension posed no such problems and a tried and tested system of double wishbones, coil springs, telescopic dampers and anti-roll bar was adopted very early on in the 928's development, along with the power assisted rack and pinion steering and the disc brakes front and rear. Somewhat surprisingly the rear brakes were not mounted in-board to save un-sprung weight but retained in the conventional position.

Weight saving was, however, a definite feature of the body and bonnet, door and the bolt-on front wings – all in alloy rather than steel (all of which saved just under 70 lb/ 31 kg). Nevertheless, despite alloy engine, alloy transaxle casing and some alloy body panels the original 928 was by no means a light car for a 2+2, weighing in at 3290 lb (1490 kg); that indicated just how massive was the unitary steel shell of the 928.

At first the omens for the 928 were good; reaction at the '77 Geneva Show was good (leading one overly nationalistic German weekly to claim that the 928 '...was no longer a car, it is a throne for the Gods...') and it was Car of the Year for 1978 but many people had reservations about the shape, and the performance. To some it looked too egg-like, too bland and soulless while not being fast enough to make such objections seem mere quibbling. What was really the point of the styling when the drag coefficient was a fairly ordinary 0.39 and the car slower in acceleration and top than all of the top of the line models from Ferrari, Lamborghini, Maserati, Aston Martin and Jaguar, not to mention Porsche's own Turbo?

> **'...top speed climbed to 156 mph and the 0-60 time dropped to 6.6...'**

Perhaps had Porsche not been so conservative to begin with the car's reputation now would be far higher. In truth the original 928 was nowhere near realising its true potential. When the English motoring press got their hands on the manual version for road test they found that it needed 7.5 seconds to reach the magic figure of 60 mph (the factory had originally claimed 6.8) and that the top speed was around 144 mph (232 kph) with the standing quarter mile taking just under 16 seconds. Fast yes, but not incredibly so.

What Porsche had built was a car with such high standards of roadholding and handling that the de tuned (and disappointingly mundane sounding) V8 almost spoilt

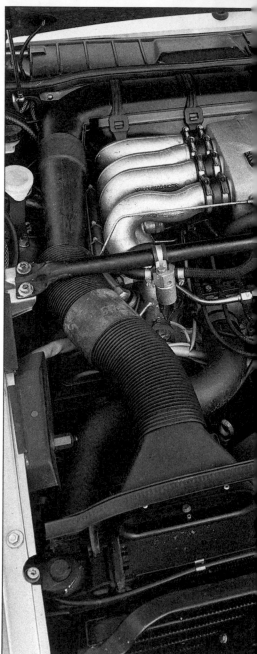

the fun and the clamour for more power soon began; Porsche's response came in 1979 with the 928S.

The engine was overbored slightly to increase the displacement from 4.5 to 4.7 litres and at the same time the compression ratio was increased to what one might expect, to 10:1. The result was a significant increase in power and torque. Power went up 60 bhp to 300 bhp at 5900 rpm and torque increased 24 lb ft to 2841 lb ft at 4500 rpm. Just as significant was the extra speed generated; top speed climbed to 156 mph (251 kph) and the 0–60 time dropped to 6.6 seconds.

The 928S was actually built alongside the ordinary 928 from 1979 to 1982 when the smaller engine was dropped. By 1983 the 928S Series 2 had appeared with another, albeit slight, increase in compression ratio (up to 10.4:1) and a switch to Bosch LH Jetronic injection. Once again power and torque increased, to 310 bhp at 5900 rpm and torque to 2951 lb ft at 4100 rpm.

The improved power to weight ratio (10.7 lb/hp or 4.8 kg/hp) helped drop the 0–60 time yet again, to 6.2 seconds and gained a fraction more top speed so that the 928S was nudging 160 mph (258 kph). The orginal 215/60VR15 tyres had given way to even more low-profile 225/50VR16 Pirelli P7s but

> *'… it was impossible to fault the suspension or anything else…'*

the press regarded the most significant change to the Series 2 928S to be the incorporation of anti-lock brakes – it wasn't that the original brakes were poor, far from it, but that the other prestige companies had them so why didn't Porsche? Of course, when they appeared in '83 they worked very well indeed; to begin with they were only standard equipment on UK cars but by 1985 Porsche decided that every 928 should have them.

Did Porsche's revisions eliminate all the 928's drawbacks and turn it into one of the world's greatest cars? The short answer is yes, particularly when some of those perceived drawbacks were simply a result of not fully understanding the car. The ride, for example was criticised, for in fact it was one of the things that led *CAR* to favour the Jaguar XJS over the 928 when it compared them in 1981. The combination of large low profile tyres (without much sidewall compliance)

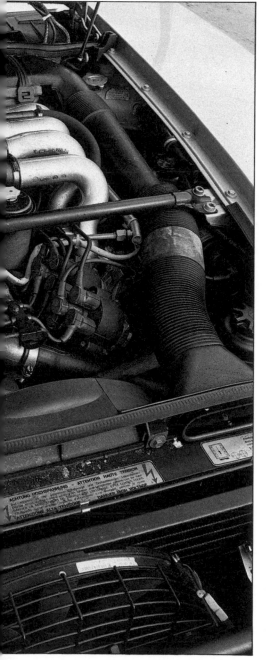

Views of the latest in the line, the 928S Series 2. By 1986 the engine displacement was 4664cc (the 4.5-litre 'ordinary' 928 having been discontinued in 1985) and power and torque had increased significantly by 70 bhp to 310 bhp at 5900 rpm and 295 lb ft at 4500 rpm thanks to a higher compression ratio and Bosch LH Jetronic fuel injection. The interior too shows some changes from the original car's shown on p 1773

and firm suspension inevitably means the ride will suffer but the carping over the 928's ride occurred because the Porsche's smooth (some would say bland) shell and unstressed engine led road testers, perhaps subconsciously, to expect soft coupé like comfort and silence rather than uncompromising efficiency. At low speeds the driver was conscious of some harshness (although certainly not to the same degree as in one of the big Astons or the latest in American V8s like the Z28 or Corvette) and that was at odds with the car's otherwise easy and flexible nature.

Once the driver began to use the performance, however, it was impossible to fault the suspension, or indeed anything else for that matter. The 928 would shrink to fit the driver; from feeling enveloped and slightly claustrophobic inside the bulbous egg-like body he would begin to feel in total command, as in tune with the car as one could be in a Frogeye Sprite. That sounds a ludicrous analogy – the 42 bhp Sprite and the 300 bhp Porsche but the 928 would generate the same sort of driver confidence that the little Austin Healeys were famous for.

The steering is precise, the car perfectly balanced and the information fed to the driver from the chassis completely reliable. *CAR* eventually realised the same thing. Observing that oversteer could really only be generated with too much right foot in slippery conditions they went on to note how '…the tail can be banged back into place with a flick of the wrists, much as you would shut a refrigerator door. In fact if you're determined to go off the road backwards in a 928 S2, the only realistic way is to arrive at your chosen corner about 40 mph too fast…'. Perhaps the 928 works too well; there is little challenge to driving the Porsche fast, it doesn't have to be treated with suspicion like a 911 or mastered like an Aston Martin Vantage it simply goes on responding faithfully to the driver's wishes. KB

ROLLS ROYCE
SILVER GHOST

In 1907 the Silver Ghost
began a journey that was to
establish Rolls-Royce as
builders of the undisputed
'best car in the world'

THE SOCIAL STANDING of Rolls, the engineering ability of Royce, and above all the commercial acumen of Johnson, had by 1905 made the Rolls-Royce company and its cars well enough respected. The 30 hp six-cylinder R-R was not as good as Johnson – a brilliant propagandist with a flair for telling lies in the most charming manner – maintained: like so many other early sixes, it suffered such severe torsional vibrations of the crankshaft that the miserable component too often broke. Something better was needed, and by 1907 it was ready – and so much better that it was kept in production, with periodic and rather reluctant changes, until 1925. Indeed it was so much better than anything else that it really earned its reputation of being the best car in the world. That accolade was originally bestowed by a journalist (not even Johnson would have had the nerve), and no other Rolls-Royce car ever deserved it. This one, the 40/50 horsepower model which later became known as the Silver Ghost, certainly did – at least until the advent of the new Hispano-Suiza in 1919. By that time, conditions were very different, and some of the factors influencing the original design were less important.

There was nothing superficially outstanding about the design; Royce deliberately avoided innovation whenever he could. What was outstanding was the attention to

‘ every highly stressed part was examined by magnifying glass ’

mechanical detail, the uncompromising search for constructional perfection. It was revealed in many beautiful felicities of design; it was backed by a quality control more stringent than any practised in the motor industry before or since.

The skills of the artisans at the factory could be taken for granted: Royce would summarily dismiss any worker seen mishandling a tool. That he understood tools and materials was beyond question: his designs proved it. For example, forgings were designed so that the grain flow of the finished machined piece should be most favourable. Thus a forging weighing 106 lb in its raw state ended up as a beautiful brake drum weighing 32 lb. Even more extreme was the connecting rod, finished at 2 lb from a raw forging weighing 8 lb, with only the perfect dense core remaining and the entire surface polished.

R-R claimed that every component of the car, if not machined, was filed and polished all over to find cracks or other flaws in the metal, and every highly stressed part was examined by magnifying glass to discover surface cracks. Flaw detection was in its infancy then, and in fact R-R were somewhat behind the times in their detection methods, as they still were 30 years later; but they were ahead of their time in the measures they took to prevent flaws.

ABOVE *The original Silver Ghost was actually the 13th car in the 40/50 series. Its name came from its silver paint finish and silver fittings and was soon adopted to refer to all 40/50s*
LEFT *Gear and brake levers were mounted outside, above the running-board*
BELOW *The 50 bhp 7-litre side-valve engine*

MODEL

Rolls-Royce Silver Ghost, 1907
UK price when announced: £985
(chassis only)

ENGINE

Location: Front, longitudinal
Type: Water cooled straight six, in
two groups of three cylinders
Cubic capacity: 7046 cc
Bore × stroke: 114 mm × 114 mm
Compression ratio: 3.2:1
Valve gear: One two-jet Royce
carburettor
Ignition: Coil and magneto, two
sparking plugs per cylinder
Maximum power: 50 bhp at
1500 rpm

TRANSMISSION

Layout: Clutch and gearbox in unit
with engine driving rear wheels
Clutch: Four speed manual with
reverse

1st 2.83:1	3rd 1:1
2nd 1.66:1	4th 0.8:1

Final drive: Spiral bevel drive
Ratio: 2.708:1

SUSPENSION

Front: Forged axle on semi-elliptic
leaf springs
Rear: Live axle supported on semi-
elliptic leaf springs and transverse
leaf spring

STEERING

Type: Worm and nut

BRAKES

Type: Rod-operated drums at rear

WHEELS AND TYRES

Type: Wooden spoked, with
875 mm × 105 mm tyres at the
front, 880 mm × 120 mm tyres at
the rear

BODY/CHASSIS

Type: Ladder type U-section steel
chassis with six cross members.
Special Roi-des Belges touring style
body built by Barker & Co.

DIMENSIONS AND WEIGHT

Length: 180 in (457 cm)
Width: 62.5 in (159 cm)
Wheelbase: 132.5 in (344 cm)
Track – front 56 in (142 cm)
    – rear 56 in (142 cm)
Weight: 3685 lb (1671 kg)

PERFORMANCE

Maximum speed: 55 mph
(88.5 kph)
Acceleration 0–60 mph: not
known
Fuel consumption: 20.8 mpg

The bare bones of the original Silver Ghost. The six-cylinder side-valve engine was made up of two, three-cylinder monobloc units. Note the rear suspension which featured a transverse leaf spring along with the more conventional longitudinal semi-elliptic leaf springs. The high armchair-style seats were the distinctive feature of Roi-des-Belges coachwork

Every hole, whether bored for clearance or for lightening, was carefully machined to a smooth finish lest any surface asperity act as a stress-raiser and start a fracture. The common practice of stamping the chassis number on one of the main frame members was shunned because the indentation might weaken the piece. Good stress distribution in the axle casing was sought by assembling it with a large number of small studs rather than a few big ones. Bolts had square heads above circular thrust faces, not the usual hexagonal heads; like their matching nuts, and everything else possible, they were made by Rolls-Royce themselves.

Royce was very distrustful of other people's methods. Every bolt-hole was checked for squareness with the abutment face, and all spring washers were tested and if necessary retempered; they were in any case only

perfection was sought. The quality would still be appreciated, as Royce remarked, long after the price had been forgotten.

The customer, who could certainly see the price, might not recognize such quality; but Royce appeased him with a superb and obviously durable finish. In particular, the nickel plating was unique in the motor industry, thanks to a Sheffield technique known as close plating: Royce despised the microscopically thin layer deposited by electroplating such as other firms used, instead employing craftsmen to cut to shape pure nickel sheet about 0.006 in (0.15 mm) thick and then soldering it onto the part to be plated. It kept its colour permanently, did not scrape off, and gave the impression that it would last forever.

Such standards were more necessary then than today. Most people were abysmally

ignorant about machinery. Reliability had to be faultless because competent diagnosis and repair of a fault was rare, and because the wealthy classes who bought such cars as these were intolerant of failure.

Because of these things, engine performance was best left mediocre; a good car had to be a gentle car. If it had any pretensions to performance, speed should be sought with a large engine rather than a notably efficient one. If it had any pretensions to elegance, it would probably have to carry a body

ABOVE *The year is 1907 and the event the 15,000 mile trial. The rest stop is the Cat and Fiddle – near Buxton – and the original Silver Ghost is the car on the left. After the trial only the minutest wear was found in a handful of parts*
BELOW *A 1912 Ghost, stately and solid*

> **'There were… seven main bearings for the crankshaft …a robust piece '**

used for locking external nuts, internal ones always being castellated and locked with cotter pins or by similarly positive methods. All rotating parts were balanced, not just the wheels, crankshaft and flywheel but also all gearwheels and even the bevel gears in the final drive. Copper pipes were brazed, not merely soldered. Rods and tubes in tension were always straight. Everything ferrous was steel except the cast iron cylinders, piston rings and handbrake linings; and the steel parts were always rolled or forged, except for four pieces which could only be cast. In every little detail, masked or manifest,

custom-built by craftsmen still relying on horse-carriage methods, with no understanding of the interaction of high speeds, bad roads, coarse springs and flexible chassis. The body would be excessively heavy, structurally precarious, aerodynamically indefensible, and likely to promote or aggravate instability of the vehicle. It would provide little or no insulation against noise or vibration from engine or chassis, and its adverse effects on the behaviour of the car would be identified by most customers as

BELOW *This Silver Ghost was built towards the end of Ghost production, in 1923. It was built by Rolls-Royce America Inc in Springfield, Massachusetts, with a body by Brewster. Although R-R America was shortlived, North American examples were often more elegant than the British*

the fault of the chassis manufacturer.

In this context the R-R 40/50 made very good sense. Its chassis was broadly similar to that of the earlier 30-hp car, but the engine which gave it its title was completely new. The 40 was in round figures the horsepower according to the RAC taxation rating, determined according to piston area and thus the product of six cylinders each of 4½ inches (11.4 cm) bore, disregarding with splendid theoretical assurance the stroke which was also 4½ inches. The 50 was in ever rounder terms the actual output of the engine in brake horsepower, the product of 7036 cc running at a compression ratio of 3.2:1 and a brake mean effective pressure under 70 psi.

Unlike the earlier six-cylinder R-R, the 40/50 engine appeared as a brace of threes in line, rather than as three twins. The two cast iron blocks had integral heads, and

were perched on a long aluminium-alloy crankcase within which the couples of two mirror-image threes were lost in mutual cancellation, only the extra long centre main bearing testifying to the uneven distribution of loads typical of the type. There were altogether seven main bearings for the crankshaft, itself a particularly robust piece of work by the standards of the time although it was devoid of balance weights; Royce, who farmed out most of his mathematical tasks, never mastered the intricacies of engine balance. The old 30 hp problems were attacked first by adopting the basic layout just described, and then by making the main journals and crankpins nearly twice as thick as before. This entailed something better than the rudimentary lubrication system previously used: oil was fed under pressure through the hollow crankshaft of

> **'It was in its ancillaries that the 40/50 displayed its class'**

the 40/50, as Royce had done in his abortive V8 engines a little earlier.

Another change was in the valve apparatus. Royce discarded his overhead inlets and pushrods, preferring side valves. When compression ratios were perforce so low, when cam profiles were necessarily gentle, and when cylinder head gaskets were so treacherous, such a layout was attractive. Without those pushrods it was also quieter, especially because there was provision (not always to be found in those days) for adjusting the tappets which, like the valve springs, were exposed along the left-hand side of the

engine. The timing drive to camshaft and ignition was by gears, for Royce was utterly opposed to the use of chains; and only the cooling fan remained to be driven by a link belt from a pulley on the crankshaft.

It was in its ancillaries that the 40/50 displayed its class. The electrical apparatus was of outstanding quality, recalling the origins of the company. The distributor, trembler coils and magneto were Royce's own, abetted by 4V accumulators serving the coils. Two spark plugs served each cylinder: the drill then was to start on the coils and thereafter (to avoid draining the accumulators) run on the magneto. When running slowly both were kept switched on, for magnetos performed poorly at low rpm. When it could be deferred no longer (that is, in 1919) Royce grudgingly gave the car a dynamo so as to maintain the stored charge for lighting and starting; with the normal coils which then supplanted the tremblers, running with both ignition systems switched on became the normal practice.

Control mechanisms were as refined as the electrics. The governor system was often criticized as being too fancy, but those who learned to use it appreciated that the complication and expense were justified by the pleasure and assurance it brought to driving. Very delicate and precise, the centrifugal governor was interlinked with the accelerator pedal so as to supplement it but be overridden by it; it was much more subtle than the simple constant-speed governor that some other engines borrowed from steam practice. It could control the tickover, or maintain a constant cruising speed regardless of gradient. Some drivers used it as an aid to achieving a smooth and silent gearchange without any need for skillful coordination of feet and hands; this trick was taught at the R-R drivers' school, to compensate for a rather difficult gearbox.

In fact the car was designed to be driven mostly in top gear, and in other respects was very forgiving of incompetence at the wheel, while rewarding skilled drivers with surprisingly high performance. It fared well in competitions such as the Alpine Trials, and in long-distance record-breaking over such routes as Monaco to London. First of all it distinguished itself in sundry officially-observed trials of roadworthiness, speed,

flexibility, reliability and economy, all organized for publicity by the ambitious Johnson. Thus is proved itself able to go from 3.5 to 53 mph (85 kph) in third (direct) gear, to 63 mph (101 kph) in overdrive fourth, and to average 17.8 mpg between London and Glasgow – repeating the trip until it had done 15,000 miles (24,150 km), when a complete strip-down revealed only the faintest wear in a handful of minor parts that could be replaced for £2 2s 7d.

The 4430 lb (2009 kg) car that did all this was the thirteenth chassis, fitted with a silver-painted touring body on which all appropriate metal fittings were silver-plated. On the scuttle gleamed a cast plate identifying this particular car as *Silver Ghost*; as it rapidly became famous, the car lent its name to the whole series, even the company eventually condescending to follow the public in adopting the model name. The fame was what mattered, and it was enough to encourage full production, four cars per week.

The rate was to grow, as was the fame. In the course of 18 years, R-R built 6173 examples, at an average of seven per week – including the war years, when the car did sterling service on the Western Front and quite amazing service (as armoured fighting vehicle, long-range reconnaissance intruder, staff car and dragoon-bearer) in the deserts of the Middle East. In all those years the design did not go unchanged, of course; the most notorious alteration was made within

The 1910 Silver Ghost on these two pages has Roi des Belges bodywork, a style named after the coachwork the King of Belgium had built for him on his Panhard by the Paris company Rothschild & Fils in 1901. Seat elevation intimated status

> **'The high altitude and the high bottom gear were…too much for it'**

two years of production beginning.

It seemed logical to Royce to substitute a three-speed gearbox with direct top for the previous four-speeder. People expected to drive everywhere in top gear, and were incapable of understanding that direct third was to be treated as top, and that an overdrive fourth was something different. That indirect ratio could not be as quiet as the direct top, but they could not understand that either. To keep them quiet, they were given a three-speed box with revised ratios, while the engine was enlarged to 7428 cc by adding a quarter of an inch to the stroke.

Everybody was happy until one of the cars competing in the Austrian Alpine Trial of 1912 failed to restart on a 1 in 4 gradient. The high altitude and the high bottom gear were together too much for it: two passengers had to get out. It was a disgrace (if only to a Rolls-Royce) and so in 1913 a normal four-speed gearbox was installed, first in the so-called Continental model and later in the standard chassis.

Four cars were entered in the 1913 Austrian Alpine event, redeeming the firm's reputation by making mincemeat of all opposition. They were not perfectly standard (neither, presumably, were many of their rivals), for they had aluminium alloy

pistons, and they were sprung at the rear by the cantilevered half-elliptics that had been introduced on the London-Edinburgh cars.

The London-Edinburgh stunt grew from a challenge by Napier to drive from London to Edinburgh in top gear, then return to Brooklands for a speed test, fuel consumption also being measured. A Rolls-Royce with tapered bonnet, raised compression and larger carburettor as well as the new rear springs did

---

> *That the Ghost did have rivals was by this time beyond question*

78.26 mph (125.9 kph) and 24.32 mpg, beating the Napier fair and square. It was then stripped and fitted with a higher axle ratio and a narrow single-seat racing body, in which it was timed at 101.8 mph (163.8 kph).

A few London-Edinburgh types were offered for sale, and it was from them that the Continental model was developed. This in turn became the standard model after the Great War ended in 1918. There was no time to prepare something new, least of all by the painstakingly slow R-R methods: people were avid for cars in the post-war euphoria, and would not wait. It was the same in the USA, where the firm was prompted to set up a satellite factory at Springfield: perversely the Americans wanted to buy the genuine English car, although the American one was made to the same standards and was often better bodied, but they managed to dispose of a further 1703 Ghosts, a respectable total when compared with the Derby figure quoted earlier.

By this time there had been some further changes. The adoption of relatively modern electrical gear – the dynamo, starter and revised ignition equipment – took place in 1919, rather a long time after most of the car's rivals had followed the example set in America by Cadillac. That the Ghost did have rivals was by this time beyond question, though Johnson always maintained the pretence that R-R were in a class of their own. He was always disappointed that he could never get the King to use one for personal travel, even though the Prince of Wales became an enthusiastic R-R owner. The King remained faithful to his silent sleeve-valve Daimlers (always extremely conservatively bodied, with the radiators painted instead of being plated), and many others thought that the Daimler offered superior ride comfort. Those who went abroad knew differently, however: on the roads of France, especially, the R-R was supreme (a result of extensive testing on that country's demanding highways) whereas the Daimler was grossly inferior. There were others to consider, too, but such debate should have ceased after the appearance of the Hispano-Suiza at the Paris Salon in 1919; Royce's limitations began to show more clearly.

There remained one more change, and this again was an example of R-R delaying

the adoption of something modern until they had been able to make sure that it worked really well. This was the change, in 1923, to four-wheel brakes, accompanied by a brake servo of Hispano-Suiza type for which the necessary energy was derived from a power take-off at the gearbox. That servo was to remain a feature of Rolls-Royce brakes for no less than 42 years!

The firm did not like innovation. They did not even like modification, though sometimes a customer would force them to do it, and sometimes one of their own mistakes would be discovered and start a conscientious panic to get it righted. As such times it was convenient that customers had grown used to the idea of the travelling inspectors who would call from time to time to see that the car was still healthy: it was easy for modifications to be made during such visits without the customer ever knowing – and much less embarrassing than a recall!

Keeping the design up to date was a different matter. R-R simply never managed it, and the Ghost gradually ceased to be

competitive. As it grew slower and heavier (as much the fault of the bodybuilders as of the unsympathetic customers) it was easier to dismiss. Finally came the inevitable day, in May 1925, when a successor was announced: the New Phantom was about the same size, but it had a long-stroke engine with overhead valves. It was faster and noisier, and it was much more popular among the Americans than the old side-valve car had been. It

---

> *…faster and noisier… it was much more popular among the Americans*

---

also gave the company an occasion on which to ratify the long-popular unofficial name for the old car: not until the New Phantom was on the market did Rolls-Royce themselves call the old model the Silver Ghost.

The old car sired a long line of distinguished successors, even though none of

them was ever the best car in the world, as the Silver Ghost had for a while been. What might have succeeded it was a different matter: had the little 20 hp car, which was added to the catalogue in 1922, enjoyed the twin-overhead-camshaft specification originally intended for it when the design was begun in 1919, R-R history might have taken a very different course. As it happens, an overhead-camshaft version of the Ghost engine did put the firm on a new course, during the Great War: by copying the layout of the 1914 GP Mercedes cylinder head and the details of its single-camshaft valve gear, and superimposing this on the lower half of the Ghost engine, Royce made his first aero-engine (later to be very effective in the naval blimps used for submarine-hunting) and – very much against his will – started the firm on a new career in aviation. If it was any consolation, Rolls (killed in a flying accident at Bournemouth in 1910, a month after becoming the first Englishman to fly the Channel) would almost certainly have approved. LJKS

The Silver Ghost series lasted a long time, perhaps too long. By 1925 when it was replaced by the New Phantom, other manufacturers had improved on the 40/50 design. Nevertheless this 1921 Torpedo Tourer by Barker is a splendid device

PC 5553

Rolls-Royce

When dated design urged a successor to the Silver Cloud, the revolutionary Silver Shadow was born, embodying striking innovations; twenty years on, the Shadow theme continues...

BY THE EARLY 1960s, demand for the traditional Rolls-Royce Silver Cloud declined as new cars appeared from Mercedes, Jaguar and Daimler which offered better performance, handling and ride comfort at lower prices.

The slide was slowed, but not halted with the 1959 introduction of the all-alloy V8 engine (which in true Rolls-Royce tradition, had been in active development since 1953) which at least brought the performance more nearly up to scratch, but it was obvious that the only answer was a completely new car. In fact such a car had been in its later stages of development under the code-name Project Burma ever since 1958, but it was only at the 1965 Motor Show that the public realised how revolutionary a design it was, by Rolls-Royce standards.

The new car, the Silver Shadow, was a complete break with so many Rolls-Royce traditions. Here at a stroke the separate chassis, live rear axle and massive drum brakes gave way to a unitary body, all-independent suspension with hydraulic ride height control, and disc brakes all round with high-pressure hydraulic operation reminiscent of Citroën's.

The Shadow got off to a bad start in some ways. It was not only that the name was chosen at the last moment to replace the intended Silver Mist (when somebody pointed out late in the day that Mist is German for manure, or worse...). Despite the 1965 launch, cars were not available for sale in any quantity until mid-1966, leading to accusations of premature announcement

and to the inevitable lunatic black market in 'low mileage used' cars.

Worse still, when the fuss caused by its 'advanced' engineering had died down, some question arose as to what had actually been gained. For one thing, the Silver Shadow offered no significant performance advantage over the V8-engined Silver Cloud 3; in fact the original *Autocar* Shadow road test of 1967 showed the test car to be just 1 mph slower in maximum speed (115 instead of 116 mph) and 0.1 sec slower to 60 mph (10.9 instead of 10.8 sec) than its predecessor. It was also, oddly enough, 0.1 mpg less economical (12.2 instead of 12.3 mpg). Worse still, it emerged that while the Shadow was generally considered to look more 'ordinary' and less impressive than the Cloud – which had been three inches longer in its wheelbase, and nine inches longer overall – it was just as heavy! And to crown it all, a picture soon emerged of a soft and soggy suspension, massively understeering handling and under-geared, feel-less steering. In developing the Silver Shadow, it was said in some quarters, Rolls-Royce engineers led by Harry Grylls had their eyes far too firmly fixed on the other side of the Atlantic.

It was also true that however much Rolls-Royce had moved into line with general motor industry engineering in some respects, in others the Silver Shadow (and the inevitable Bentley T-series stablemate) remained old-fashioned. By 1965, after all, radial-ply tyres had become commonplace on high-performance cars but the Shadow

SILVER
SHADOW
& SPIRIT

MODEL
Rolls-Royce Silver Shadow (1966)

UK price when introduced:
£6669 19s

ENGINE
Location: Front, longitudinal
Type: All-alloy V8 with wet liners.
Five main bearings
Cubic capacity: 6230 cc
Bore × stroke: 104.1 mm ×
91.4 mm
Compression ratio: 9.0:1
Valve gear: Two valves per
cylinder operated via pushrods,
rockers and hydraulic tappets by
single camshaft mounted in centre
of vee
Fuel supply: Twin SU HD8
carburettors with twin electric fuel
pumps
Ignition: Mechanical by coil and
distributor
Maximum power: Approximately
200 bhp

TRANSMISSION
Layout: Transmission in unit with
engine, driving rear wheels
Gearbox: Four-speed Hydramatic
automatic
   1st 3.820:1   3rd 1.450:1
   2nd 2.630:1   4th 1.000:1
Final drive: Hypoid bevel
Ratio: 3.080:1

SUSPENSION
Front: Independent with
wishbones coil springs telescopic
dampers and automatic self
levelling
Rear: Independent with semi-
trailing arms, coil springs telescopic
dampers and automatic self
levelling

STEERING
Type: Recirculating ball. 3.5 turns
lock to lock

BRAKES
Type: Discs all round, 11 in
(27.9 cm) diameter with twin
calipers, three independent circuits
and servo

WHEELS AND TYRES
Type: Steel wheels 8J × 15 in with
8.45 × 15 in crossply tyres

BODY/CHASSIS
Type: Integral steel monocoque
with subframes front and rear. Four-
door, five seat saloon body

DIMENSIONS AND WEIGHT
Length: 203.5 in (5169 mm)
Width: 72 in (1829 mm)
Wheelbase: 119.5 in (3035 mm)
Track – front: 57.5 in (1460 mm)
      – rear: 57.5 in (1460 mm)
Weight: 4556 lb (2067 kg)

PERFORMANCE
Maximum speed: 120 mph
(193 kph)
Acceleration 0–60 mph:
10.9 seconds
Fuel consumption: 15 mpg

This superb cutaway of the exclusive Rolls-Royce Silver Shadow shows all the car's major components. The body/chassis is an integral unit, but the engine and suspension are mounted on separate front and rear subframes. By fixing these frames to the body via specially designed resilient mountings, the transmission of noise to the car's interior can be cut to a minimum. A unitary construction body/chassis unit tends to be much stiffer than one comprising a body bolted to a separate chassis. The Silver Shadow's engine is a 6750 cc V8, which produces 'adequate' power. The company will not disclose how much power, but this series I Shadow's two tons can hurtle along at a speed of 120 mph and can accelerate to 60 mph in little more than ten seconds.

was shod with 6.45–15 crossplies. Automatic transmissions had moved almost entirely away from the fluid flywheel to the torque converter, but the Shadow retained – in right-hand-drive form at least – the 1940s four-speed Hydramatic, a GM transmission built under licence at Crewe.

Within a few years, the car which had suffered such a doubtful start enabled Rolls-Royce's car division to turn in its first genuine profit. It went on to become the most prolific Rolls-Royce of all time, since some 35,000 Shadows were built in all compared with 28,000 Rolls-Royces of all types built up to 1939: In other words, there was more to the Silver Shadow than first met the eye.

> *... boost the production rate to over 3000 cars a year – a figure unheard of...*

What people failed to realise was that the purpose of the Silver Shadow was not only to replace the Silver Cloud with something more acceptably modern-looking, but also to reduce production costs and increase volume. The switch from chassis-plus-body construction to unitary may not, in the event, have saved the weight many were hoping for but it was a cheaper form of construction. With complete shells emerging from Pressed Steel Fisher's plant at Cowley at whatever rate (within limits) was needed, the Rolls-Royce factory at Crewe could be reorganised to boost the production rate to over 3000 cars a year – a figure unheard of earlier.

Of course, it was no good building that many Shadows if they could not be sold. That was, in a sense, why the car was so disappointing in many European eyes: Rolls-Royce *had* been looking across the Atlantic, and proceeded to ship off cars at a considerable rate to a market whose standards and demands had been carefully observed and catered for.

The Silver Shadow was virtually all-new, since although the engine and transmission

LEFT *is a Rolls-Royce Corniche convertible while* **BOTTOM LEFT** *is a stately 1976 Silver Shadow, retrospectively known as Series I* **ABOVE** *The 1978 Bentley T2* **BELOW** *A 75-year anniversary model of the Series II Rolls-Royce Silver Shadow*

were carried across from the Cloud they were substantially changed on the way. The engine retained the Cloud dimensions of 104.1 mm bore, 91.4 mm stroke for a capacity of 6230 cc but its cylinder head layout was completely changed to make servicing – and in particular, access to the sparking plugs – much easier. The two big SU carburettors were retained. As for the Hydramatic transmission, the original cast-iron casing gave way to aluminium and the mechanical selector gave way to an electrically-operated system.

Rolls-Royce had already adopted the tradition of not quoting outputs for their engines, claiming simply that the power was 'sufficient'. There is however general agreement that the V8 produced no more than 200 bhp, making it very lightly stressed and therefore quiet and reliable if not efficient in any overall sense. Where the transmission was concerned, the company knew its precious American market was unlikely to accept a 20-year-old unit at all gratefully, and

a deal was struck with General Motors to supply the excellent GM400 three-speed torque converter unit directly from Detroit for fitment to all left-hand-drive Shadows from the outset. Crewe's involvement was limited to converting the transmission from mechanical to electric selection. So successful was the GM400 that by 1968 Crewe had ceased production of the Hydramatic and the Detroit-built transmission became standard on all Shadows. It remains the standard Rolls-Royce transmission to this day.

The car's unitary construction had been adopted for the sake of cheaper and quicker production despite fears about vibration and noise levels which are more easily filtered out if an unstressed body sits on a separate chassis (it is worth noting that the Cadillacs of the day were being built with perimeter-frame chassis). The Rolls-Royce answer was to fit the Shadow with front and rear sub-

> *... what was original was the provision of automatic ride height control...*

frames, the first carrying the engine and front suspension, the latter the final drive and rear suspension. Filtering was then achieved by attaching the frames to the body by specially developed pads of stainless steel mesh, unkindly likened to Brillo pads by some observers. This technique worked well enough but it was far from being a good engineering solution. Certainly it failed to provide enough sound insulation to allow radial-ply tyres to be fitted; it would also have allowed the frames to move relative to the body had they not been located by their own little Panhard rods.

The all-independent suspension was hardly original in concept since it used double wishbones at the front and semi-trailing arms at the rear, with coil springs all round. What *was* original was the provision of automatic ride height control, using a high-pressure hydraulic ram sitting above each damper. This was not an active system of the Citroën variety – no hydropneumatic

EVOLUTION

The Silver Shadow was introduced at the 1965 Motor Show at Earls Court and pioneered unitary construction for Rolls-Royce

1966 The Shadow entered production

1967 The Silver Shadow Convertible introduced

1968 The GM400 three-speed automatic transmission replaced the old Hydramatic on UK cars – it had been standard equipment on US spec cars from '66. Revisions were made to the suspension to improve handling. The front anti-roll bar was stiffened and a rear bar added

1969 Higher ratio steering was introduced and the long-wheelbase version was introduced

1970 The V8's stroke was lengthened to 99.1 mm to give a displacement of 6750 cc and 10 per cent more torque

1971 The Corniche convertible was introduced

1972 The front suspension was redesigned with more compliance, allowing radial tyres to be fitted for the first time. The front track was increased and the front discs ventilated

1975 The very expensive coachbuilt, and Pininfarina-styled Camargue was introduced

1977 Sufficient changes were made to rename the Shadow the Shadow II. Rack and pinion steering replaced the recirculating ball system, the aerodynamics were revised, as was the front suspension and interior

1980 The Shadow was replaced by the Silver Spirit in short and long-wheelbase versions. The Bentley version was introduced as the Mulsanne

1982 The Bentley Mulsanne Turbo was introduced

1984 The Bentley 8 was introduced with a slightly low level of equipment such as the low profile tyres and alloy wheels of the Turbo but with the stiffer suspension

1985 The Mulsanne Turbo was replaced by the Turbo R which featured even stiffer suspension and greater feel to the steering. Late in '85, Avon tyres replaced the Pirelli P7s which became an option

1986 The Rolls-Royce Camargue was discontinued

by Rolls-Royce standards but the engineering decision was forced by the sheer size of the drums which had become necessary to stop cars of such weight and performance: the Silver Cloud's drums were 11.25 in (28.5 cm) in diameter and 3 ins (7.6 cm) wide. What was more adventurous was the adoption of high-pressure hydraulic operation, much more in line with Citroen practice, using a 2500 psi pumped supply and an accumulator to store energy.

Although the Shadow started to sell well, there is no doubt that Rolls-Royce's feelings were rather hurt by the criticism levelled at the car by the more enthusiastic European drivers. To some extent the company had not reckoned with the emergence of this kind of driver but was more attuned to the age of the chauffeur; the early Shadows felt much better when one was sitting in the back than they did from the driving seat. Gingerly, therefore, the developers sought to overcome some of the car's drawbacks without risking noise problems or 'spoiling' it in American eyes.

There were four main objections to the steering and handling of the early Shadow. First, the car was very soft in roll especially at the front. Second, it understeered to excess. Third, its steering was too low-geared (originally there were 4¼ turns of the wheel between extremes of a far from impressive lock). Fourth, there was almost no steering 'feel'.

There had been a front anti-roll bar from the beginning, so the first corrective move

---

> *'...a rear anti-roll bar was also fitted... improving roll stiffness...'*

---

was to stiffen it. By itself, however, this tended to increase the understeer still further, so a rear anti-roll bar was also fitted with the advantage of improving roll stiffness still further as well as balancing the handling. These changes were made (but not to American-market cars!) in 1968. Rather later, the steering ratio was reduced in two stages to a more reasonable 3½ turns between locks, but the only gesture towards improved steering feel (for a long time, at least) was the fitting of a smaller steering wheel in European-market cars. One measure which could still not be contemplated was the fitting of radial-ply tyres even though they would have cured many of the handling problems.

Other parallel changes to the car were being made all the time, including the fitting of a viscous-coupled fan, the substitution of an alternator for the generator, and the

standardisation of the previously optional air conditioning – all improvements which came in during the last two years of the 1960s. A bigger change, in every sense of the word, was the 1969 creation of the long-wheelbase version by letting 4 ins (10 cm) into the floorpan and lengthening the rear doors and roof to match.

By the late 1960s it was evident that huge engineering effort would have to be devoted to safety and exhaust emissions work if Rolls-Royce was to stay in its precious American market without which survival was not really possible. One of the problems caused by anti-emission measures was loss of power, with which the Shadow was not over-endowed anyway. The solution was typical of the Rolls-Royce approach. Instead of tuning the engine, they lengthened its stroke to 99.1 mm for a capacity of 6750 cc, for fitting to all Shadows from 1970 onwards. Almost as typically, that increase was devoted more to higher torque output than to extra power. The *Autocar* test of a 1972 Shadow with the bigger engine and GM400 transmission showed it to be only 2 mph faster than the original, but over half a second quicker to 60 mph. The fuel consumption remained stuck at 12.4 mpg.

The early 1970s were a traumatic period

springs or front-to-rear linking – but worked slowly when the car was on the move to compensate for any trim change caused by emptying of the fuel tank, and more quickly at a standstill to adjust against the entry of passengers and the loading of luggage. Eventually it was realised that the front units achieved little beyond extra complication since the rear rams could always level the car on their own, and in 1969 they were deleted.

The disc brakes really were an innovation

*Compare the lines of the Corniche convertible, **ABOVE RIGHT**, and the stunning Pininfarina-styled Camargue of 1983, **RIGHT**. Both vehicles use the same Silver Shadow chassis and floorpan and offer much the same performance*

for Rolls-Royce not only because of the American regulations but also because in 1971 the Aero Engine division overstepped the mark with its RB211 turbofan and brought the whole company to bankruptcy. By this time the Car Division was making a healthy profit and was thus in a position to be sold off when the Derby-based aero engine facility was nationalised, but the confusion and uncertainty led to delays in a number of planned improvements. By 1972, however, a new front suspension layout was fitted which took advantage of the then-new art of 'compliance' – the technique of allowing a suspension to deform in some directions, to absorb shock and vibration, while keeping it stiff in others to retain accurate handling and good stability. By redesigning the Shadow front suspension along these lines, Rolls-Royce at last found the way to fit radial-ply tyres – 205VR15s to begin with, 235/70-15s by the mid-1970s – without suffering a noise and vibration penalty. At the same time the front track was widened and the front brake discs were ventilated; the Shadow had taken a large stride down the road towards the best European standards of handling.

One of the biggest problems raised by the switch from separate chassis to unitary construction for the Shadow was the future of Rolls-Royce's traditional coachbuilding operations. Although the post-war British coachbuilding trade was a pale shadow of its former self in the 1930s when every Rolls-

> *'...In its new guise the indisputably handsome car began to sell better...'*

Royce had some kind of bespoke body on a Derby-supplied chassis, two companies (James Young and Mulliner Park Ward) had continued to build special versions including the Bentley Continental. Sadly, James Young was not well equipped to face the change to the more complicated production techniques needed to build 'special' bodies unitary-fashion on Shadow floorpans and scuttles supplied by Pressed Steel Fisher, and that left Mulliner Park Ward alone in the business.

Very early in the life of the Shadow, MPW created a two-door saloon version, following up a year later in 1967 with a matching Convertible. Production of these models ran to a few hundred a year until in 1971 when a small stroke of marketing genius increased their appeal. A discreet collection of restyling measures, plus some mild engine tuning (Rolls-Royce admitted to a 10% gain without disclosing actual figures) was allied with a new name: Corniche. In its new guise the indisputably handsome car began to sell better. It continued to parallel the mechanical developments of the standard Shadow and indeed often led the way as with the introduction of ventilated front disc brakes. Eventually it became clear that the Corniche

Convertible was becoming relatively more popular than the Coupé, and in 1980 the latter was dropped to leave the Convertible alone in production.

A less successful venture was the Camargue, styled by Pininfarina again on a standard Shadow floor pan, built originally by MPW alongside the Corniche and later at Crewe from panels supplied by Motor Panels of Coventry and launched in 1975 as 'the ultimate owner-driver's car'. In the event, the next ten years turned up no more than 500-odd ultimate owner-drivers. Part of the problem no doubt was the sheer price of the Camargue, plus the fact that it offered nothing significant in the way of a performance margin over the Corniche. In a sense it was put under further pressure in 1984

> *'...rack and pinion steering which gave better response and improved feel...'*

when the Bentley-badged Corniche became the new Continental, and early in 1986 Rolls-Royce announced that the Camargue had been withdrawn, leaving the other coachbuilt models to continue.

In 1977 Rolls-Royce announced the Silver Shadow II with changes which further improved the car's road behaviour. The main change was a switch from recirculating-ball to rack-and-pinion steering which gave better response and improved feel. Stability was also improved through revision of the front suspension and some subtle aerodynamic tweaking of the body shape. Inside, the panel and control layout was completely revised and made more logical, while the Shadow II also received as standard the comprehensive split-level air conditioning system first seen in the Camargue and later put into the Corniche. With these changes, the Shadow matured into a model which managed to please all but the most demanding European drivers without offending the most sybaritic American ones: and it ran for a further three years before being replaced.

The replacement took the form of the Silver Spirit which at first glance was little more than a rebodied Shadow II. There was more to it than that, however, because the engineering improvements were there too, especially in the rear suspension, even if they were too subtle to be obvious. The Spirit brought with it a longer-wheelbase Silver Spur (replacing the Silver Wraith as the LWB Shadow had latterly been christened). More significantly the range included new Bentley models of genuinely different character, a refreshing change after so many years in which the Bentley T had been nothing more than a rebadged and socially slightly inferior Shadow. The differences became even more interesting when the new Bentley Mulsanne gained massive extra power and performance with the aid of a twin-turbo installation on the V8. Today, interestingly, there are five listed Bentley

models from the 'budget priced' Eight through the Turbo R to the Continental, while the effective Rolls-Royce range has shrunk to three with the deletion of the Camargue. Certainly there is an air of balance between Rolls-Royce and Bentley today which has not existed for years – and it has been achieved despite the fact that all the models are based on that same floorpan which in its earliest form underpinned the original Silver Shadow of 1965.   JD

The Bentley Mulsanne Turbo, RIGHT, is as fast as it is handsome, thanks to a twin-turbocharged version of the revered V8 engine. The Turbo is a far cry from the original Shadow of 1966 with its 'adequate' performance and soft handling, for it also has greatly stiffened suspension and alloy wheels with low-profile tyres

TRIUMPH TR 2/3

They were the models which established the TR line and proved that the company could make high-performance cars

SOME CARS ARE LUCKY, and some are not. Some succeed after a rather rocky start and others fail. The Triumph TR series undoubtedly ralls into the first category, for its launch could not have been less favourable. Yet for nine years the same well-known range of sports cars sold strongly – more than 80,000 were built – and the car put the Triumph name firmly back on the motoring map.

It all started in the early 1950s, when Standard-Triumph's chairman, Sir John Black, was inspired to produce a sports car for export. Standard had bought the corporate remains of the bankrupt and bombed-out Triumph company in 1944, and in the first few post-war years had offered several undistinguished Triumphs such as the 1800/2000 Roadster, the Renown saloon and the quaint little Mayflower.

In the meantime, MG produced the TC and TD sports cars, and Jaguar produced the famous XK120. Both took the United States by storm, and consequently Sir John Black took the attitude that if they could succeed in the States, so could he – and that was the way it looked to his colleagues.

It couldn't be done overnight, however. First Sir John encouraged his chief styling engineer, Walter Belgrove, to produce a new Roadster (the TRX) on a Standard Vanguard chassis, but it had a bulbous shape, too many complicated electro-hydraulic controls and never got beyond the prototype stage. Next, Sir John tried to take over the Morgan company, but after being rebuffed at the end of 1951, he decided to have another attempt 'in house'.

Thus the real TR story began early in 1952, on a minimum-cost/minimum tooling basis. The engineers and chief designer Harry Webster were encouraged to use as many existing Standard components as possible, while Walter Belgrove was offered a mere £16,000 budget for body tooling, a ludicrously low figure even in 1952. The result was that the design used an obsolete

RIGHT *The interior of a 1960 Triumph TR3A, a model first introduced in 1958. It had a wide grille and front disc brakes*

BELOW There was nothing in the least pretentious about the TR3. Its simple chassis owed its robustness and rigidity solely to its bulk, the live rear axle was located only by its semi-elliptic leaf springs and the damping was by old-fashioned lever arm units. At least the front suspension, with its double wishbones, coil springs and telescopic dampers was more modern — there were even disc brakes at the front. Triumph had not aimed for sophistication, however, and the engine was a development of a rugged Standard unit as tough as the chassis. The result was a fast and cheap sports car, albeit one that demanded a certain respect from its driver

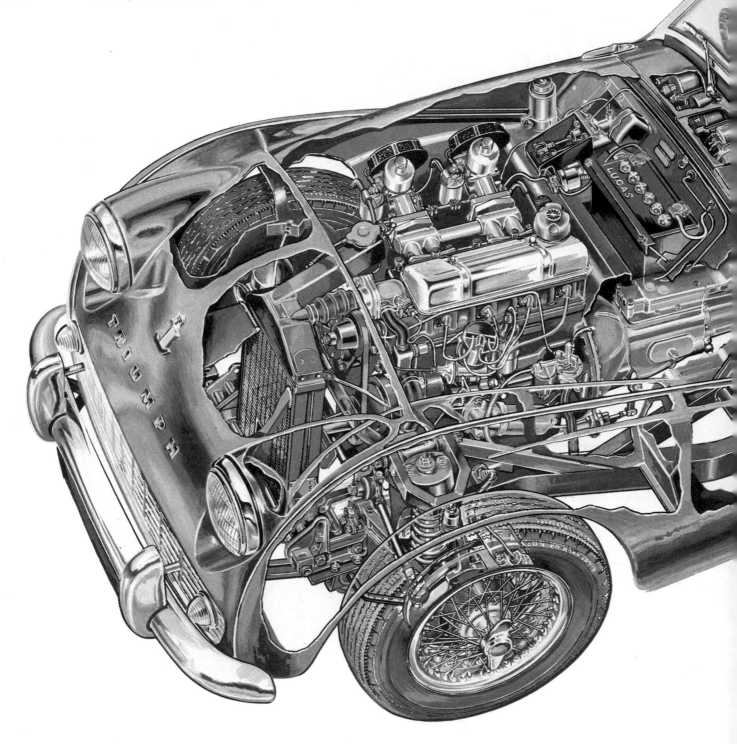

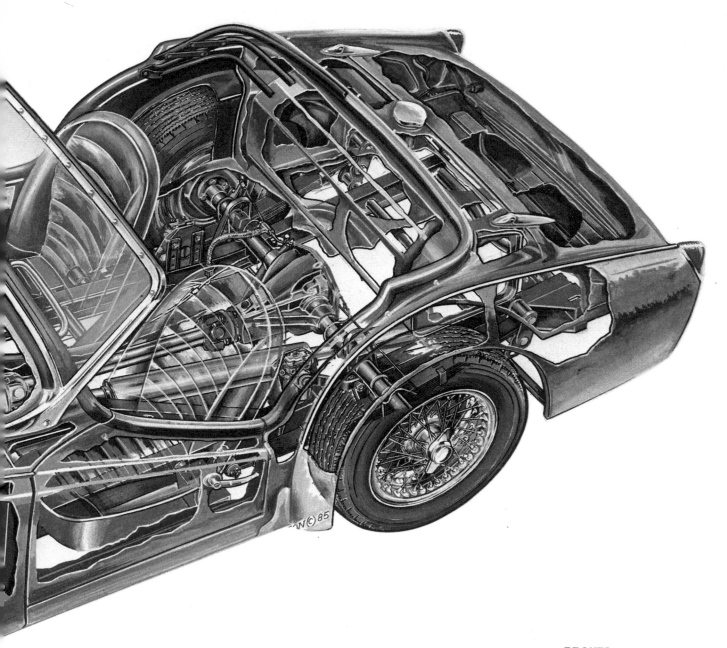

MODEL
Triumph TR3 (1957)
UK price when announced:
£1137 12s (inc. tax)

ENGINE
Location: Front, longitudinal
Type: Water-cooled in-line four
with cast-iron block and head
Cubic capacity: 1991 cc
Bore × stroke: 83 mm × 92 mm
Compression ratio: 8.5:1
Valve gear: Two valves per
cylinder operated by single block-
mounted camshaft, pushrods and
rockers
Fuel supply: Two inclined SU H6
carburettors
Ignition: Coil and distributor,
mechanical
Maximum power: 100 bhp at
5000 rpm
Maximum torque: 117 ft lb at
3000 rpm

TRANSMISSION
Layout: Clutch and gearbox in unit
with engine, driving rear wheels
Clutch: Single dry plate, 9 in (23 cm)
diameter
Gearbox: Four-speed manual
gearbox with synchromesh and
overdrive (ratios in brackets) on
upper three gears

1st 3.38:1	3rd 1.32:1
2nd 2.00:1	(1.08:1)
(1.64:1)	4th 3.70:1
	(0.82:1)

Final drive: Hypoid bevel
Ratio: 3.7:1

SUSPENSION
Front: Independent, with coil and
wishbones and telescopic dampers
Rear: Non-independent, with live
axle, semi-elliptic leaf springs and
piston-type hydraulic damper

STEERING
Type: Cam and lever

BRAKES
Type: Girling disks front, drums rear

WHEELS AND TYRES
Type: 15 in wire wheels and 5.50–
15 tyres

BODY/CHASSIS
Type: Steel two-seat sports car
(available as hardtop or convertible)
built on box-section ladder-frame
chassis

DIMENSIONS
Length: 150.25 in (3816 mm)
Width: 56.5 in (1435 mm)
Wheelbase: 88.5 in (2248 mm)
Track – front: 46.5 in (1181 mm)
    – rear: 46 in (1168 mm)
Weight: 2212 lb (1003 kg)

PERFORMANCEE
Maximum speed: 110 mph
(177 kph)
Acceleration 0–60 mph: 11.4
seconds
Fuel consumption: 27 mpg

1936–39 type of Standard Flying Nine chassis frame (of which more than 500 examples were in stock in the Spares department!) to which a Triumph Mayflower's coil-spring independent front suspension and live rear axle were grafted. The wet-liner Standard Vanguard engine was reduced in size from 2088 cc to 1991 cc by using smaller bore pistons, and was slightly tuned by the addition of twin SU carburettors, while the Vanguard's three-speed gearbox was converted to a four-speed with a central gear change.

Belgrove's style was surprisingly close to that finally used in production, except that there was a short, tucked-in tail, with an exposed spare wheel, and with the fuel tank's filler protruding through its centre.

Even Harry Webster now agrees that the original 20TS concept was not a success, and although the prototype shown at the 1952 Earls Court exhibition was one full step further advanced, it was still no beauty. That first car was built in just eight weeks, with an improved (though still not rigid enough)

> **' ... the most awful car I've ever driven in my life ... a death trap '**

chassis frame, and with a remote-control change. Almost before it had run on the roads it was shown to the world, with a provisional price tag of £555 (basic), and a 75 bhp engine; its top speed was claimed (but not measured) to be 90 mph (145 kph).

Immediately after the show, a seasoned driver/tester/mechanic, Ken Richardson, who had long been involved with the V16 BRM project and who was a confidante of Raymond Mayes, was invited to try the car and offer his opinions. This he did, and after a relatively short outing was so appalled by the car's behaviour that he returned and told the startled Standard directors: 'I think it's the most awful car I've ever driven in my life. It's a death trap!'

As *The Motor* wrote at a later date: 'At this point the Standard company might well have

thanked Richardson politely for his expert opinion, but pointed out that questions of production made it impossible to carry out any fundamental alterations to the design. And if they had done so, the TR would have died very soon after its birth…'.

However, the directors not only listened, but acted: Richardson was invited to join the company to develop a better TR, and Harry Webster's team was given a mere three months to transform its behaviour.

Thus it was that the definitive TR – the TR2 – was first seen at the Geneva Show of March 1953. The TR1, by the way, is a name retrospectively given to the original 20TS prototype.

The TR2, rapidly prepared for production, was a much more rugged car. The engineers had produced an entirely new box-section chassis frame, allied to an improved and tuned 90 bhp engine, and Belgrove's team had reworked the rear of the body, slotting the spare wheel away out of sight under the boot and squaring and lengthening the tail. Most important of all, Ken Richardson had put in many high-speed hours at the industry's MIRA proving ground, testing the components.

Thus, from its origins as an evil-handling 90 mph 'mongrel', the project had moved rapidly, so that the TR2's handling was much more predictable and the top speed was comfortably over 100 mph (161 kph). The development engineers were also delighted to discover that the engine was extremely fuel-efficient; if the optional Laycock de Normanville overdrive were fitted, the car could be driven hard and still over 30 mpg.

There was still, however, a major marketing problem. Whereas the MG, Jaguar and Healey sports cars already had established reputations, the Triumph TR2 had none. Sports car customers would sign an order for one of the aforementioned without even taking a test drive, because they knew and trusted the heritage. But what did they know about the TR2, and Triumph? Nothing – the car had no pedigree.

Standard-Triumph could, at least, prove a point by showing that the car was fast, so Ken Richardson took a prototype (MVC 575)

to the Jabbeke motor road in Belgium for speed trials. On 20 May 1953 he drove a mechanically standard car, with nothing but an aeroscreen and a full-length undershield to improve the aerodynamics, at 124.9 mph (201 kph). Even in full touring trim, with hood, screen, and side-screens erect (though still with the undershield in place) the car achieved 114.9 mph (185 kph).

Production of the TR2 got under way slowly in the summer of 1953 (the Austin-Healey 100, also previewed at the 1952 motor show, beat it to the showrooms by several months), and only 248 cars were actually delivered before the end of the year.

> **' ... a very favourable road test, in which their car achieved ... 103 mph ... '**

Nevertheless, that did not disappoint the factory hierarchy, for the original plan had been to produce only 500 cars a year.

Things improved early in 1954, especially after *The Autocar* published a very favourable road test, in which their car achieved not only 103 mph (166 kph) and 0-60 mph (97 kph) in 11.9 seconds, but the quite remarkable fuel consumption figure of 32 mpg overall. Both at home and in the USA, the TR2 offered very good value for money. By mid-1954, when its reputation was becoming established, the TR2's all-in UK price of £887 compared very favourably with that of £780 for an MG TF, £1064 for an Austin-Healey 100 and £1602 for the Jaguar XK120.

Its pedigree, too, was rapidly refined, for not only did the TR2 establish itself as a

robust and reliable club rally car, but it achieved major competition successes. In March 1954, privately-owned TR2s took first, second and fifth places overall in the RAC International rally (John Wallwork driving the winning car, and Peter Cooper – now chief executive at the RAC's Motor Sport Association – runner up). In May, Ken Richardson and Maurice Gatsonides finished 27th overall in the Mille Miglia, at an average speed of 73 mph (117 kph). A month later Edgar Wadsworth's privately-owned car finished 15th (at 74.7 mph/120 kph in atrocious conditions) in the Le Mans 24 hours, while at the next big event in the calendar, the French Alpine rally, the TR2s won the manufacturers' team prize, and Gatsonides won a Coupe des Alpes for a clear run.

That did it. In Europe the TR2 had made its name as a strong, robust, 2-litre sports car, while in the USA it was rapidly being seen as an obvious alternative to MGs and

Austin-Healeys. Even though the MGA of 1955 was a vastly better car than the TF which it replaced, and the Austin-Healey was gradually improved, the TR family never looked back.

The TR2 had a very definite character, but not all of it was likeable. By the end of 1954 it could be ordered with overdrive, centre-lock wire wheels, and a removable hardtop, but less attractive was its very barky and boomy exhaust note, its hard and bumpy ride, its drum brakes which tended to grab when abused, and the way that the car would suddenly swop ends on slippery corners, especially if the optional Michelin X radial tyres were fitted.

But it was so reliable, and such good value, its owners seemed to forgive it anything. Spare parts were cheap and rarely seemed to be needed, and the engine was so rugged that it seemed to go on and on for years needing nothing more than routine

attention. It was surprisingly economical even when used for rallying, and unless you bent the chassis frame when crashing the car, it was quite cheap to repair.

From 1953 to the end of 1962, when the very last of this TR series was built, the cars were always recognisably the same. Badges changed, engines were slightly improved, grilles came, altered, and widened, but the TR went on and on. At its peak, in 1959, a total of 21,298 cars was delivered, the vast majority of them going overseas, and only 638 spared for the home market. The British sports car makers relied very much on the USA for sales, and the best year for TR sales in the UK was 1955, when 1730 were made available.

It is worth looking at the TRs specifications to see why they appealed so much to the enthusiasts of the day. At first the cars had what the aficionados now call 'long doors', but these were soon shortened so that they could, at least, be opened against a high kerb, and thereafter it was easy to get into or out of a TR2 or TR3. The seating position was low, necessitating a straight-legged posture. The gear-lever was short and stubby, with a quite delightful short-action change, and if the overdrive was fitted it was controlled by a switch on the instrument panel, close to the steering wheel rim. The handbrake, to the left of the transmission tunnel, had a fly-off action and was very powerful.

The Motor admitted that no '…pretence could be made that the chassis and suspension are at all advanced, and the result of orthodox layout is the expected compromise between comfort and road-holding.' They found that the TR3's back end would slide quite easily and was extremely sensitive to the type of tyres and their inflation pressures, finding that softer tyres at the front, '…serve to increase the understeering tendency which is inherent but not objectionable.' Overall the verdict was that the TR had '…shortcomings but no vices; the TR3 offers a great deal at a modest price…'.

very snug in winter. All these factors helped make it an extremely satisfactory rally car.

It was one of those cars which got better, season after season, because the changes all seemed to have been done with the enthusiast, and performance, in mind. All, that is, except the arrival of the full-width grill in 1958, which was strictly for American no-

---

> *'… the changes all seemed to have been done with performance, in mind '*

---

tions of taste… .

By 1955, when it evolved into the TR3, the original TR2 had been much improved. The TR3 now had an egg-box grille in the nose instead of the open air-intake, while the engine power had been pushed up from 90 bhp to 95 bhp. That, incidentally, was the start of the process which showed that as the power went up, the fuel efficiency went down. The '56 was a good car, but the 1957

model was even better, for that particular TR3 became one of the first British series production car to be fitted with front-wheel disc brakes as standard.

Now that even the humble Metro, or Fiesta, has servo-assisted discs, it is difficult to recall just what a stir this innovation made. At a stroke, it seemed, the spectre of high-speed brake fade had gone for good, and the car which had been a good rally car now became a truly formidable machine.

In 1958 it became even more attractive. The TR3A (although the car was never actually badged as such) was given a new nose-panel with full-width grill, the 100 bhp engine recently phased in for TR3s was standardised and lockable handles were fitted to the doors and boot lid. American sales soared – over 300 cars were exported every week – and the TR3A became as typical a British sports car as any MG. This, by the way, made the Abingdon-traditionalists furious, and inter-marque rivalry intensified.

In the meantime, Triumph had set up a works competition team, which notched up more and more successes. In 1955 a trio of

The engine was extremely torquey, and most TR drivers learned to keep it booming away between about 3000 rpm and 5000 rpm. With overdrive they had no fewer than seven forward ratios, for overdrive was available on second, third and fourth gears.

It was even a joy to top up with fuel, for with 30 mpg (which dropped to about 26 mpg on later derivatives) the running costs were not high. Behind the cockpit, centrally located, was a fat, chrome-plated, snap-action filler cap, and nothing – not even the flow from modern electric pumps – could ever overload that amply-proportioned neck.

Most enthusiasts liked to drive their TRs with the hood down and the side-screens stowed, but even with all the weather-protection in place (especially if the optional hardtop was fitted), there was excellent all-round visibility. Heaters were not standard (but usually fitted), and made the interior

EVOLUTION

Introduced at the 1952 Earls Court Motor Show, the Triumph 20TS prototype (retrospectively known as the TR1) was an open two-seater based on a stiffened Standard Flying Nine chassis and fitted with a moderately tuned 75 bhp, 2-litre Standard Vanguard engine. Its top speed was claimed to be 90 mph (145 kph). When Ken Richardson, an experienced driver and engineer, test-drove the 20TS, he found it to be extremely dangerous, and the car underwent extensive modification

1953 The TR2 was unveiled at the Geneva Motor Show in March, an open two-seater with redesigned and smoother body, a new box-section chassis frame and the engine improved to produce 90 bhp. It had a maximum speed of 103 mph (166 kph), a 0–60 mph time of 12.6 seconds and an overall fuel consumption of 31 mpg

1954 The TR2 hard-top version became available (the roof was made of glassfibre), and other options included overdrive and wire wheels. Modifications included larger drum-brakes at the rear, stiffer sills and increased kerb-clearance for the doors

1955 The TR3 was announced, with its engine further tuned to produce 95 bhp, Girling disc brakes fitted to the front wheels and an egg-box grille. Maximum speed was 110 mph (177 kph) and the 0–60 mph time was reduced to 11.4 seconds. Average fuel consumption was 27 mpg

1958 The TR3A was announced, fitted with a new nose panel with full-width grille, and engine power was increased to 100 bhp

1961 The TR3B was built for the American market, fitted with the forthcoming TR4's all-synchromesh gearbox and a choice of its 2 and 2.2-litre engines

LEFT & BELOW *Views of a 1960 TR3A, a car which was built to satisfy the enthusiast, being fast, attractive, reliable and relatively easy to maintain; the engine was very accessible and rarely gave trouble. The boot rack was a popular option, for boot space was limited, and with one the TR became a good tourer*

cars entered, and finished, at Le Mans, but in the main the works TR was a rally car. There were many stirring performances, and highlights included five Coupes, the manufacturer's team prize in the 1956 French Alpine rally, third overall in the gruelling Liège–Rome–Liège, victory in the Circuit of Ireland in 1958 and second in the 1959 Tulip rally.

The important feature of the 1958 French Alpine was not just that the works cars beat the works Austin-Healeys, but that they used the enlarged 2138 cc engines for the first time, a unit that soon became optional on production cars (although very few were built), and was later standard on the early '60s TRs.

The TR3A's production-line performance peaked in 1960 and tailed off rapidly thereafter. From about 1957, Standard-Triumph had been casting around for a replacement style for the car, but it was not until the autumn of 1961 that the TR4 was ready to go on sale. That car retained the same basic chassis

---

' … there was a special American-specification TR3B, effectively the same… '

---

design, but the Michelotti-styled bodyshell was completely new.

When the American dealers first saw the TR4 they apparently commented that it looked too smooth, too modern and too comfortable, and asked that the TR3A be continued. This request was granted, for one more season, and explains why there was a special American-specification TR3B, effectively the same structure as the TR3A, but with the TR4's new all-synchromesh transmission, and a choice of 2- or 2.2-litre TR4 engines.

The death of the TR3B, however, was not the end of this type of Triumph sports car, for it was progressively changed and improved until 1976. In 1965 a new chassis was introduced, in 1967 a new engine and 1969 a major facelift. But all that, as they say, is another story.   GR

The all-time best-selling car has captured the hearts of millions with its rugged charm. Despite dated design, it is still manufactured forty years on

THREE PERSONALITIES are responsible for the Volkswagen Beetle being the most popular car in the history of the automobile. They are Adolf Hitler, who conceived the idea of a car cheap enough for the German working man to afford, Ferdinand Porsche, who created the distinctive air-cooled rear engined design while in the post-war years Heinz Nordhoff turned the Hitlerian dream into a reality. To date over 20 million Beetles have been built and production continues in Mexico and Brazil.

The starting point of the Beetle project was 30 January in 1933 which was when Adolf Hitler became German chancellor. Determined that Germany should once again become a world power, he was also intent on building a web of special roads, designed for the needs of the motor car. But this was only the first part of Hitler's grand automotive plan. The all important second stage was for the government to initiate the production of a Volkswagen or People's car. These ideas had been exercising Hitler's thoughts ever since he had been imprisoned in Landsberg Castle, near Munich in 1924 after his unsuccessful attempt to overthrow the German Government with his National Socialist, or Nazi party. Already a committed anti-semite, Hitler was attracted to the writing of Henry Ford, who was not only of the same persuasion but had also put the world on wheels with his famous Model T. While in prison Hitler read Ford's ghosted autobiography *My Life and Work*. It was early in 1924 that Hitler received a visit from a young Munich lawyer named Hans Frank. Hitler confided that he had conceived a plan for mopping up the nation's unemployed; they would be set to work building a network of motor roads.

This idea was clearly inspired by the Italian *autostrada* which Mussolini had recently initiated, but this was not all. A Hitler-lead government would then mass produce a car that would be within the reach of the man in the street; once Hitler had come to power he wasted little time in pursuing these objectives. The *autobahnen* programme was announced in February 1933, only weeks after he had taken office, and work on the first section, between Frankfurt and Mannheim, began eight months later, in September. By 1943 there would be over 2300 miles of motorway in Germany and they were by far and away Europe's finest roads. With the

RIGHT *This is a 1953 Volkswagen Beetle which was built for the export market*

MODEL
Volkswagen Beetle 1300 (1970)
UK price: £585

ENGINE
Location: Rear, longitudinal
Type: Air-cooled horizontally-opposed, four cylinder with aluminium cylinder blocks, cast-iron liners and alloy cylinder heads. Four main bearings
Cubic Capacity: 1285 cc
Bore × stroke: 77 mm × 69 mm
Compression ratio: 7.3:1
Valve gear: 2 valves per cylinder operated by pushrods from one central camshaft
Fuel supply: 1 Solex downdraught single-choke carburettor
Ignition: Mechanical by coil and distributor
Maximum power: 44 bhp DIN at 4100 rpm
Maximum torque: 69 lb ft (SAE) at 2600 rpm

TRANSMISSION
Layout: Gearbox in front of engine driving rear wheels
Clutch: Single dry plate
Gearbox: Four-speed manual
  1st 3.800:1 3rd 1.260:1
  2nd 2.060:1 4th 0.890:
Final drive: Spiral bevel
Ratio: 4.375:1

SUSPENSION
Front: Independent twin swinging longitudinal trailing arms with transverse laminated torsion bars, anti-roll bar and telescopic dampers.
Rear: Independent swinging semi-axles with longitudinal trailing arms, transverse torsion bars and telescopic dampers

STEERING
Type: Worm and roller. 2.6 turns lock to lock

BRAKES
Type: Drums all round

WHEELS AND TYRES
Type: Steel perforated wheels with 5,60 × 15 in tyres

BODY/CHASSIS
Type: Backbone platform and integral bodyshell. 2-door, 4-seat saloon

DIMENSIONS AND WEIGHT
Length: 160 in (4070 mm)
Width: 61 in (1550 mm)
Wheelbase: 94.50 in (2400 mm)
Track – front: 51.57 in (1310 mm)
    – rear: 53.15 in (1350 mm)
Weight: 1676 lb (760 kg)

PERFORMANCE
Maximum speed: 75 mph (120 kph)
Acceleration 0-50 mph: 14 seconds
Fuel consumption (approx): 33 mpg

A cutaway view of the legendary Beetle, which Hitler commissioned as the 'people's car'. Although the car has been much modernised over the years, the basic, distinctive shape and the flat four air-cooled engine have always remained. Interesting is the adoption of torsion bar suspension all round which allows separation of chassis and bodyshell without disturbing any of the running gear; the Beetle chassis has proved to be the most widely used base for kit cars for this reason. The early '70s saw much revised suspension units introduced on the 1302 model, incorporating MacPherson struts at the front and semi-trailing arms to locate the rear hubs

autobahnen programme well under way, Hitler turned his attention to the Volkswagen project. He was already acquainted with one of Germany's most famous car designers, Ferdinand Porsche, and in the autumn of 1933 he met with him at Berlin's Hotel Kaiserhof to discuss the project.

Porsche, like Hitler, was not German but had been born in the small town of Maffersdorf in the old Austro-Hungarian empire. In 1905 he had joined Austro-Daimler and did not leave until 1923. He left to take one of the prime jobs in the German motor industry: that of technical director of Daimler-Benz. But in 1929 he was on the move again and returned to Austria and the Steyr company. Unfortunately, the Depression had hit Steyr and in 1930 Porsche found himself without a job, deciding, rather than work for others, to set up in business in Stuttgart to offer a design facility for motor manufacturers. The firm, established at the end of 1930, was staffed exclusively by Austrian engineers whom Porsche had met during his working life.

Ferdinand Porsche was therefore the ideal person to take on the Volkswagen project though when he heard that the car was to have a selling price of less than RM (Reichsmarks) 1000 (£86), have a top speed of 100 kph (62 mph) and a fuel consumption of seven litres of petrol per 100 km (around 42 mpg), he nearly turned the project down. Hitler was also insistent that the car have an air-cooled engine. Fortunately these specifications came fairly close to two designs that Porsche's design bureau had already created. The first, designated Type 12 in the

---

> **❛** *... model boasted a rear mounted air-cooled four-cylinder boxer engine...* **❜**

Porsche register, had a rear mounted water-cooled five-cylinder radial engine with backbone chassis and all independent suspension. Although Zündapp, who were motor cycle manufacturers, expressed interest in the idea, they did not pursue it and the similar Type 33 produced for NSU suffered much the same fate. This model boasted a rear mounted air-cooled four-cylinder boxer (horizontally-opposed) engine and Porsche's patented torsion bar suspension.

It was this later experimental car that formed the basis of the Volkswagen that was alloted the designation Type 60 in the Porsche design register in 1934. However, on the grounds of cost the four-cylinder boxer

TOP LEFT *The 1932 Zündapp, predecessor to the Beetle*
ABOVE CENTRE *This 1936 VW30 was purely experimental*
LEFT *The first production topless VW appeared in 1949*
ABOVE RIGHT *This military amphibian has an enclosed Beetle chassis with crank-driven propeller*

motor was dispensed with. Instead a series of experimental engines was built. There was a vertical four, which alas, broke its crankshaft and then a variety of twins with sleeve and overhead valves. While the design team were wrestling with the problem of trying to produce a cheap, relatively quiet power unit, Franz Xavier Reimspiess, a new Austrian recruit, came up with a four-cylinder boxer motor of such simplicity that, when costed, it was found to be cheaper than the twins then under development. This over-square four is substantially the same design which is still in production today though, of course, it has been considerably refined over the years. In addition to making this immeasurable contribution to the Volkswagen, Reimspiess was also responsible for the world famous VW badge.

With the all important matter of the engine resolved, work could now proceed on testing the prototypes. Two had been built in the double garage of Porsche's Stuttgart home in 1935 and a further three were made in 1936. These cars were then handed over to the German Automobile Manufacturers' Association for a rigorous 30,000 kilometre test programme. The most serious problem encountered was the continual breaking of the cast iron crankshafts and they were replaced by conventional forgings. Minor problems were also experienced with the front suspension and cable

brakes and practically every car broke its gear lever.

The Manufacturers' Association issued a 100 page report in January 1937 as a result of these trials. It was generally in favour of the project but felt that the RM 990 selling price could not be realised. Nevertheless the Association offered to take the Volkswagen over but Hitler had other ideas. From May 1937, the VW became a state-funded project and the responsibility of the German Labour

---

‘… it should look like a beetle… look to nature to find streamlining… ’

Front which replaced the abolished trade unions. This resulted in an immediate cash injection of RM 50,000 (£42,918) and Daimler-Benz was commissioned to produced a further batch of 30 cars. Hitler, speaking of the Volkswagen's appearance, said on one occasion: 'it should look like a beetle, you've only got to look to nature to find out what streamlining is'. This new series of experimental cars certainly did look beetle-like, accentuated by the fact that they still lacked a rear window. There followed yet another series of exhaustive tests with the drivers recruited from the SS and

the cars based at their barracks at Kornwestheim.

There was just one more series of experimental cars to be produced. At long last a divided rear window was introduced and the number and frequency of the louvres in the engine bay lid were reduced as the output of the engine's cooling fan was boosted. In addition, running boards were introduced and a one piece bonnet replaced the divided versions that had hitherto sufficed. The capacity of the engine was upped 1 cc to 985 cc and the remaining mechanical features, the backbone chassis and all independent suspension by transverse torsion bars, were confirmed. Here, in 1938, was a Beetle that would have been instantly recognisable today.

With the car's design at last resolved, the German government had to find somewhere to build it. They chose a green field site in the north about 50 miles east of Hanover, near the village of Fallersleben on the banks of the Mittelland Canal which joins the River Rhine to the Elbe. This followed a visit by Porsche and a small team to America and the motor city of Detroit in 1936 and 1937.

Work on the factory began in 1938 and in May of that year Adolf Hitler ceremonially laid the foundation stone. It was then that he announced that the car would henceforth be known as the KdF-Wagen (Strength through Joy car) which was the name of the Labour

Front's leisure section. Then, in August, Front chief Robert Ley announced that the KdF-Wagen could only be bought by a unique hire purchase arrangement whereby prospective buyers would be issued with a savings book and savers would be commited to a minimum payment of RM5 (58p) per week. However, unlike the more usual hire purchase arrangement, the car would be delivered on the completion of payments rather than at the outset. Price of the two-door saloon was set at RM 990 (£85) while a version with a roll-back sun roof was RM 60 (£5.15) more. There was just one colour available: blue grey.

In 1937 Ferdinand Porsche, with his traditional love of fast cars, decided to approach Labour Front officals with a view to producing a sports version of the KdF-Wagen. But the idea was turned down as it was felt that a utilitarian vehicle such as this should not have a glamorous image. So Porsche pushed ahead with his own design and came up with a streamlined coupé with a mid-mounted water-cooled V10 engine. The authorities then had a change of heart and Porsche was given the green light to build three special Volkswagens, which were alloted the designation Type 64 in the Porsche design register, as it was intended to enter them for a race from Berlin to Rome, scheduled to take place in September 1939. Although the outbreak of war put paid to the project, the streamlined cars were built and represented the first stirrings of the Porsche marque that emerged with the 356 in 1948.

The first stage of the KdF-Wagen factory was completed by the spring of 1939. It was to be capable of producing 150,000 cars in its first full manufacturing year. Further ex-

pansion would result in the plant being able to produce 1.5 million cars in 1942 which would have challenged the American automotive giants. But, of course, it was not to be. On 1 September 1939 Hitler invaded Poland and World War II began. As all the tooling had been delivered, a pilot run of KdF-Wagens was produced from 1941 though only 630 examples were built during hostilities. Made in rather larger numbers was the Kubelwagen, the military version of the Volkswagen, which entered production in 1940 and by the end of the war 50,435 had been manufactured. By contrast, the Americans built over half a million Jeeps.

When the war came to an end in 1945, the KdF-Wagen plant fell within the British military zone. In July 1945 the Royal Electrical and Mechanical Engineers moved in to the works and the following month Major Ivan Hirst took charge of the factory.

One of the first things that the British did was to give the settlement that had grown up around the Volkswagen factory a name. The Nazis had called it KdF Stadt (town of Strength through Joy) but the community was renamed Wolfsburg after the nearby 14th century castle. Incredibly, for a short time, Kubelwagen bodies continued to ar-

*A 1947 Beetle, **LEFT**. The engine, **FAR LEFT**, is essentially unchanged to this day, this unit being of 1131 cc. **BELOW CENTRE** is the austere 'people's' accommodation while the weird creation **BELOW** is a Porsche-developed Type 60 streamlined coupé of 1939. Three were prepared for the 1939 Berlin-Rome-Berlin marathon with 32 bhp engines giving a top speed of 80 mph (130 kph)*

rive at the plant so for the rest of 1945 these were assembled from spare parts and by the end of the year 522 examples had been produced; 58 saloons were also built in the same year.

As Wolfsburg fell within the British military zone, inevitably it received a visit from the Society of Motor Manufacturers and Traders who were investigating the activities of the German motor industry during the war. They were clearly impressed by what they saw. 'It can be said that the Volkswagen is most advanced and interesting for quantity production...both the car and factory in which it is produced are wonderful achievements in their respective spheres.' The car's importance was reflected in it becoming the subject of a second report, published in 1946. Conducted by Rootes, it consisted of a road test between a Volkswagen and a Mark III Hillman Minx. The British car proved to be a good 6 mph (10 kph) faster, with a top speed of 61.5 mph (100 kph) for the Beetle could only manage 56.3 mph (90 kph). In addition it incorporated a war-time report, undertaken by Humber, on a Kubelwagen that had been captured in North Africa, following General Montgomery's triumphal victory at El Alamein. The Kubel was dismantled and 100 lb (46 kg) of sand removed in the process. The subsequent report completely failed to appreciate the ingenuity of the Porsche design and one paragraph, in particular, has echoed down the years. It reads: 'We do not consider that the design represents any special brilliance, apart from certain of the detail points, and it is sug-

gested that it is not to be regarded as an example of first class modern design to be copied by the British industry'. Inevitably history has had the last word for Humber and Rootes have disappeared and the Volkswagen has gone on to become the most popular car in the history of the automobile.

The other difficulty facing Volkswagen was the ever present danger that it might be taken as reparations by the victorious allies. The French government were all for moving the entire facility, *en masse*, to France although the French motor industry was united in opposition to this project. Then, in

---

> *'...Heinz Nordhoff...*
> *set about turning the*
> *Beetle into a world beater...'*

February 1948, Henry Ford II took a look at the Wolfsburg facility. There were thoughts about buying Volkswagen and Ford even drove a Beetle but complications about the firm's ownership and the air-cooled rear engined vehicle flew in the face of practically every law in the American automotive design canon.

Transport was a major problem in post-war Germany, and Hirst was fortunate to receive a request for 10,000 cars from the British army; there being also a valuable order from the German Post Office. Amazingly out of the chaos (the factory had been heavily bombed in 1944) cars began to

appear; no fewer than 7677 were made in 1946. With great difficulty output was maintained for the next two years, then, in January 1948, Heinz Nordhoff took over as General Manager. A former Opel executive, he had run that company's Brandenberg lorry plant, which was Europe's largest, and he immediately set about turning the Beetle into a world beater. In July 1949 he introduced a greatly improved export model and in 1947 Ben Pon, a Dutch motor trader, signed up as Volkswagen's first overseas agent. The cars sold well enough in his native Holland and at Nordhoff's behest he took one across the Atlantic to America in January 1949 with a hope of awakening interest in the car there. But Pon had little luck as did Nordhoff himself who arrived, not with a car, but photographs. Convinced of the potential of the American market, in 1955 Volkswagen of America was established and that year the Beetle became the continent's best selling import. Sales peaked in 1968 when 423,008 cars were sold; by contrast, only 601 Beetles had been registered there in 1950.

The Volkswagen was becoming a world car, following in the wheel tracks of its famous Model T forebear. Manufacturing plants were established in South Africa in 1951, Brazil two years later, Australia in 1957 and Mexico in 1964.

Meanwhile the VW was being progressively refined. During the war, the car's capacity had been increased from its original 985 to 1131 cc to bring it in line with the Kubelwagen's specifications. In 1954 the

EVOLUTION

Introduced in 1945, the Beetle was first available as the VW 1200, equipped with an engine of 985 cc capacity and a four-speed manual gearbox. It offered comfortable accommodation for four in a compact body combined with frugal fuel consumption

1949 The export model was introduced, sporting high-polish finish, chrome decorative strips and a bonnet lock operated from inside

1950 Draft-free ventilation was achieved via recesses in the side windows; sunroof production commenced

1951 Side ventilation flaps were fitted

1952 Tyre size was changed to 5.60 × 15 in and quarter lights were also added further to improve ventilation. The bumpers were modified and two brake lights were incorporated into the rear light/reflector units

1953 The small, two-part rear window was replaced by one larger single one

1955 New rear light clusters were installed higher on the rear wings while the exhaust system received two outlet pipes. PVC was first used for the sunroof

1957 The rear window was further enlarged and the windscreen glass area was also increased. A new shape of engine compartment lid was first seen

1958 A larger outside mirror was fitted

1959 Pushbutton fixed door handles were introduced

1960 The Beetle was equipped with a windscreen washer unit, asymmetric dipped beams and turn signals

1961 Dual chamber rear lights replaced the previous units

1963 The front turn signals were modified, a steel sunroof was made available and the licence plate lamp received a wider housing

1964 saw enlargement of the window area while the windscreen wiper rest position was moved to the left and the engine compartment lid was fitted with a pushbutton catch

1965 The VW 1300 first saw the light of day and perforated disc wheels with flat covers were introduced

1966 The VW 1500 was launched, with a wider rear track, modified rear lid and licence plate light, thinner decorative strips and new door locks

1967 saw better fresh air ventilation introduced on the Beetle and three-point safety belt anchorages for all seats. Plastic control buttons, heavy-duty bumpers and an outside fuel filler neck on the right-hand side also featured

1969 Road wheels were changed

1970 The through-flow system of ventilation was adopted and an additional 1302 saloon was introduced featuring a larger boot and increased engine power of 50 bhp. The suspension was completely revised with MacPherson struts replacing the front torsion bar system and semi-trailing arms the rear swing axles

1971 The ventilation was even further refined while the engine lid received more air slats

1972 The VW 1303 was launched offering a 'panorama' windscreen and larger rear lights

1974 The turn signals were integrated in the bumpers

1975 The VW 1200 had its bumpers painted black and black mudwing beading was fitted. The VW 1200L was given chrome bumpers with rubber bump strips, chromed wheel covers, reversing lights and forced air ventilation

1977 saw a VW 1200L version from Mexico, featuring chromed bumpers and wheel covers, reversing lights, upgraded equipment with padded dashboard, adjustable front head restraints, three-point inertia reel safety belts, lap belts in the rear, a heated rear window and radial tyres.

---

car's capacity was upped to 1192 cc and although this had little effect on the Beetle's 62 mph (100 kph) top speed, acceleration perked up somewhat. However, it was not until the 1966 model year that capacity again increased, to 1285 cc, for an additional 1300 model while a 1500 model arrived for 1967.

Volkswagen sales were by this time soaring. The 100,000th car had been built in 1950 with the millionth example produced in 1955. Output continued to rise and in 1965 Wolfsburg had its first million Beetle year and between 1968 and 1971 the feat was again repeated. Alas, Heinz Nordhoff died in 1968 and the mighty Volkswagen factory stopped work for one minute in silent tribute to the man who had built Volkswagen up to be not only Germany's largest car company but also one of Europe's.

The Beetle's refinement continued for 1971 with the arrival of the 1302 with a new 1600 cc engine. This car marked the first departure from Porsche's original specification with MacPherson struts replacing the intrusive transverse torsion bars to increase luggage accommodation while semi trailing arms took the place of the rear swing axle. These changes were made to improve sales on the all important American market. It was replaced for 1973 by the 1303 with its new distinctive curved windscreen but this did not prove a success. In February 1972 the Beetle finally overtook the record of 15,007,033 Model T Fords produced to become the best selling car in the history of the automobile. (Ford subsequently revised its T output figure to 16.5 million but Volkswagen overtook that in 1973). But VW was in danger of repeating the very same mistake that Henry Ford had made when he kept the T in production for too long. The Beetle was

getting long in the tooth and attempts to replace it by a 1500 car in 1961, the 411/12 of 1968 and the front wheel drive K70 in 1970 proved unsuccessful. Then, in 1974, the impossible happened and Volkswagen recorded a loss, the first in its history. In May of that year the German motoring press were treated to a preview of the car that Volkswagen and the country were waiting

LEFT Karmann's stylish Beetle Cabriolet is a desirable car which is beginning to fetch extraordinarily high prices. The first Karmann Cabriolet was built in 1949 and production continued to 1980 and inspired the Golf Cabriolet
BELOW This VW 1303 is seen tackling the rigorous Land's End Trial of 1984

for, the front-wheel-drive Giugiaro styled Golf which had nothing in common with the Beetle apart from its wheelbase. At last a replacement had been found. The last Wolfsburg-built Beetle left the factory in July 1974 though production continued at the firm's Emden factory and was maintained until 1978. This was not quite the end of the Beetle in Germany for the Karmann-built cabriolet, introduced back in 1949, continued until 1980. The European market was serviced with spare parts from Volkswagen's Mexico plant though deliveries ceased in 1985.

To date over 20 million Beetles have been produced, an astounding success story for a 40 year old plus creation that still looks and sounds like no other.   JW